Swindon Town
THE FANS' CHOICE

Swindon Town
THE FANS' CHOICE

DAVE WALLIS

SwindonAdvertiser

First published in Great Britain in 2007 by
The Breedon Books Publishing Company Limited
Breedon House, 3 The Parker Centre,
Derby, DE21 4SZ.

All pictures courtesy of the

Swindon Advertiser

ISBN 978-1-85983-574-6

Printed and bound by Cromwell Press,
Trowbridge, Wiltshire.

Contents

For Dad

No one ever had more confidence in me.

Acknowledgements

Trying to pull together all the facts and statistics for a project like this necessitated relying on the help of many sources.

My own, surely unhealthy, penchant for cutting out and keeping just about anything that relates to Swindon Town has caused much frustration for my long-suffering wife, but has formed the backbone of much of what this book has been built around. Thank goodness all the inexplicable hoarding finally proved it had a purpose.

As much of this material consisted of back pages torn from the *Swindon Advertiser*, I offer my thanks for the excellent coverage the local paper has given my club. Without that, there would have been little for me to file away over the last 30 years, although my loft would have been significantly less cluttered.

Groaning shelves of football-related books, such as the indispensable tome still known purely as the *Rothman's Yearbook*, regardless of fresh sponsorship, have also been crucial. The invaluable help of the many books of Dick Mattick were a comforting cross-reference when things needed to be verified, and the excellent website www.swindon-town-fc.co.uk was a constant source of corroboration.

Thanks also to *Swindon Advertiser* photographer Dave Evans for agreeing to allow me to use pictures he has taken over many years covering Town, to club photographer Chris Adams for his help supplying photographs of the most recent seasons, and to Dunwoody for granting me access to their own excellent picture library.

I'm grateful to Steve Caron at Breedon, who held on to the belief that deadlines could be met when I seriously wondered whether I could pull this project off, and to fellow Town supporters Mike Judd and Mike Rogers for agreeing to proof read the manuscript from a Swindon supporter's view point.

The feedback and support I received from the players whom I've had so much pleasure watching and writing about, brought a serious shot in the arm if I started to doubt the quality of what I was putting together, and the boost I received when Shaun Taylor agreed to pen some words for a foreword was a major bonus. Thanks Shaun.

Most of all I have to thank my wife Mel, who continues to put up with the unreasonable behaviour of someone who has allowed his affection for Swindon Town to grow totally out of sensible perspective.

Introduction

Each Swindon Town season produces someone who is considered a hero, whatever the outcome of the campaign's endeavours. He might be the long-serving, one-club man, or a journeyman player passing through Wiltshire as his career takes him elsewhere. A flamboyant creator who captures the imagination of the crowd, or a workhorse whose game is epitomised by blood and sweat.

Telling the club's story since 1990, this book details the careers of the 13 most recent winners of the prestigious Swindon Town Player of the Year award and the part they played in the season in which they won it. They are those players who the fans themselves adjudged to have made the outstanding contribution to the trials or successes of each campaign.

Seventeen seasons, a baker's dozen worth of Player's of the Year. Eleven managers, four divisions and two spells in administration.

The period has been one of constant flux; the only consistency has been change. There have been tears of joy, frustration and despair. Following a football club tests all of the emotions, and Swindon Town are exponents of the art of keeping their supporters on their toes. Things are rarely boring at the County Ground.

One man each season is deemed by the fans to be the most significant contributor. Here are their stories.

Foreword

I would like to take this opportunity to thank Dave for being able to say a few words about this book that you are about to read.

When Dave asked me if I would like to produce this foreword, I had no hesitation whatsoever. It is an honour to put my name to this publication associated with Swindon Town's Player of the Year Awards.

My best years and the highlight of my career were definitely with Swindon Town. The rapport I achieved with the fans was unbelievable and the making of some unforgettable memories for me.

My aim when I played for the Town was always to give my best at all times, thinking that the fans when they watched were in some ways playing themselves, and would have given anything to be in my shoes (boots). I was lucky enough to have the opportunity to do it, and intended not to let anyone down or let any moment pass me by.

I could not have achieved what I did without playing with a lot of very good players during my time at the club, so I feel this book is a tribute to all Swindon players of the past.

Dave has achieved an excellent collation of facts and stories and I hope everyone who reads this book will enjoy it as much as I did.

Shaun Taylor

Duncan Shearer

(1990–91) ~ A season of turmoil

The season of 1990–91 couldn't start quickly enough for everyone connected with Swindon Town. As the summer progressed, England had tried to keep the Town's mind on football as Paul Gascoigne wept his way out of Italia '90, but for Swindon supporters it had been difficult to concentrate on matters on the pitch.

The previous May had ostensibly seen Town claim promotion to the top flight with a Division Two Play-off Final victory over Sunderland at Wembley. A single goal from midfielder Alan McLoughlin from a shot that deflected wildly past Rokermen 'keeper Tony Norman had settled a hugely one-sided match and, after a dash back along the M4, the whole town prepared to celebrate.

A sign outside the Fountain Hotel in Old Town, Swindon, proclaimed the score to the returning fans. 'Swindon Town 1, Sunderland absolutely bloody nothing' it told supporters fresh from Wembley, hell bent on enjoying the evening to the full.

The notice was accurate in fact and sentiment. Sunderland had rarely threatened Swindon, while Town had carved out a multitude of chances. That the match ended with just one goal separating the teams did little to demonstrate the gulf between the two sides on the day. Town's reward was to be elevation to the top division, then still called Division One, for the first time in the club's 109-year history.

The party lasted late into the night, but eventually many supporters made their way home to relive the entire event on video, as the match had been transmitted by Bristol-based television company HTV. Presenter Roger Malone, often derided by Swindon fans who were suspicious that he was a Bristol City supporter, was magnanimous in his praise of Ossie Ardiles's side.

Duncan Shearer.

An open-top bus ride was staged the following day as the town came out to acknowledge their heroes, but clouds were gathering to rain on the parade. Rumours of financial irregularities at the County Ground had been rumbling on for months and the Football League had let it be known that they would be fully investigated.

The charges related to the way Swindon had both paid their players and conducted their transfers. It had been suggested that players had received more remuneration than their contracts determined, and that this had helped Town capture the signatures of transfer targets ahead of other clubs. As such, the Inland Revenue was another interested party.

Furthermore, the mechanism that football used to calculate a transfer fee when a tribunal was necessary factored in details of the buying club's contract offer to the player. In short, by understating the salary offered, it was alleged the fee would be set too low.

The press had made much of the behind-the-scenes activities at the County Ground and everyone with a love for the club had been preparing themselves for some sort of punishment from football's authorities.

On the last day of April, just days before the end of the regular season, former chairman Brian Hillier, ex-manager Lou Macari, captain Colin Calderwood and club accountant Vince Farrar had all been arrested and taken for questioning as the inquiry gathered pace. Calderwood was released without charge, but the uncertainty continued.

Ten days after the victory, the Football League took the decision not only to deprive Town of their newly-won place in the top flight, but also to drop the club another rung down the ladder into Division Three. The whole town was stunned. One word was heard from all quarters and it was the one that most succinctly summed up the mood of everyone concerned. That word was 'devastated'.

The club immediately lodged an appeal with the Football Association, which as the highest authority, had the power to overturn the judgement. Campaigners swung into action as a petition containing 44,000 names of the dissatisfied was quickly raised and deposited at Villa Park, where the lawmakers were gathering to pontificate their actions.

There was a mixed reaction when the decision was made to reduce the sentence to allow Town to kick-off the new season back in Division Two. Many still felt the club had been harshly treated, while others heaved a sigh of relief that at least the status quo had been restored. The reduction in punishment gave the club the chance to try to regain the prize of top-level football 12 months later, and fans looked to their players to right what they perceived to be a massive wrong at the earliest opportunity.

One man had done more than any to take Town to Wembley in the first place.

Duncan Shearer had been signed by Lou Macari from Huddersfield Town in June 1988 for a club-record £230,000. Both Jimmy Quinn and Dave Bamber had departed Wiltshire and the loss of the striking pair, who had hit 34 League goals between them that year, left a hole to fill. Forming a new strike partnership with Steve White, Duncan quickly settled at his new club.

He earned the unusual nickname of Postman Dunc. Some thought it was due to his similarity to the legendary TV mailman Postman Pat. Others believed it was a reference to his ability to despatch a ball swiftly into the net. Whatever the truth, there was never any mention of a black and white cat.

It had been Shearer's 21 Division Two goals in 45 appearances that had contributed hugely to Town's progression to the 1990 Division Two Play-offs, where he registered once more against future employers Blackburn Rovers in the semi-final. Now, in the aftermath of the swingeing punishment meted out for Town's fiscal lack of wisdom, the 5ft 10in Scotsman was among those whom supporters were pinning their hopes on to steady the ship as 1990–91 approached.

Born on the west coast of Scotland at Fort William on 28 August 1962, Duncan had joined Chelsea from Highland League team Inverness Clachnacuddin. He made two appearances for the Blues and scored on his debut in a 2–2 home draw with Leicester City on the first day of February 1985. Unable to repeat the feat a week later, Duncan's Stamford Bridge career was prematurely over as the Terriers of Huddersfield beckoned. Thirty-eight goals then came from 83 League games at Leeds Road before Lou Macari made his move on behalf of Swindon Town.

Shearer settled quickly and top scored for Town with 14 in his first season. With Steve White chipping in with just one fewer, sixth place in Division Two was claimed along with a 1989 Play-off semi-final with Crystal Palace. Defeat over the two legs was a disappointment, but everyone found it easier to accept inferiority on the pitch than the distressing experience they would suffer after the Sunderland match 12 months later.

By 1990–91, manager Macari had been replaced by ex-Tottenham Hotspur and Argentine legend Ossie Ardiles. It took Shearer just 30 minutes to open his goalscoring account in a 2–1 opening-day victory at Charlton Athletic, but that wasn't quick enough to beat Paul Bodin to the honour of Town's first goal of the season. Three days later and Duncan was at it again, scoring the only goal of the match at home to Ipswich Town. Town had been stung by the League's punishment and time appeared to be of the essence. It was certainly a relief for supporters to be able to concentrate on footballing matters once more, rather than scanning the front pages of the newspaper for the next bad news, off-the-pitch story, but the feel-good factor looked short-lived.

In September came news that brought dread to the hearts of Swindon supporters. The *Daily Telegraph* published fresh allegations of financial irregularities at the County Ground, claims which the FA confirmed would be fully investigated. More sleepless nights for Town fans. Then in December, the feeling of injustice was compounded when Exeter City, themselves found guilty of financial irregularities, were slapped on the wrist and the directors concerned made to carry the financial can rather than the club and its supporters.

The outcome did little to dispel the belief that Swindon Town had been made an example of by the authorities, and that having served that purpose other clubs found to be acting similarly would be treated leniently. Many felt the FA were exercising double standards, but a spokesman was quoted as saying 'The two cases were not comparable'. At the same time, Chelsea were under investigation for alleged illegal payments and Town supporters awaited the outcome of the First Division giant's case with more interest than most.

A Shearer effort hits the post at West Bromwich Albion in Town's victory in December 1989.

It was to be three days before the new year before the FA announced that they were satisfied they had thrown enough books at Swindon Town. Serving manager Ossie Ardiles was told he could not be held accountable for any of the financial misdeeds, all of which had taken place before his arrival at Swindon. The fresh charges were to be 'placed on file'. Ardiles, who had feared a ban himself, had indicated he might have to leave Swindon Town if the clouds had continued to hover. It was heavily rumoured that old club Tottenham would link up with Terry Venables.

As September entered its third week, a trip to Oxford United brought a 4–2 win and left Town fourth in the table. The game was notable for the appearance of a new boy. Ex-Coventry City FA Cup winner and winger Dave Bennett had signed just two days before from Sheffield Wednesday for a reported £60,000 fee. Oxford claimed their two-goal lead inside the first five minutes but Town fought back, with Shearer striking twice to take his tally to five. The striker suggested they were not unnecessarily concerned by Oxford's start to the game. 'We were not too worried when they went two up as there was still plenty of time left and we knew we could pull it back.' Talking about the new boy Bennett, Duncan had this to say: 'Dave did well until his legs gave out on him, but once he gets a few games under his belt it is going to be interesting to see what kind of service he can provide.'

April 1989 and Duncan Shearer shows his technique against Blackburn Rovers.

It was both sad and ironic then, that the winger was to take to the pitch just once more in a Swindon Town shirt. Three days later, a shattered leg saw Bennett stretchered from a 3–0 League Cup defeat at Darlington and a lengthy period of recuperation lay ahead. It would have been of no consolation whatsoever to Bennett that, 10 days later, Town surprisingly turned the tie around with a 4–0 win in the return match at the County Ground.

The result at Oxford left Town fourth in Division One and raised hopes that Swindon could indeed reclaim the promotion they had been denied months earlier. Then eight games without a win blew that belief out of the water. On 28 September the midfield was bolstered with the arrival of Micky Hazard from Portsmouth for £130,000. The fee surpassed the £110,000 Ardiles had spent bringing David Kerslake to Swindon, making ex-Tottenham teammate Hazard Ossie's most expensive signing. Hazard scored on his first full game for Town in a 3–2 defeat at Oldham. The loss left Town fifth in Division Two after nine games, but a further six would pass before Town next tasted victory.

An embarrassing 2–0 home defeat by Bristol Rovers in the middle of October coincided with an injury to Shearer, one of just two League matches he would miss that season. A hamstring strain had brought about his replacement by Shaun Close in a 3–3 draw at Brighton the week before. The next was surrendered too, this by a goal to nil and inflicted by West Ham United, also at the County

Ground. Worse was to follow, as a massive 5–1 humiliation at the hands of Barnsley at Oakwell as the month concluded saw Town drop below mid-table.

A 3–0 home win over Portsmouth on 10 November might have signalled better fortunes, and the match was notable for the arrival of a World Cup finalist in the ranks of Swindon Town. Argentine Nestor Lorenzo, who had been presented with a loser's medal in the 1–0 defeat by West Germany less than five months earlier, joined forces with fellow countryman Ardiles and took just 30 minutes to hit the net. Not bad for a defender!

It was a false dawn. It was to be three days before Christmas before the next victory, over West Bromwich Albion, produced the next three points. But slowly the tide was turned as defeats were turned into draws. Confirmed as a Division Two club rather than among the big money of Division One, Town were forced to balance the books and on 13 December 1990, Wembley hero Alan McLoughlin left Town for Southampton in return for £1 million. It was the sort of fee that was impossible to turn down and the fans' disappointment was tempered with realism. They might have expected to have lost more of last season's squad by then.

A creditable point at Newcastle United on Boxing Day was followed by a 2–2 draw at Watford in the last game of 1990. Duncan was first on the score sheet after seven minutes, but a shot stopped by Hornets' goalkeeper David James two minutes earlier was controversially cleared from around the goalline. Duncan said 'It was definitely over. If the ball did not go over I would be the first to say so because I would like to think I am an honest person. There was no doubt in my mind.' Always a straightforward man, Duncan's protestations were enough for Swindon fans.

Had his first effort been allowed, Town's half-time two-goal lead would have been extended to three. Instead, in the last minute and with Town still a goal to the good, Duncan headed for the corner flag to waste time when a goalscoring chance looked on. 'We were still 2–1 up and had I been given the ball again I would have done exactly the same', said the front man. The ball was lost and in the time remaining Gary Penrice grabbed the goal that gave the home side a point. Shearer could have had a hat-trick, but Town had to settle for a share of the points.

It was also in the last minute of the match, this one on New Year's Day, that Town's Steve Foley notched the goal that brought a 1–1 home draw with Plymouth, the seventh drawn match in the last eight League matches. Then, in the middle of January, old wounds were reopened. Chelsea, found guilty of making irregular payments to players, were fined £105,000. 'No comment', said chairman Ken Chapman diplomatically, but former director Lionel Smart admitted to being puzzled. 'I think that what people will be asking, is why, when the two cases seem so similar, is there such a difference between the decisions.' Lionel was correct. Swindonians were asking just that.

Former Swindon chairman Brian Hillier was also nonplussed. Serving a three-year ban from football as a result of Town's financial situation, he announced 'My sentence was prejudged and

Swindon were also made a scapegoat.' Even Exeter City weren't happy. 'It stinks', secretary Stuart Brailey told the *Daily Mirror*. That Chelsea chairman Ken Bates was a member of the League management committee hardly helped stem accusations of a cover-up, and his resignation from the committee followed.

Adding grist to the mill, Lou Macari then attacked Town after his appointment as manager of Birmingham City. Along with Hillier, Macari still faced potential tax charges through his connection with the County Ground and had already been fined £1,000 for his involvement. 'I had five happy years at Swindon. What I have been through in the last 12 months has made me a lot harder about the facts of life', said the ex-Town boss.

Meanwhile, Duncan's form in front of goal had been consistent. After five goals in the first five weeks of the season, he had been missed during his absence through injury in October, but came back with a goal in a 2–2 draw at Leicester. By the last game of 1990, Shearer had hit 11 in the League, half his total for the season, and a strike at Ashton Gate in the middle of January completed a satisfying 4–0 rout of Bristol City. A week later, two Shearer goals brought a home win over Hull City, but just one win in the next nine left Town nervously looking at the wrong end of the table.

A major feature of Shearer's season so far was the absence of a barren spell in front of goal, and a run of five games without a goal after that match with Hull constituted something of a crisis for the Scotsman. It did little for Swindon either, with just one victory claimed over the period. This wasn't what fans had expected when Swindon had set out to force the League's punishment back down their throats. All the off-field wrangling was taking its toll as players fought to keep their concentration on the pitch.

A 2–1 home win over Sheffield Wednesday on 19 February brought the only maximum points haul in 10 weeks of trying. Mid-March brought a 2–2 home draw with Oldham and a goal from Town's top scorer. The results might still be faltering, but Duncan was determined to do his stuff. On 6 March it was announced that another of last season's Wembley heroes was flying the Robins nest, when full-back Paul Bodin moved east to Crystal Palace for a fee of £500,000. Bodin was sad to leave Wiltshire after three years, but the move reflected the ongoing financial difficulties.

Shortly after the Welshman's departure, the club made an announcement. It was estimated that demotion from the First Division had cost the club almost £1 million, with £150,000 still owed to the Inland Revenue. Town were continuing to pay the price of enforced demotion.

Shearer's name was one of those in the referee's goalscorers book in a 3–2 win in the last match in March when Town entertained Newcastle United. A Micky Hazard penalty, Shearer's 18th League goal of the season and a Colin Calderwood close-range stabbed shot claimed Town the 3–2 win. Calderwood's goal was the icing on the cake for the well-respected centre-back. Forced out with knee ligament damage in the 1–0 victory over Wolves back in September, 24 League games had passed before Colin had recovered sufficiently to return to first-team action. His goal in his fourth game back was indicative of the influence the skipper had on the team.

Colin's return was a well-timed boost. A week earlier another cheque had been dangled in front of the Town board, resulting in central-defensive partner Jon Gittens making his way back to former club Southampton. £400,000 came Town's way, but another member of the playing staff had been sacrificed at the altar of financial pressures. Then came another bombshell, as the win over Newcastle United was superseded as the biggest story of the weekend. Jim Smith's resignation from St James' Park had brought denials from Town chairman Ken Chapman that Ossie Ardiles's name was in the frame to replace him, but on April Fool's Day and after tendering his resignation in Wiltshire, new Newcastle manager Ardiles watched his side lose 2–0 at home to Bristol Rovers.

The move might have been considered a little unusual, as Ardiles had been connected with spiritual home White Hart Lane back in November when Tottenham Hotspur's managerial scene looked unstable. Instead, a move to the North East, taking Tony Galvin as his assistant, opened the way for ex-teammate Glenn Hoddle to replace him at Swindon on 4 April. Ardiles said 'The selling of players played a big part in my decision.' Finances and unrest had cost Town their League position, key members of the playing staff and their manager in the space of just eight months.

The draw with Newcastle left Town 17th with nine games to play, and with six of those lost, Town's 21st-place finish was just about safe, but massively disappointing when compared with the pre-season determination to reclaim what had been taken by the authorities. When the final League table was published, it showed Swindon two places and two points clear of the drop zone. A restructuring of the top flight saw the numbers in Division Two reshuffled and just two teams, Hull City and West Bromwich Albion, took the plunge into Division Three. The events of the

Shearer heads home his first and Town's second equaliser in a 3–3 draw at Plymouth in April 1991.

Another goal modestly celebrated.

previous summer had produced an unhealthy persecution complex among Swindon supporters and there were many who felt the authorities had been conspiring to ensure the club suffered the relegation to Division Three that the Football League had always wanted.

A 2–2 draw at Leicester City back in October had seen David Kerslake sent off just three minutes into the match, and three minutes of seemingly unwarranted injury time was enough for City to grab the goal that shared the points. It was Duncan's first game back from injury and it was he who opened the scoring. After the 5–1 loss at Barnsley three days later, during which central defender Jon Gittens was dismissed, Town assistant manager Chic Bates said 'It just makes you wonder if truth were known – have the League got it in for Swindon this season? These comments could get me into trouble, but when you get decisions like we have had, something has to be said.'

Unsurprisingly, the club were called before the League to explain their comments.

The season had been one long roller coaster of emotions for everyone connected with the club. Town had been associated with Divisions One, Two and Three and staved off the threat of on-the-pitch relegation that the Football League had wanted in the first place. It seemed every week had brought a new story about the cash situation at the County Ground and fresh rumblings of new, behind-the-scenes allegations. Ready to feel bitter, paranoid fans and officials eyed every referee's decision with suspicion.

A new transfer record was set as McLoughlin left for Southampton, and a new manager was installed months afterwards. Results had swung wildly as the club tried to keep its mind on the action on the pitch. The one steadying influence had been Duncan Shearer, who had calmly gone about his business of scoring goals, and at the end of the season he was rewarded with the Player of the Year trophy for 1990–91. Typically downbeat as the season had generally been, the presentation took place before defeat at the County Ground at the hands of Barnsley. A week later the season came to a close with a 3–1 defeat at Port Vale. What a contrast to the euphoria of the previous May.

Twelve months on and enough progress had been made by new manager Glenn Hoddle during 1991–92 to challenge for a promotion place once more. Duncan was still doing his stuff and as Town threatened to grab a Play-off place, Blackburn Rovers were downwardly mobile from the top spot they had occupied most of the season.

An offer that was too good to refuse came in on transfer deadline day from the team who were bankrolled by steel magnate Jack Walker, and terrace hero Duncan Shearer's Swindon career was over. The loss of his goals cost Town a Play-off place and helped cement Rovers' eventual elevation to Division One. In return, Town received a cheque for £800,000 and Duncan's 22 League goals still left him Town's top scorer once more by a 12-goal margin.

Always ready to feel hard done by, Town fans noted that he played just six League matches for his new club and just once in the Play-offs themselves, scoring only one goal in the blue and white of Rovers. Then he was sold on again, back to familiar territory with a return to Scotland and Aberdeen in July 1992. Replaced at Ewood Park by namesake Alan Shearer, there were wry comments that Rovers manager Kenny Dalglish might have initially bought the wrong one. Town supporters were in little doubt, though, that by depriving Swindon of their top scorer, Blackburn had achieved everything they needed to clinch a Play-off place.

Back in Scotland under Aberdeen manager Willie Miller, things continued well for Duncan. Twenty-two League goals, a number that Duncan seemed to make a habit of throughout his career, left him the Dons' top scorer by a comfortable margin in a season that saw his team finish second to Glasgow Rangers. Coupled with appearances in both the Scottish FA and the Scottish League Cup Finals, even defeat by two goals to one against Rangers in both would not have tasted too sour. Duncan played in both Finals and scored in the League Cup version.

The following year brought Groundhog Day. The same League position, again behind Rangers, with Shearer top marksman again. The success brought the Dons a UEFA Cup place, and while that was a new experience for Duncan, it was a slightly bitter one. A preliminary two-legged win tie with Latvian side Skonto Riga brought elimination on the away goals rule at the first hurdle.

Nothing lasts forever. Just nine goals in 1994–95 left Duncan second in the goalscoring pecking order behind Billy Dodds and left Aberdeen ninth, avoiding relegation in a Play-off match with

Dunfermline. That looked like heralding the beginning of the end of Duncan's playing career. Half of his 30 appearances in 1995–96 saw him come off the bench, but Aberdeen were resurgent with a third-place finish, and a goal in a 2–0 win over Dundee claimed Shearer a League Cup-winners' medal.

But his swansong as an Aberdeen player was near. The 1996–97 season saw him make just two starts from 21 outings and 1997–98 produced a move to upwardly mobile Second Division Inverness Caledonian Thistle.

At a new club there, was life in the old dog yet. Twenty-four appearances, five goals and a new role as youth development officer followed under boss Steve Paterson. Twelve months later and at the age of 35, Duncan was still scoring. Twelve goals in 30 appearances helped Thistle to second place and promotion, and in 1999 big Duncan was installed as Paterson's number two, his last League appearance coming in a 3–2 defeat at St Mirren on 21 August 1999. Then, in December 2002 and after two near misses with promotion to the top flight in Scotland, the management duo were tempted to Pittodrie to take the reins at Shearer's old club. It was not to be the most successful of moves and 12 months later they were both gone.

Duncan Shearer Prestige Hospitality was formed to offer corporate hospitality packages, but a return to football management took Duncan to Highland League side Buckie Thistle and brought an upturn in the Jags' fortunes at Victoria Park. The season of 2006–07 saw Thistle challenge for both the League title and a Highland League Cup double under Duncan's command, but Keith pipped the Jags to both trophies to claim their own double.

It had not been until Duncan transferred his talents from England to the Scottish Premier Division that he was called to the world stage. After returning to his familiar stomping ground it was perhaps easier to attract the attention of the national team manager. Craig Brown selected Duncan to represent Scotland in a friendly with Austria on 20 April 1994, where he replaced John McGinlay in Vienna. Unable to get on the score sheet in the 2–1 victory that day, it wasn't to be long before Shearer made his international goalscoring mark.

Five weeks later, a trip to Utrecht saw the Scots take on Holland, where again McGinlay made way for Duncan. The result might have gone against the Scots, but the 3–1 loss was notable for Duncan's first-ever international strike with nine minutes of the match remaining. Brown was plainly testing the water with his new striking option.

On 7 September Scotland travelled to Finland as the 1996 European Championship qualifiers commenced and, 29 minutes into the game, Duncan added to his international goalscoring record. His strike gave his country the lead, which when added to a second from John Collins, gave Scotland a good start to the qualifying campaign. In March 1995 Duncan was off to Russia, where he took to the field in place of Darren Jackson. A 0–0 draw kept the qualifying campaign on course and a month later Shearer was again involved in a 2–0 win in San Marino.

Duncan Shearer lifts the Player of the Year award of 1991.

But there was a pattern developing. Substituted by John Spencer in the second half, the bench was featuring prominently in the ex-Swindon star's international career and Craig Brown appeared to harbour doubts about his suitability for his side. A trip to the Faroe Islands a month later secured another 2–0 win, bringing Scotland closer to qualification for Euro '96 in England and also bringing Duncan's sixth international cap.

Thus far Duncan's international caps had all been gained on foreign soil, but the 1–0 win over Greece in August at Hampden saw Duncan finally play international football in his home country. Sadly, his substitution by Ally McCoist in the 71st minute saw him leave the field and brought his career to a close. He had played a role in taking his country to the Finals of a major football competition, but he was to be discarded before the final tournament in the home of the Sassenachs would take place.

It is interesting to compare Duncan Shearer's Swindon career with that of the man who was bought to replace him. Craig Maskell cost £225,000 in the summer of 1992 and scored 20 goals in his first season. The fees and goalscoring records are similar to those of Duncan. Like Duncan, Craig had played for Huddersfield, where he scored 43 times in 87 League appearances, eerily similar to Shearer's 38 in 83 matches. And the two are again almost twins in that they both played for Town at Wembley, with Maskell trumping his predecessor by getting on the score sheet.

Yet Duncan won the Player of the Year and Maskell didn't. Football supporters are a fickle bunch.

Paul Bodin

(1992–93) ~ Fixed penalty

After Duncan Shearer's success as the fans' favourite, for reasons that will become clearer later it is necessary to jump a season to 1992–93 to pick up the story of Swindon Town and the destination of the club's Player of the Year award.

Paul Bodin signed for Town on 7 March 1988, and the deal spoke volumes about the depth of knowledge manager Lou Macari had of the game that existed outside the glare of publicity that the top stars inhabited.

Born in Cardiff on 13 September 1964, left-back Paul had started his footballing life as a junior at Chelsea. Released by the Blues in January 1982, he was snapped up by Newport County, who brought him back to his South Wales roots. County were to face major problems in the future, but at the time were playing their football in Division Three, and, it has to be said, doing so somewhat more successfully than Swindon Town. At the end of the season Town faced relegation to Division Four, while County finished six places and six points higher, but by August of that year Paul had moved on to home-town club Cardiff City without making an appearance at Somerton Park.

There, despite playing almost 90 times for the Bluebirds, during which time he helped City to promotion to Division Two, Paul was allowed to leave on a free transfer to Gola League side Bath City in the summer of 1985. There seemed little indication that his career was to reach the heights that his ability would eventually justify. Three seasons of non-League football followed, but just before Macari made his move Newport County decided they might have been a little hasty and threw their hat into the ring once more. £15,000 changed hands in January 1988 and Bodin was back in the Football League. County's finances were so precarious, though, that six weeks later, when Lou offered twice what Bodin had cost Newport, the deal was forced through to bring the Welshman to Swindon.

Paul Bodin makes a challenge on Alan Shearer of Blackburn Rovers.

Paul spoke about his rapid elevation through football's ranks to Division Two. 'It's going to be tough but I can't wait. The last few weeks have restored my confidence.' His impact was not immediate and it wasn't until January 1989 that a

Paul Bodin signs for Lou Macari in March 1988.

consistent run in the first team was forthcoming. Then, with regular left-back Phil King's sale to Sheffield Wednesday in November the door was open for Paul to claim the number-three shirt on a permanent basis.

By the start of 1992–93 Bodin had been through the transition of an ill-fated £500,000 move to Crystal Palace. Eagles manager Steve Coppell was the man who had taken him to London, and after just nine starts he appeared to change his mind about his acquisition. The deal contained a clause that sent extra cash back to Wiltshire after Paul had played 15 times for Palace, and with Bodin on 14 appearances and the pen poised over the cheque, Coppell seemed to decide that he did not want to part with any more money. A loan spell at Newcastle United under ex-boss Ossie Ardiles preceded a return to Wiltshire in January 1992 for Paul, and the fee agreed was just half of that which had taken him to Palace in the first place.

The man who gloried in the nickname of Zippy (believed to be because of his speed getting forward rather than any connection with the *Rainbow* character of the 1970s) was back in a Swindon shirt, and the best was yet to come.

Ironically, after all those years of trying and after the denial of the prize of First Division football in 1990, Swindon kicked off 1992–93 in Division One after all. Not satisfied with the majority of football's cash, the top teams broke away from the Football League to form the FA Premier League, taking even more of the money with them. That left Swindon as one of the most senior teams, as Division Two was renamed Division One.

Pre-season had been marred by Dave Bennett breaking his right leg in a comeback match at Yeovil. It was the fourth break of his career and he had only been on the field of play for 10 minutes. The unlucky Bennett would never again take to the professional field and he was released at the end of the season. Town's season proper started with the visit of Sunderland – beaten FA Cup finalists just months earlier and the side who had taken Swindon's place in the top flight despite being beaten in the Play-off Final of 1990. The game was won by a classic Glenn Hoddle strike from 30 yards, his first for the club. Four days later and Bodin scored from the penalty spot, the odd goal in seven that was responsible for a win over Bristol Rovers. His initial successful kick had to be retaken after someone strayed into the box. The second attempt was despatched and Town were 3–0 up at Rovers' temporary home of Twerton Park, Bath. It seemed a sweet homecoming for the ex-Bath City player.

But Rovers fought back and with the score at 4–2 and the match in the 88th minute, 'keeper Fraser Digby was adjudged to have handled a back pass. With the rules amended only that week to make such actions illegal, a free-kick crashed home as Town defenders lined the goalmouth. That made the last few minutes a little nervous for travelling Town fans, but six points were successfully claimed from the first six available. A 2–2 draw at Wolverhampton Wanderers was followed by a 4–1 home win over Cambridge United. A hat-trick from Craig Maskell, added to Shaun Taylor's third strike in four League games, left Town second in Division One as the first month of the season closed.

Then things slipped a little. Successive 2–2 home draws with local rivals Bristol Rovers and Oxford United put a dampener on the start, and it was 29 September before a win over Grimsby Town brought the first win of the month. Town had dropped out of the top half a dozen and their confidence was dented. The slip didn't appear to damage Bodin's reputation, though, and a call up for Wales' World Cup qualifier against Cyprus came through from manager Terry Yorath. But Paul's good news was followed by bad. A knee-ligament injury during Town's 3–1 defeat at Portsmouth the weekend before the international took place forced the unlucky defender to withdraw from the game in Limassol. A young Kevin Horlock came off the bench to fill in at left-back at Fratton Park.

A lengthy spell in the treatment room was on the cards and it would be the new year before Bodin was to pull on a first-team shirt again. Just to add insult to injury (in the most literal sense), former Town hero Alan McLoughlin, now at Fratton Park, scored Portsmouth's opening goal in the defeat.

October had generally brought a return to winning ways, with that loss at Fratton being the sole occasion that Town didn't claim maximum points. Home wins over Watford and Barnsley, coupled with a 5–1 victory over Notts County, were trumped by a marvellous 1–0 win over West Ham United at Upton Park.

The result would have been sweet for West Ham lad Martin Ling, whose charge on goal had drawn the free-kick from which Craig Maskell won the game. Another man with a smile on his face would have been stand-in left-back Horlock, who was an ex-Hammer trainee. Over the month Town had cemented their place at second in the table behind Newcastle United and things looked rosy.

At the end of October, though, came a familiar story, with the news that Town were in debt. The publishing of the annual accounts showed Town now owed a variety of creditors the hefty sum of £2.5 million, but with the playing staff valued at £3 million the books were considered acceptable. Clubs were blind to the now familiar effect of the Bosman ruling that stripped clubs of the opportunity to count their players as part of their financial assets by allowing them to walk away for nothing at the end of their contracts.

November saw a mixed bag of results. A home win over Southend brought the only three points from the five matches played. Balanced against the single defeat, again at home but this time against Brentford, Town slipped a little, but greater damage was done in December. Just two League matches were played during that month. Both were lost by four goals to two, and strangely Micky Hazard and Craig Maskell scored goals in each game. The second of those defeats came at Leicester City, five days before Christmas. By the time 1993 kicked off, Town had slipped out of the Play-off zone and Paul Bodin was back to match fitness.

During Paul's injury-enforced absence, Kevin Horlock had done his own reputation no harm at all as he gained valuable first-team experience. Deputising effectively at left-back, Kevin made 10 League appearances and might have had Paul wondering how long it would take to get his place back. Those two defeats as 1992 came to a close may have hastened his return.

A win over local rivals Oxford United is always celebrated by Town fans and the new year started with just that, Steve White claiming a 34th-minute goal that secured a win at the Manor Ground. The pause button had been pushed on Paul Bodin's season. Starting well but then losing almost three months through injury, he was about to launch into a run that would make his and Swindon's campaign. A goal at Grimsby on 26 January couldn't prevent defeat, but his 69th-minute strike at home to Wolves four days later was the only goal of the game and won the match.

As Paul said to the *Swindon Advertiser* afterwards, 'They could have snatched a draw at the end and maybe it was our turn for a bit of good fortune. There was an element of good luck with the goal – my first ever with my head – but it does not matter how they go in. I was not quite in the right position when Martin Ling first attempted to cross the ball, but it hit a defender and gave me a few extra seconds to get into the penalty area. In the end it was a tremendous cross and all I had to do was keep the ball down.'

A week later he did it again. A solitary 53rd-minute goal claimed Town's first-ever three-point haul at Roker Park, where Sunderland fell victim to the in-form, goalscoring defender. The game had seen 'keeper Fraser Digby save one penalty and then a second, after 95 minutes and awarded after the ball had struck Bodin's hand, was blasted wide for a hugely-important win. As Paul had suggested, perhaps luck was turning in favour of Town and when his goal put Town two goals to the good at home to Millwall in the middle of February, it provided the comfort zone to help produce a 3–0 victory.

Four games and a goal in each. Not all fullbacks are so prolific.

The month ended as it had started, Bodin's 88th-minute winner in a 1–0 win over promotion

rivals Portsmouth at the end of February again proving decisive. Pompey had fallen victim to a scrappy goal from a goalmouth mêlée and Bodin had laid the ghost of his injury against the same opposition back in October. The result allowed Town to leapfrog Pompey and Swindon were back to fourth in Division One.

Paul, however, was unassuming. 'It was a typical top-of-the-table clash with not too many chances around, and looked to be heading for a 0–0 draw. I just happened to be at the right place at the right time. After that it was a case of just making sure I hit the target and hoping for the best.' The goal was a bit of a collector's piece. 'It was on my wrong foot so I could hardly believe it when the ball hit the back of the net. I've scored a few recently, but this could be the most important of the lot.'

Everything seemed to be going well, so it was time for some bad developments. News from chairman Ray Hardman that Town were losing £12,000 for every home game they played brought a reality check, when a cheque was what was really needed. He estimated that crowds, at that stage averaging over 9,000, needed to increase by a further 5,000 to make up the difference.

There was plainly too much good news emanating from the County Ground. But performances on the pitch continued to be unreflective of the financial scene. As the season entered its last third, Town were more than handily placed to challenge for an automatic promotion spot. Newcastle United, under the leadership of Kevin Keegan, had set the pace all season. Hitting the top spot by the middle of September, the Magpies were destined to stay there until the end. When March commenced, United had just 14 matches to wait before they would reclaim the top division place they had vacated in 1989. A dreadful period for the North East club had seen them drop into the third tier of the Football League, but Keegan was guiding them home.

Hot on Newcastle's tails, West Ham United had consistently challenged for the top and had sat second in the table since the end of January. Both teams needed to visit the County Ground before the campaign was out, as did Play-off contenders Leicester City. Swindon had yet to travel to Tranmere Rovers, a team who also fancied their chances to finish strongly.

There was much to play for, and Town's destiny was in their own hands. An impressive 4–0 win at Watford brought a hat-trick for Steve White and continued the push for the top, and a week later it was Keegan's Magpies who were due to fly south to the Robins' nest. But before that and just ahead of Town's trip to Southend United came a furore that threatened to lose Town their manager. The board's decision to sell right-back David Kerslake to Leeds United led the *Western Daily Press* to proclaim that Glenn Hoddle was about to walk out. The deal brought in £500,000 for the Town's coffers but Hoddle was unhappy. It was believed that he would leave, taking assistant John Gorman with him, if any more of his squad were similarly disposed of.

Twenty-one-year-old Nicky Summerbee slotted into the right wing-back role for the game at Roots Hall and Town came away with a 1–1 draw. In light of the uncertainty regarding their manager, it might have been difficult for everyone to concentrate on footballing matters, but Newcastle United were in town and almost 18,000 packed into the County Ground to see the top-of-the-table clash. One man in particular could be relied upon to keep his focus. Paul Bodin hadn't scored for over two weeks. He ended that 'drought' with a 12-yard spot-kick, which, when added to a goal from skipper Colin Calderwood, bettered the one scored by United's David Kelly.

Keegan's side's defeat did little to damage their promotion party and they would win eight of the remaining 11 matches before the curtain came down on the season. A home win over Bristol City was achieved on 24 March and brought the usual kudos associated with a triumph over a near neighbour. The game, which finished 2–1, was again won from the penalty spot, so that was another to add to Bodin's tally, but the show was stolen by home debutant Brian Marwood, who scored a spectacular diving header to open the scoring. The home win was Town's sixth on the trot. The season was about to enter its last full month of regular action, and there were to be two extraordinary matches that might never be forgotten.

On 27 March Swindon took the short trip along the M4 to Brentford. The Bees had struggled all season and were desperate to claim the points that would lift them away from the wrong end of the table. Thirty-two goalless minutes into the match, striker Steve White was dismissed from the field for the use of an elbow on Keith Millen. Fellow striker Dave Mitchell felt the Brentford man had overreacted to elicit a response from referee Vic Callow and minutes later, his own foul on Millen brought the Aussie a yellow card. Two minutes before half-time, Mitchell made another reckless challenge on the same man and red was flashed again. Nine-strong Swindon had 45 minutes to play, without a striker on the field.

The second half was one long exercise of backs to the wall. Without a man to find up front, Town used speedy counter-attacks whenever they could break out of defence. With time running out and still no goals for either side, Hoddle combined with Shaun Close and Paul Bodin was released down the left. His rocket shot was an inch or two wide of claiming what would have been an astonishing victory, but Town supporters celebrated the point as though the game had been won. The following week Bodin was back on target with the goal that sealed a 1–0 win over Peterborough. Played through by Hoddle, Paul raced into the penalty box to fire past 'keeper Ian Bennett from 15 yards, but the trip to Tranmere to play promotion rivals Rovers three days later ended 3–1 to the home side and allowed the Prenton Park side to make up some ground on Hoddle's team. On Easter Monday came the second of those memorable away matches that punctuated the 1992–93 season.

Like Brentford before them, Birmingham City had not been enjoying a good season. Nineteenth in the table and with five games remaining, there was the real threat that the Blues might drop into Division Two. Meanwhile, Swindon travelled to St Andrews in the fourth place that they had occupied for much of the last two months. The game turned out to be a classic.

Typical concentration by Paul Bodin.

The match was 25 minutes old and central defender Shaun Taylor was off the pitch receiving 10 stitches to a head wound, when a slip by Ross MacLaren allowed City to take the lead. Four minutes later and Town were two down, the ball cleared from a Swindon corner allowing City to break from defence to double their lead. Then, with Taylor back on the pitch, the brave centre-back powered home a header to bring the team back into the match. At half-time it was 2–1 to Birmingham.

Six minutes into the second half and the home team had added two more goals. Losing by 4–1 away from home, what chance did the team have with promotion on their minds? On the hour Craig Maskell pulled one back, and five minutes later Dave Mitchell, back from suspension, headed home to make it 4–3. Then, with less than quarter of an hour remaining, MacLaren, Martin Ling and Maskell put together a move that gave Mitchell the opportunity to square the match at four goals apiece. Twelve minutes from the end a Paul Bodin corner found Maskell's head and incredibly Town were in the lead. With the game in its last minute, Mitchell beat both defender Trevor Matthewson and 'keeper Andy Gosney to complete his hat-trick. Birmingham City 4, Swindon Town 6.

Breathless travelling Town supporters could hardly believe what they'd seen and feverishly acclaimed their heroes at the final whistle. How on earth could a team able to come back from such a position not claim promotion at the end of the season? It is impossible to tell whether the pressure on Hoddle's team had taken its toll, or whether his players started to feel too confident after showing such invincibility, but only two points were taken from the remaining four matches of the season.

A 1–1 home draw with Leicester City was followed by a similar score at Notts County as Bodin notched his 11th goal of the season, typically from the penalty spot and in the 40th minute. In May came the last two matches of the Division One season. Both were lost, the last at home by three goals to one against West Ham United, but Town had confirmed fifth place in the table and claimed a Play-off place. The season had still to reach its dramatic climax.

Before that, though, Paul Bodin had the honour of accepting the supporters' Player of the Year award. 'The goals have been flowing in but I never expected this,' said Town's favourite of the season. 'It's my first award of this kind and it really does mean a lot to me. It's something else to be chosen for an award by the fans. People pay a lot of money to watch us play and it's nice to think they appreciate what they see.'

'I still can not explain the goalscoring phenomenon,' he continued, but showing a focus for the task still to be completed, he finished 'It's great to pick up individual awards but this is a team game and promotion remains the biggest prize of all.' The presentation came ahead of the home game with West Ham, but Paul missed the match, having been injured in a previous midweek game for Wales. Town supporters, though, needn't have worried that their goalscoring fullback would be either injured or distracted before the big test of the Play-offs.

As expected, the United's of Newcastle and West Ham took the automatic promotion spots, leaving Portsmouth, Tranmere Rovers, Swindon Town and Leicester City to fight it out through the Play-offs for the prize to compete with English football's elite. With Town finishing fifth and Tranmere Rovers fourth, the two teams were to face each other to decide who went to Wembley for the Final. The two League fixtures between the clubs had seen the points shared equally. A Dave Mitchell brace in February gave Town a 2–0 victory at the County Ground, and a hat-trick from Rovers' Kenny Irons wrapped up the points at Prenton Park in April, despite Mitchell's third strike against them.

On 16 May 14,230 gathered at the County Ground to watch the first leg of the Play-off semi-final. At stake: a place at Wembley to contest the last promotion place for elevation to the new Premier League. The TV cameras were in Swindon to capture the action and anyone arriving late would still be kicking themselves. The game was just two minutes old when Tranmere defender Steve Vickers forced the ball from Dave Mitchell. From the resultant throw-in, Nicky Summerbee swung in a cross that Vickers, under pressure from Mitchell, headed powerfully past his own 'keeper Eric Nixon.

Within a minute, Vickers knocked another Summerbee cross straight to Ross MacLaren, whose parried shot was turned into the net by Mitchell. If Town supporters felt sorry for the unfortunate Vickers, it was hard to tell. John Aldridge then had a headed 'goal' ruled out before Craig Maskell intercepted a Vickers ball in midfield to put Mitchell through. One on one with Nixon, he squared to Maskell to put Town 3–0 up. Just before the hour John Morrissey pulled a goal back to give the away team hope, but a 3–1 defeat was the best they could muster. Given the chance, Swindon fans might well have voted Steve Vickers Town's Man of the Match.

Up on Merseyside three days later, the drama continued in the second leg. A Martin Ling run allowed John Moncur to restore Town's three-goal aggregate advantage before a wounded Tranmere came storming back. Mark Proctor reduced the arrears before Pat Nevin netted from a Fraser Digby fumble. At the other end, Craig Maskell's attempt was saved before he composed himself to crash home the loose ball. It was 5–3 to Town overall, but when Glenn Hoddle made an uncharacteristic challenge in the box, Kenny Irons's successful penalty-kick left Town with a very nervous last seven minutes. Fingernails were chewed but the score remained the same. Swindon were through to meet Leicester City at Wembley with a Premier League place to be awarded to the winners.

And what a day it was to be.

The following is a piece I did for Swindon Town's match day programme in 2003, as the club and fans spent the season remembering the events of 10 years earlier.

'On Saturday 31 May 2003 I raised a toast in commemoration of the day 10 years earlier when Glenn Hoddle's team fulfilled the dream of all Town supporters. The events at the national stadium in 1993 laid the ghost of a similar day in 1990 which had given me sleepless nights for far too long, and Swindon were finally installed in the top flight.

Town, of course, had qualified for the First Division 1992–93 Play-off Final through a high-scoring aggregate win over Tranmere Rovers and 12 days later, most of north Wiltshire were Wembley bound to face Leicester City.

My memories are still vivid and are replicated by 30,000 other Town supporters. Red and white ribbons tied around car aerials. Coach after coach on the M4, all displaying Town flags. The early start to spend as much time enjoying the day as possible. The pre-entry wander around the stadium to soak up the atmosphere. The chants of 'Red Army…Red Army…Red Army.' Forty-two minutes of sparring, tit for tat, then Craig Maskell's back heel…Glenn Hoddle's precise finish. Half-time wondering, praying, wishing for the score to stay in our favour.

Only three minutes into the second period, and John Moncur's ball to Craig Maskell wide on the left. Craigo's fantastic finish in the top right-hand corner. Another five minutes. Nicky Summerbee's toilet paper-encased right-footed corner. The poor Leicester clearance. Moncur's return into the box. Shaun Taylor's lunging, neck-straining header. 3–0! Surely! Four minutes later 'and Joachim buries the rebound', as the TV commentary put it. Ten minutes more and Steve Walsh has made it 3–2. A minute later, I've still got my head in my hands and Steve Thompson's made it 3–3.

On the rack. Leicester's tails up. Chalkie White on for Maskell after 78 minutes and slowly but surely, Town turn it around again. Ling has a shot well saved by Kevin Poole. Shaun Taylor's header from the corner is headed off the line. Dave Mitchell comes off second best in a one-on-one with the 'keeper. Then Hoddle's through ball to Chalkie. Over he goes. Referee David Elleray. PLEASE! Of course it was a penalty. After all, Geoff Hurst's shot was over the line wasn't it?

Paul Bodin steps up…YES!!! Still Town press. Hazard on for Moncur. Martin Ling sends in a 30-yard screamer. The clock ticks down. Then the whistle. The euphoria. The air-punching. The tears. The hand shakes. The presentation. The celebrations.

The game was heralded as the classic it was. Three goals in an 11-minute spell for Swindon had been matched by three in 12 by Leicester City. After a magnificent performance by John Moncur, the Man of the Match award was shaded by Martin Ling. The media, predictably, only had eyes for Glenn Hoddle and after a sprint back to Swindon the celebrations began in earnest. Old Town was one big party as traffic was forced to a standstill deep into the evening. It was de rigueur to include the passing police cars in the jubilation as smiles from citizens and law enforcement officers alike turned the area into a carnival.

I still can't pass under the motorway bridges close to Swindon without glancing up and visualising the flags and the waving, chanting, smiling throngs who didn't make the trip but greeted our return as though we personally had achieved greatness. I thank you if you were one of those on those bridges that made me feel that way. I defied the world to wipe the smile off my face.'

Cometh the hour, cometh the man. Paul Bodin had been scoring goals all season and it was his penalty with five minutes to go that settled the game that took Town to the Promised Land. The two teams had contested a high-scoring game in December when Leicester had run out winners by four goals to two. This time, and ultimately more importantly, Swindon had grabbed the four and secured the prize of promotion that went with it, and this time Swindon were allowed to keep it. Up where we belonged, as a celebratory record put it. The FA even changed the name of their flagship competition from the Premier League to the Premiership as if to join in the fun.

During Swindon's single season in the Premiership, Bodin finished as the club's second top scorer with seven. His dependability from the 12-yard spot was confirmed when five of them came through penalties. In the summer of 1996 Paul was handed an exit permit from the County Ground via a free transfer by manager Steve McMahon, despite announcing his readiness to slash his salary demands to stay with Town. He went on to make 41 appearances for Reading and five on loan at Wycombe Wanderers before returning to Dr Martens Premier League side Bath City. There he assumed the position of manager, appointing ex-colleague and fellow Wembley hero Steve White as his deputy. However, in May 2001, after three years at the helm, Bodin quit as boss at Twerton. He returned to Swindon, where a coaching position with another ex-teammate Tom Jones at Dr Martens League Swindon Supermarine followed, and then went back to the County Ground as manager of the Under-15s team.

On the world stage, Paul's international career had begun with an Under-21 call up against Yugoslavia in 1983 while he was at Cardiff City, but his full international record spanned four years. Starting with a 1–0 win over Costa Rica in a friendly in May 1990, it ended as a non-playing substitute in a 1–1 win with Albania in Tirana in an European Championship qualifier under Mike Smith in September 1994. The last brought his 23rd cap for his country, 16 of which came while he also wore the red of Swindon Town. He scored three times in all for Wales. Terry Yorath, manager of Wales between 1988 and 1994, valued the Town fullback so highly that he awarded him all but one of his full caps.

A proud family man shows off his Welsh caps.

On 17 November 1993, the day that England conceded in nine seconds in San Marino in a

Paul Bodin is awarded the Swindon Town Player of the Year award.

group from which qualification was already impossible, Wales faced Romania at Cardiff Arms Park. A win would have taken Wales to the World Cup Finals in the US, but with the score at 1–1 Bodin's penalty hit the bar. The game finished 2–1 to the visitors and Wales were out. The defeat cost manager Terry Yorath a renewed contract and heralded the end of Bodin's international career. Welsh readers may be excused a grimace when hearing comments of Paul's accuracy from 12 yards!

Who would have thought, back at the end of the 1980s, that Bodin, plying his trade at the Conference level of English football and hoping to re-establish himself in the Football League, would one day be representing his country and holding the hopes of his nation in his hands from the 12-yard spot? It's difficult to overestimate the importance of Paul Bodin's contribution throughout the season of 1992–93. Starting in the second match of the season, his penalty at Bristol Rovers turned a match that could so easily have finished in a draw into a victory for Town, and in a run of four goals in four matches during January and February, his strikes produced two 1–0 wins.

From then until the end of the season, further goals from the defender were responsible for victory on four occasions, and a point was rescued by his spot-kick at Notts County as the regular season neared its conclusion. His haul left the Welshman with 11 goals over 46 Division One matches, a total that made the defender Town's second top scorer behind Craig Maskell.

Altogether, 15 points would have slipped through Town's fingers if Paul hadn't hit the net in the games that he did. That would have left Swindon marooned in mid-table, and any striker would be proud of such an influence on his club's fortunes. And perhaps the most important strike of all, surely the most important spot-kick in the club's history, came at Wembley, after the fans had already voted Paul Bodin their chief man of the season.

John Moncur
(1993–94) ~ Premiership star in waiting

After over a century of trying and a false start in 1990, Swindon Town had finally made it to the top flight of English football. The partying was to go on throughout the summer, but soon after promotion had been confirmed a dampener was placed on proceedings with the news that manager Glenn Hoddle was to quit Wiltshire.

Chelsea chairman Ken Bates had recently parted company with club manager David Webb, and as he scanned fellow clubs for a replacement his eyes alighted on the highly rated ex-England midfielder. Even though the major development of Chelsea Village was still to take place, the surrounds of Stamford Bridge looked palatial when compared with the homely environs of the County Ground. Hoddle was tempted and even as the celebrational, open-decked bus tour to mark promotion took place, the boss was carefully fielding questions regarding his plans for next season.

On Thursday 3 June, just three days after victory at Wembley, Hoddle tendered his resignation at the County Ground to take up the vacant role at Chelsea. The announcement enraged many of the fans that the now ex-manager left behind. 'How could he lead Swindon to Shangri La, then walk away without ever consummating the results of his actions?' they asked. The board moved fast. Hoddle had been player as well as manager and relied heavily on a valued and trusted colleague on the sidelines, watching the field of play and advising accordingly. After initially looking as though he would accompany his friend to Chelsea, Glenn's number two, John Gorman, was collared as he left the County Ground and persuaded to step up to occupy the vacant managerial seat and steady the (Premier!)ship. A couple of weeks later, Gorman announced the appointment of David Hay as his second-in-command and a brave new era was under way.

Moncur shows a clean pair of heels against Everton.

Then, as if losing the player-manager wasn't bad enough, the long-serving and well-respected captain decided London was the place for him as well.

In July Colin Calderwood had indicated his hope that Town could match his new salary aspirations, but as his contract ran out at the end of the month, Spurs offered the deal that Town couldn't and Colin was bound for White Hart Lane. He moved to Tottenham Hotspur to replace Neil Ruddock as Razor travelled north to Liverpool.

It was a decision that disappointed everyone at Swindon, but few begrudged the Scot the opportunity to try his hand at what was undeniably a bigger club after such loyal and distinguished service. The fee would be set by tribunal at £1.25 million, but half of that sum was due to former club Mansfield Town, who made the defender the Stag's most lucrative piece of business ever. After 330 games for Swindon, the move was surely a big success for the centre-back. Another 160 matches at Spurs and a trip to the World Cup Finals in France to represent his country in 1998 proved that. But the loss of the skipper left another huge hole to fill.

The new managerial team set about rebuilding the squad in readiness for the exciting challenge ahead, signing Norwegian international striker Jan Aage Fjortoft from Rapid Vienna for £500,000 in July. Dutch midfielder Luc Nijholt came in from Motherwell for £175,000 on the day that Calderwood departed, and with the ex-captain's fee still to be set, the board took a flier by investing another half a million in Leyton Orient's Adrian Whitbread to fill Calderwood's boots.

Ready to greet the new arrivals was a man who had starred in the Wembley match that had brought promotion in May. John Moncur had been brought to the County Ground in 1992 by Hoddle himself, and there must have been times when the young Moncur cursed the fact that he had to vie for a Tottenham place with the Spurs legend. He had begun as an apprentice at White Hart Lane and turned professional in August 1984. At the time, his mentor had made over 300 League outings in midfield for Spurs, while another man occupying a midfield berth was Ossie Ardiles. Moncur must have realised the need to be patient.

And patient he was. It was a three-year wait and the last day of 1986–87 before he made his Spurs debut. Hoddle departed for Monaco in June, but even then opportunities for Moncur were few and far between, and the following season he made just one more appearance. During 1989–90, John's frustration must have been growing. A mere five Spurs games were added to his League career, but perhaps his highlight came in a 2–1 defeat at Derby where he scored Spurs' only goal of the game. The season ended with Tottenham in third place in the Division One table, but John could have been forgiven for getting itchy feet.

February 1991 finally brought him an extended run of eight consecutive appearances, so by the time the season was reaching its conclusion 12 months later and John had yet to get as much as a sniff of first-team action, it was hardly surprising that he was ready to accept the challenge of a move to Swindon. Forced to tout himself to other clubs in order to gain first-team experience,

John Moncur challenges Ipswich Town's Eddie Youds in a 2–2 home draw in November 1993.

by the time Moncur signed for Swindon he had spent loan spells at Doncaster Rovers (where he made his League debut in 1986), Cambridge United, Portsmouth, Brentford, Ipswich Town and Nottingham Forest, making 28 appearances in all. That total was more than the 5ft 7in Stepney-born player made for Spurs throughout his entire Tottenham career, so when his ex-colleague came waving an £80,000 cheque on transfer deadline day in 1992, the choice was stark. At the age of 25 it was time for John Moncur to cut the apron strings that tied him to White Hart Lane and had stunted his progress for far too long.

When it came to evaluating a midfielder, Glenn Hoddle could surely be considered something of an authority, and it must have been quite a fillip to Moncur that his abilities were obviously valued by the Swindon boss. Interviewed in the programme John said, 'When Glenn came along I had no second thoughts. It is obviously a big change but it's better to feel wanted. Spurs looked after me, however I am now at the stage where I really have to establish myself in top-class football. Glenn told me I was suited to the Swindon style, though if I don't perform he won't play me. After so long in the reserves it will take me a little time to find my sharpness.'

Injury blighted his first full season at Swindon and he made just 14 League appearances, but he was back to full fitness in time for the Play-offs and made the three-match tournament his own, with a goal at Tranmere Rovers and an outstanding performance at Wembley. By the time Swindon kicked off the Premiership season of 1993–94, Moncur was ready to make up for lost time. The season started on 14 August with an away match at Bramall Lane as Town faced Sheffield United for their historic first-ever game as a top-flight team.

The Blades had finished the previous season just three points off the relegation zone and, while there was some disappointment that Town's long-awaited campaign should start away from home, there was a feeling that United just might offer one of the least testing challenges that Swindon would face over the next 10 months. A point or three would be a morale-boosting start to the campaign.

Oh, that it should have been so.

Forced to wear socks from the United club shop to avoid a colour clash, Swindon fell behind from a free-kick after 21 minutes. But as the second half began, Town scored their first-ever goal as a Premiership side. Craig Maskell was brought down outside the Blades penalty area and as the home side organised their defensive wall, Moncur elbowed his teammates out of the way and fired the free-kick past 'keeper Alan Kelly. Moncur told the *Advertiser* 'I asked the ref before I struck the free-kick if I could take it, and he nodded.' Demonstrating the inconsistencies of football, John added 'I scored one like that when I was on loan at Brentford and the ref disallowed it.'

By the end of the afternoon, though, Sheffield United had scored twice more and Swindon had lost their inaugural match at the top level by three goals to one. Four days later almost 12,000 filed into the County Ground to witness Wiltshire's Premiership debut. Oldham Athletic were the opposition and with the game tied at 0–0 and in its 90th minute, Paul Bernard won the game for the visitors. The Latics had escaped the drop on goal difference the previous season and some Swindon fans were already experiencing a feeling of concern. Town had played two of the easiest

Moncur beat Arsenal's John Jensen to the ball in April 1994.

games they might expect all season and had left the pitch without a point to their name on each occasion. And next up in Swindon were Liverpool.

Ahead of the game with the Anfield giants, due to go out live to a watching Sky TV audience, manager John Gorman moved to spice up his forward line. Twenty-nine-year-old Andy Mutch was separated from his long-term strike partner Steve Bull at Wolverhampton Wanderers, splitting up a prolific forward line and giving the England B international the chance to prove he could do it on his own. The deal cost Town £250,000 and a baptism of fire awaited. By half-time Liverpool were two goals to the good. Neil Ruddock forced home from close range before Steve McManaman doubled the lead. If the margin slightly flattered the visitors, then there could be little complaint when McManaman added his second and Ronnie Whelan and Mike Marsh completed the scoring.

So, 5–0 to the away side and Town were bottom of the table on zero points, while the margin of victory left Liverpool top on goal difference with nine. Then came another trouncing, as Southampton became the next team to stick five past 'keeper Fraser Digby. Ex-Saint Craig Maskell scored a late penalty at the Dell, but it was small consolation as Matthew Le Tissier ran riot with two goals and a commanding display in midfield. The last game of the month produced Town's first-ever Premiership point in a goalless draw at Norwich City. Already anchored to the bottom of the table, everyone agreed that this Premiership lark was going to be tough. It was not what anyone who had cheered Town on at Wembley three months earlier had hoped for.

On the first day of September, Swindon slipped to another home defeat, this one at the hands of Manchester City. One nil up through a Nicky Summerbee strike on the hour, Town conceded three times in the last 15 minutes. After that Swindon's defence was reinforced with the acquisition of Terry Fenwick from Tottenham, and he came off the bench as a replacement for Kevin Horlock as Town claimed a goalless draw at Upton Park against West Ham. Seven games into the season and Town had collected just two points. The statistics showed why.

That opening-day strike by Moncur, coupled with the penalty by Craig Maskell at the Dell and the goal from Summerbee against future employers Manchester City, comprised the entire haul in front of goal. In contrast, Town's defence had been breached a massive 17 times. Neither newly-signed strikers Jan Aage Fjortoft or Andy Mutch had managed to get on the score sheet, placing greater pressure on the rearguard. With figures like that any improvement would be welcomed, and eventually a slight change for the better in front of goal was about to start turning defeats into draws. In a home game with Newcastle United that saw Paul Bodin's penalty saved before the visitors scored from their own spot-kick minutes later, Martin Ling and Andy Mutch scored the brace that cancelled out a two-goal deficit.

The last game of the month brought the toughest challenge so far – the match that would have been the first to look for when the fixtures were published. On 25 September Town travelled to Old Trafford to take on champions Manchester United. After 77 minutes the footballing world was proceeding to order. United had scored three times and Swindon were on course for another harsh Premiership lesson. Then Andy Mutch glanced home a Micky Hazard cross, and 10 minutes later Paul Bodin netted past Peter Schmeichel from the penalty spot after Steve White had been felled. White, though, was convinced referee Joe Worrall had denied Swindon the chance of a goal after Gary Pallister had upended the veteran striker in the penalty area minutes before. In the dying seconds Mark Hughes hit another to end the match 4–2 to the home side, and for most of football's followers the score was all they would notice. Manchester United had humbled little Swindon Town as expected, but after a battling performance Town left the pitch with their heads held high.

But no points.

It had taken striker Steve White 34 years to make an appearance at Old Trafford, and his career total was just short of 500 League games by the time Swindon kicked off at the top. In contrast, John Moncur's total was just 64, but his 21 games at Tottenham Hotspur, while being sparse in number, had been made against some quality opposition. Who was the better prepared for the challenge?

October came and went with Gorman's men still searching for that first elusive win. Creditable consecutive 1–1 results at home to Everton and a satisfying homecoming for John Moncur at Tottenham Hotspur brought more points. The game at White Hart Lane saw David Kerslake and Colin Calderwood feature for the home side and Moncur named Town's Man of the Match. John remained upbeat. 'The whole team showed great character and it's surely only a matter of time before we improve our League position,' he said. 'John Gorman and David Hay have always said there is no problem when we have the ball – our troubles start when we have to defend. But if we can keep going like this there should not be too much of a problem. Our midfield needs the ball – if we don't get it we don't tick.'

But after such a terrible start, drawn matches were never going to be enough to enhance Swindon's Premiership survival chances. Manager Gorman continued to search for an answer to Town's ills and on 18 November he moved for Wycombe Wanderers' striker Keith Scott. His patience had finally run out with the big-name, highly-priced front man Jan Aage Fjortoft, who had played 15 games and had yet to find the target.

It was a big step up for Scott, who had been playing non-League football just six months before, and the fee of £300,000, while big by Swindon's standards, reflected the gulf between the top and bottom teams in the Premiership. The 26-year-old made his debut in place of Fjortoft in the home game with Ipswich Town two days later, and it took the new man just 45 minutes to do what the Norwegian international had failed to do in over three months. His header on the stroke of half-time equalised a John Wark opener, but it was Wark's second-half penalty that gave the visitors the lead once more. Then Paul Bodin showed huge nerve by smashing home his own spot-kick with seven minutes to go, just 72 hours after missing that penalty for Wales in the World Cup qualifier. Two goals apiece.

Four days later came the event that Swindon supporters had almost stopped hoping for, and again Scott was the hero. Queen's Park Rangers came to town on Wednesday 24 November, lying eighth in the table and already 20 points ahead of Swindon. When Luc Nijholt was sent off for dissent after just 18 minutes, however, there appeared little likelihood that history was about to be made. Eight minutes before half-time, Keith Scott forced the ball home from an Andy Mutch knock down, and, despite the numerical disadvantage and well over half the match still to play, Town held on to a lead for the first time in 1,440 minutes of Premiership football.

Cue a pitch invasion more suited to a team who had clinched a trophy, than one who were now 'just' six points from safety. Christmas was approaching when Swindon took a trip to another of those destinations that would have had supporters licking their lips in anticipation at the beginning of the season. Anfield.

Moncur goes down from a challenge at Sheffield United.

With less than five minutes to go, and with the score Liverpool 1 Swindon Town 2, there was a real chance that Town's season might even yet be retrievable. Just how morale-boosting would it be to beat the former European champions on their own pitch and expunge the memory of that 5–0 home reverse back in August? Such a result would make huge inroads to rebuilding the shattered confidence of so much earlier heartbreak and there might just be enough of the season still left to turn things around.

Against a side that contained Neil Ruddock, Jan Molby, Ian Rush, Robbie Fowler and the emerging Jamie Redknapp, the score had remained at 0–0 into the second half. Then Moncur raced into the box after a move involving Keith Scott and Nicky Summerbee, sliding the ball past Bruce Grobbelaar from Summerbee's cross. John Barnes hit back soon afterwards to bring the two sides level, before an Andy Mutch header from a Kevin Horlock centre was blocked by Grobbelaar for Scott to net the rebound. With Town fans ready to party again, Mark Wright headed home a Steve McManaman corner in the 86th minute. An amazing victory had been snatched from Town's grasp and the *Adver* described the performance of Moncur, named as their Man of the Match, as 'simply magic'.

A week later and Town were back at the County Ground. This time it was the turn of Southampton to make the short trip from the south coast, no doubt with the Saints supporters ready to take three points home to the Dell to ease their own relegation fears. Seven days before Christmas came the chance to avenge the earlier 5–1 defeat in August. Could the belief of such a good performance against Liverpool raise Town's game?

John Gorman made the unusual move of switching left-back Paul Bodin to midfield and it paid almost instant dividends as the Welshman rattled a left-foot strike past Dave Beasant in the 12th minute. Just before half-time Matt Le Tissier added to his haul against Town with an equaliser, but 20 minutes into the second half Keith Scott continued to justify his purchase with the goal that gave Town their second victory of the campaign.

Santa had arrived early to bring some premature celebrations to the festive season.

The win took Swindon's points total to 14, level with vanquished Southampton and a point behind Chelsea. While hardly comfortable, Town were one win away from lifting themselves not just off the bottom of the table, but to within a point from fourth-from-bottom Sheffield United and on course for safety.

The period turned out to be something of a purple patch and over a nine-game spell, the whole season was to be defined. Gorman's team had fought themselves to the brink of turning things around, and when Arsenal came to town two days after Christmas, there was a feeling of renewed hope. Just as in August Swindon faced one of the top teams in the country, but by now they were surely as prepared for the challenge as they could be. When the Gunners returned to London on the back of a 4–0 win, the nation would again have been little surprised. 'What else could a

Swindon supporter have expected?' they would have asked. A hat-trick from Kevin Campbell and a sublime 90th-minute chip from Ian Wright underlined the difference between the two sides.

With two days of 1993 left came a trip to Sheffield Wednesday, where a challenge from Owls striker Gordon Watson with 20 minutes to go left Fraser Digby grounded with a dislocated shoulder. The score stood at 2–1 to Swindon, and the defence waited for referee Phil Don to blow for the 'keeper to receive treatment, but instead he allowed play to continue and Watson himself squared the scoring. Watson netted again two minutes later, this time past replacement 'keeper Nicky Hammond as Swindon tried to come to terms with the injustice, but with the game in its last minute, Craig Maskell headed his second of the match to secure a point. It was the story of the whole season: it was brave, it was glorious, but it was too little to make a real difference.

So to 1994 and a home match with Chelsea brought a return for ex-manager Glenn Hoddle, and, disappointingly for the home fans, another loss. After 22 away games without a win, Chelsea continued their elevation from near the foot of the table with a 3–1 victory. The scoring had stood at 2–0 with the game in its 90th minute when Andy Mutch struck to restore hope for Town, before future Swindon manager Dennis Wise headed an even later finisher. A 1–1 draw at Coventry City preceded a match at Everton where John Moncur scored his third goal of the campaign, but before the trip to Goodison, news broke that seemed to herald the end of big striker and unconsummated hope Jan Aage Fjortoft's Swindon Town career.

Gorman announced his plan to ship the 6ft 3in man back to Lillestrom in Norway in the hope he could find the goalscoring form that had attracted the manager's attention before the big kick-off. Frustratingly, even in the midst of his barren run in a Town shirt, Fjortoft had scored for his country in Poland in October – the game that brought qualification for the World Cup '94 in the US. Town went to Liverpool to face Everton without the Norwegian international, and four minutes into the second half Swindon were without Andy Mutch as well, after a red card was shown when he was adjudged to have lashed out at John Ebbrell. Incredibly, 10-man Town fought back from a two-goal deficit to equalise through goals from Moncur and Paul Bodin. With less than 20 minutes to go the home team went ahead once more, and three more goals in the last seven minutes gave the score the almost surreal proportions of six goals to two.

Goalscorer John Moncur wasn't happy with referee Gerald Ashby's interpretation of Mutch's actions. 'I wonder how much he really saw of the incident. The crowd got the free-kick which led to their third goal and a linesman gave the penalty for Everton's fifth. That cost us two goals when we had just clawed our way back into the game with 10 men. It's almost as though the ref was rubbing our noses in it.'

The defeat was the heaviest so far and its manner threatened to undermine the fragile confidence that had slowly been built. Town had gone two goals behind and been reduced to 10 men, but still levelled the scoring. The travelling fans had faced the ignominy of leaving Goodison

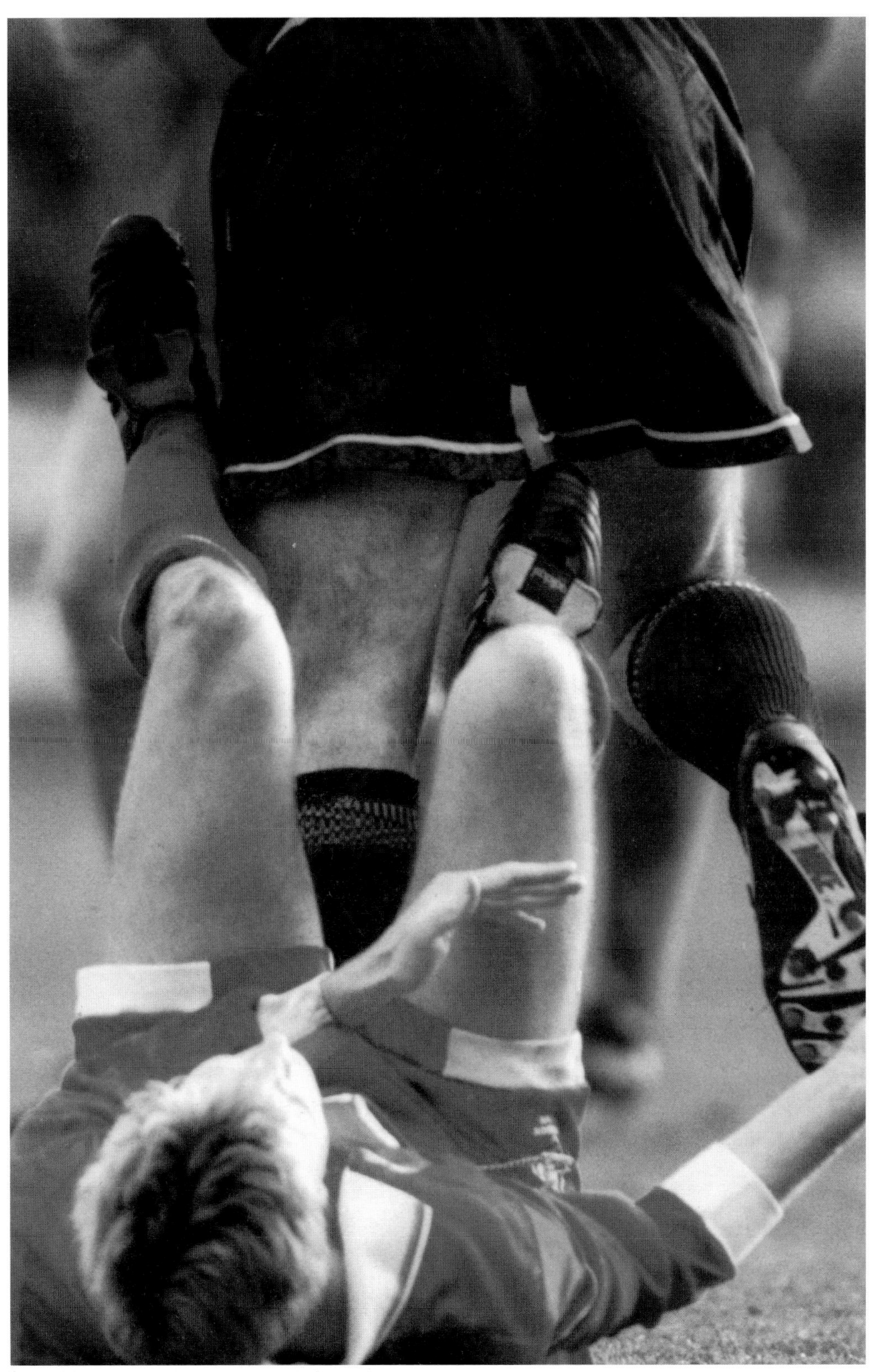

The infamous Cantona stamp, March 1994.

Park with jeers in their ears, knowing that those watching the scores coming in on *Grandstand* would once more be sniggering that their side had been put in their place by their supposed superiors.

The dismissal and subsequent suspension of Mutch brought new problems up front for the manager and fresh opportunity for Fjortoft. Gorman's striking options were reduced and he was forced to reconsider his idea of returning Jan to his native country. In an FA Cup replay at Ipswich three days later, Fjortoft drilled Martin Ling's through ball past Craig Forrest to finally open his scoring account for his team. The relief was palpable but came with complications. Jan was keen to advance his chances of playing in the following summer's World Cup, and realistically knew his chances were unlikely to be enhanced with a spell in the reserves at Swindon. A return to Norway still seemed best suited to Fjortoft's needs.

It was typical of Swindon's season that on 22 January Fjortoft scored again, and this time it brought a win. The visit of Spurs to the County Ground brought the return of ex-favourite Colin Calderwood, who was forced to return along the M4 after a 2–1 defeat by his old employers. Then, as January became February, Fjortoft went two better. A brace of penalties were included in a hat-trick, Coventry City were defeated 3–1, and for the first time all season, Swindon had won two games on the trot. Jan (who was quickly christened 'The Man') had scored five times in three games, and all thoughts of a departure to Norway had disappeared.

There were 14 matches of the season remaining and Town were just two points from safety. Finally winning at home and producing inspiring performances away, Swindon once more toyed with the hopes of their supporters. A goalscorer had at last been unearthed. How ironic it was that that wouldn't make a difference. The upturn in Swindon's fortunes ran out just as Fjortoft struck form. Over the next four games, Fjortoft was to net another four times, but home draws against Norwich and West Ham brought the only points, and a trip to Birmingham saw Aston Villa strike five for no reply.

And the worst was still to come.

On 12 March John Gorman took his side to St James' Park to take on Newcastle United and the team returned south with their tails between their legs. A goal for John Moncur could hardly gloss over the seven that the Magpies had put past Fraser Digby. Some wounded pride was restored when Manchester United were held 2–2 at the County Ground a week later, a match in which Eric Cantona was dismissed for stamping on Moncur, but Town were rapidly running out of Premiership matches. Over the next six games, just two points were collected as Town's fate was sealed. Exasperating to the last, one of them came in a 1–1 draw at Highbury. Town were capable of losing 4–2 at home to Wimbledon, the only game Moncur missed all season, but also of matching Arsenal on their own patch.

Then came a huge irony on the last day of April as Town travelled to Loftus Road to take on

Queen's Park Rangers. Swindon hadn't won away from home all season and this was their last chance. Not only that, but back in November Queen's Park Rangers had been the first team to surrender all three points to Swindon in a Premiership match. Goals by Shaun Taylor, Fjortoft and Summerbee gave Town a 3–1 win in London and gave the away supporters, who had spent all season travelling the length and breadth of the country following their team, the sort of day out that they'd been hoping for since August.

The curtain came down on the Premiership season of 1993–94 with Swindon Town entertaining Leeds United, and by the end of the afternoon the supporters who had travelled from Elland Road would certainly have felt they had been entertained. After 41 matches, Swindon Town were where they had been all season. Bottom of the table. Leeds United, meanwhile, were looking to grab a place in Europe. By the end of the day, the last match of the season eerily reflected the first month: a 5–0 home defeat. Town had capitulated as the scoreline took the total goals conceded into treble figures.

In conclusion, the season had started badly and had not got better. When the fixtures were published the thought of facing Sheffield United and Oldham Athletic in the first two matches, teams Swindon had faced on a level playing field in the recent past, who they knew well and who they might expect to reasonably compete with, had seemed a slight anticlimax. 'Bring on Manchester United' many thought. 'That's what we're looking forward to.' Then, to end those first two games without a point and to be thrashed at home by Liverpool in the third, brought the sort of clash with realism that undermined everyone's hopes. Town had failed against the teams that their players and supporters realistically thought they could live with, and then had been completely outclassed by one which they aspired to match. That both Oldham and Sheffield United eventually joined Town in the drop would only compound the feeling of wretchedness.

From then on, continued defeat coupled with the slippery slope of constant self-doubt systematically destroyed everyone's belief that Swindon deserved a place in the top flight. It soon seemed that the best chance Swindon had of winning a match was to keep the score at 0–0 and clinch the game with a strike so late that it gave the opposition no chance to respond. All Town's Premiership rivals, shocked by their temerity at scoring, looked capable of shaking their heads in disbelief, regrouping and putting the upstarts in their place.

Just as rattling a tiger's cage is tantamount to inviting trouble, if Swindon took the lead, their fans learned that trying for three points only increased the likelihood that they would get none. Where can a football supporter possibly go when faced with a mindset like that? Many managers were magnanimous in their praise of Swindon's footballing principles. Gorman's team always set about playing the game in an attractive style, but it's easy to be generous with words after another three points have been added to your team's total. Certainly the opposition's supporters would often have been very appreciative of Swindon's defensive frailties.

Who knows whether Town would have fared better under Glenn Hoddle rather than John Gorman? What would have been possible had Jan Aage Fjortoft found his form before halfway through the season? And it was little good looking to Cup competition to lift the gloom. Victory over two legs over Division One Wolves in the Coca-Cola Cup brought a goal for Andy Mutch against his old club, but preceded a 2–0 defeat at Portsmouth in the second round. Then, a draw at home to Ipswich Town brought a defeat at Portman Road in the FA Cup and Swindon were out of that as well.

As for John Moncur, he had the honour of claiming Swindon Town's first-ever Premiership goal, a commodity that was sadly to prove too rare over the 10 months of 1993–94 to outweigh the problems in defence. Further strikes against Liverpool, Everton and Newcastle United were interspersed throughout the season but none of those matches resulted in a win for his side. All took place away from home, and worse, the four games included a 6–2 and a 7–1 defeat. If the form of Jan Aage Fjortoft during the first half of the season had only matched that of the second, the Norwegian would surely have pushed Moncur to the wire in the race to be voted the fans' favourite. But at the end of an historic but traumatic campaign, John had seen action in 41 of the 42 Premiership matches, a consistency that outweighed the contribution of the late-starting and frustrating Fjortoft.

Prior to the game with Leeds United, John was presented with the Swindon Town Player of the Year award. Back in October, after starring in the game at Tottenham, John had commented in the match day programme 'We are obviously concerned about the results but the pleasing factor is that we have not disgraced ourselves football wise. We have played some good stuff against quality opposition. We can open up any side on our day'.

Those days, though, had been too few and too far between.

With relegation back to the Football League confirmed, Moncur looked likely to fly the nest. West Ham United came in with a bid of £850,000 and, once more, one of Town's stars was bound for London. He had played 61 games for Swindon Town. The deal eventually rose to around £1 million with add-ons through appearances, and the Londoner went on to make over 200 outings for the Hammers. Calling time on his playing days a little before his 38th birthday, John's career may have started late but he did his best to make up for lost time.

In 1999 John's life took a new direction. Confirmation into the Christian faith took some by surprise but brought a new focus that allowed John to change some of his former ways, which had brought dissatisfaction in his life. In Paul Gascoigne's autobiography *My Story*, Gazza comments on the nights out that he used to share with his Spurs colleague in the mid-90s, most of which seemed to involve large quantities of alcohol and more often than not the discarding of items of clothing in a public place. Finding the calmness that he felt he was missing, Moncur said in 2003 that he was now more compassionate, less angry and less worried about his life.

Silverware to show for Swindon's highest ever League finish.

Due to the infancy of the Premiership, various records were set by Swindon's Premiership adventure. With just two seasons' worth of history, records were easily achieved in the competition. As the football world noted with great glee at the time, Town's 30 points were the fewest taken in Premiership competition, but while Swindon scored on just 47 occasions, that was still better than seven other Premiership teams that season, including 10th-placed Aston Villa. But Town's goal difference of minus 53 was twice as bad as next-worst side Oldham.

The record 100 goals that Town shipped has never been seriously threatened since. Plainly it was in defence that Swindon's shortcomings were most cruelly exposed.

Shaun Taylor
(1991–92, 1994–95 and 1995–96) ~ 'Ooooh, Shaun Taylor'

When Brazil beat Italy in the 1970 World Cup Final, the South Americans were allowed to keep the Jules Rimet trophy on the basis that they had won the tournament three times. If the same rules had applied to the Swindon Town Player of the Year trophy, Shaun Taylor would have made the silverware his own and been forced to tour the sports shops looking for a replacement. The first man to take the award three times, it is testimony to the respect that the centre-back commanded on the terraces that Shaun was considered the fans' favourite in 60 percent of his seasons at the club.

In the mid-90s, the supporters effectively voted Taylor their greatest-ever player. That causes a few problems for a book that is mostly a chronology of Swindon Town. Popular Taylor's award-winning spell spanned five seasons in Wiltshire, and somewhat throws a spanner in the works. It seems appropriate that it is almost as awkward to write about him as opposing forwards must have found him to play against.

Charlton, September 1994, and Kevin Morris administers his weekly treatment to Shaun Taylor.

We now jump back to the summer of 1991 when, in July, Glenn Hoddle splashed out £200,000 and Taylor was made a team member of First Division Swindon Town.

Plymouth-born Shaun had arrived late to the professional game. A qualified plumber, he was signed by Exeter City from Bideford Town on a free transfer just two months short of his 23rd birthday in December 1986. He immediately secured a first-team shirt and made 200 appearances over the next five seasons for the Grecians, claiming a Fourth Division Championship medal in 1990. Taylor told the *Advertiser* before the contract was signed 'I reported back to Exeter and manager Terry Cooper told me Southend had made enquiries. But the next day Swindon had also showed an interest. The Swindon enquiry greatly interested me so I came up and met Glenn Hoddle. A fee was agreed and I agreed terms. Hopefully everything will now go through on Wednesday. Joining an ambitious club was too good to turn down.'

Ahead of his Swindon debut in the opening game of the season, Taylor commented 'It's a new challenge because until now I have only ever played in the third and fourth divisions. It's a big game for me but I'm looking forward to it. I feel very welcome at Swindon and I seem to have gelled quite well, but I'm not letting it go to my head.'

Hoddle had few doubts about Taylor's abilities to step up. Teaming him with Colin Calderwood,

An unfamiliar looking Tommy Mooney tangles with Shaun Taylor.

one man was to provide the guile while the other brought the much-needed graft to form a successful defensive partnership. If Calderwood was Town's Bobby Moore, Shaun was Jack Charlton. A towering presence in the air at the back, when called to the opposition's penalty area for corners he completed many an aerial challenge with a net-bulging header.

The opening day of 1991–92 saw the 6ft 1in man start the match at Leicester City and a clean sheet signalled the intentions of the new defensive unit. Three games later and Taylor's far-post header from a Duncan Shearer cross was the third of four goals Town scored in a win at Ipswich. The strike began Taylor's elevation to cult status. 'It seemed to take an eternity to go in, but it's amazing where the energy comes from once you've scored,' said Taylor, after three teammates struggled to catch the goalscorer.

It was a good start for Taylor, and results helped the overall feel-good factor. Another four goals were scored without reply at Plymouth and, in the middle of September, Town went one better with five against Sunderland. By the end of the month Taylor had scored his second in a 3–1 home win over Watford and Swindon sat third in the table with 17 points from the first nine games. October brought three wins from four attempts and by the time Newcastle United succumbed by two goals to one at the County Ground at the beginning of November, Town lay second behind Middlesbrough. Then came a run of nine games without a win, and by New Year's Eve, Town's promotion drive was effectively over. Four wins in seven to the beginning of February flattered to deceive, and four straight defeats included a calamitous 5–3 loss at near neighbours Oxford United. The departure of Duncan Shearer to Blackburn Rovers in March put the nail in the coffin of any Play-off hopes and an eighth-place finish was satisfactory but functional.

Cup competition perhaps brought supporters the most interest throughout the season. A two-legged victory over West Bromwich Albion in the Rumbelows Cup, followed by a replay win over Millwall, led to a convincing 4–1 mauling of Huddersfield Town at their then home ground of Leeds Road. The fourth round brought elimination at the hands of Crystal Palace. In the FA Cup, wins over Watford and Cambridge United culminated in a 2–1 home defeat at the hands of Aston Villa in front of the BBC TV cameras.

As always, the season was punctuated with stories about Town's financial position. Burmah had signed a three-year sponsorship deal worth £500,000 in the summer and news followed in October that Town had made a profit of the same sum over the preceding 12 months. The good news had come predominantly from the £1.7 million that had been raised from transfer dealing and seemed to signal a turnaround in Swindon's fortunes. So it came as some surprise when a £550,000 bid for midfielder Fitzroy Simpson from Manchester City was accepted at the beginning of March, and when Shearer was allowed to leave for Blackburn Rovers fans demanded an explanation. Huge increases in players' wages were blamed, the legacy of the demotion of 1990 that had resulted in First Division salaries being paid to Second Division players.

Ahead of Town's last home match of the season, a 1–0 win over Plymouth, Shaun Taylor was presented with his inaugural Swindon Town Player of the Year award. At 29 and in his first season in Division Two, Taylor had won the hearts of the Town faithful. 'It's a total surprise but I couldn't have wished for a better honour', he said. As focused as ever, Shaun concluded 'All I need to do now is to make sure the team get three points against Plymouth Argyle today.' There was no room for mixed feelings regarding his hometown club for Taylor.

Professional to the last, and typically sporting a bandage covering a stitched wound that had freshly reopened, it was Taylor's 26th-minute header that won the game against the team who missed the chance to take the centre-back as a teenager.

A draw at Sunderland and a defeat at Derby brought the curtain down on Shaun's first season as a Swindon Town player. Two years later and the team had experienced the elation of promotion to the Premiership and the heartache of relegation. Season 1994–95 kicked off with changes on the horizon. Ten years previously, the top flight had been reduced to 20 clubs and then changed back to 22. As indecisive as ever, the authorities then deemed that 20 was the way for the Premiership to go once more. The method deployed to adjust the numbers was to relegate four from the Premiership and replace them with just two from Division One. Four needed to be relegated from Division One as well to keep the numbers constant, and that would turn out to be crucial.

The summer saw a major development at the County Ground. The old Shrivenham Road stand that had been bought second-hand from Aldershot Tattoo in 1958 was finally flattened to make way for a new £1.8 million structure, completed in just 14 weeks and in time for the season's start. News broke that Tottenham Hotspur were to be fined £600,000, having been found guilty of making irregular payments to players, and it opened old wounds for Town supporters. Tottenham were also ordered to start the coming season on minus 12 points and Spurs' official information line complained that the punishment was 'the most savage ever handed out'. Swindon fans disagreed.

Worse still, by New Year's Eve 1995 it was announced that the points deduction would be overturned in return for the fine being increased to £1.5 million. With Spurs owner Alan Sugar listed as the country's 47th most wealthy person, the statement only increased the persecution complex in Wiltshire. On the Swindon pitch, Nicky Summerbee was tempted to Maine Road to join Manchester City, the second time a Summerbee had taken that route, but the strangest transfer deal of the summer was only just beginning.

With Town poised to sign winger Joey Beauchamp as a replacement for Summerbee, the Oxford United man decided to join West Ham United instead. Defender Mark Robinson then signed for John Gorman from Newcastle for a club-record £600,000, before Beauchamp announced himself unable to commit to the travelling necessary to take him from his Oxford home to East London. He had been a West Ham player for little more than a month and had not kicked a ball in anger

The full force of a Shaun Taylor aerial challenge.

for the Hammers. Four days after the opening game of the season, defender Adrian Whitbread moved to Upton Park as part of the deal that saw Beauchamp sign for Swindon, a club just 30-odd miles from Oxford. Would that be close enough?

The first four games of the season brought just one defeat and raised hopes of an immediate return to the Premiership. The feel-good factor continued when a 1–0 Fjortoft-inspired win at Notts County in the first game of September left Swindon second to Middlesbrough in the early Division One table. A top six place was held until the end of October, when news came that the local council were threatening to call in the bailiffs to reclaim a £200,000 unpaid rent bill. The argument rumbled on for a month before a deal was thrashed out. Then a 3–1 defeat by eventual champions Middlesbrough, in which Fjortoft scored Town's goal at Ayresome Park, started a slide that was to have great consequences.

Through November, three successive defeats at the hands of Bolton, Millwall and, annoyingly, Bristol City dropped Town down the table and destroyed the earlier good work. The downturn coincided with a broken left arm for Shaun Taylor, suffered in a collision with his own 'keeper Fraser Digby in the defeat by Middlesbrough. But, as had been shown many times before, he was made of stern stuff. By the middle of December, he was back in the middle of defence. Town had taken just two points in his absence, and a goal on his return helped secure a draw at Port Vale. It is unsurprising that Taylor was so highly regarded by the supporters.

The 3–2 defeat at Ashton Gate proved the last straw for manager John Gorman. His failure to keep Swindon in the Premiership the previous season had been viewed with some sympathy, but the thought of returning to Division Two brought panic in the boardroom. Shortly after midday on 21 November, a statement from the club announced that first-team coach Andy Rowland would take over from John Gorman in a caretaker manager capacity while Swindon Town looked for a long-term replacement. Gorman's reign had covered 72 matches and just 15 had resulted in victory. The club lay 16th in Division One.

A long list of potential successors' names was aired. Ron Atkinson, Bobby Gould and Mike Walker's names came to the fore. Chris Waddle and Gary Mabbutt were also mentioned as Town chairman Ray Hardman dismissed rumours linking the club with ex-manager Ossie Ardiles. Then came suggestions of an ex-Liverpool pairing of Steve Nicol and Steve McMahon forming a managerial duo. Eventually, as November drew to a close, Manchester City and ex-England midfielder McMahon was announced as the man to take Town forward in a player-manager capacity.

The move did not bring instant results. Indeed, after McMahon called for his side to be meaner on the pitch, a 2–0 defeat at Southend saw the new player-manager red carded on his debut when referee Steve Dunn judged that the six-stitch wound inflicted on Shrimpers' Roger Willis's nose was caused by McMahon's elbow. Fourteen games would pass as Town struggled to record their next victory, and when it came, it came by two goals to one at home to Middlesbrough. Unable to win for two and a half months, Swindon had contrived to beat the team who were still top of the table. Again Fjortoft was on the score sheet, and Boro boss Bryan Robson had taken notice.

By then, 1994 had turned into 1995 and Swindon had dropped as low as 20th in the table. It had been defeat by Bristol City that had brought John Gorman's dismissal and in the middle of February, the Ashton Gate side visited the County Ground and scored three against Town for the second time that season. Then a trip to Luton brought a further 3–0 defeat and Town were in another six-game run without a win.

The hoped for turnaround following the managerial change was not materialising.

The winless run came to an end with three points from the match with fellow strugglers Sunderland in the middle of March, then a trip to The Hawthorns brought an astonishing 5–2 victory over West Bromwich Albion, but still Town were in the bottom four and the six points made no impact on their League position. Four defeats on the trot came close to sealing Town's fate and by the time Shaun Taylor scored in a 3–1 home win over Oldham, Town were third from bottom of the table and Jan Aage Fjortoft was a Middlesbrough player. Fjortoft had scored 26 times in all for Town, but transfer deadline day saw the Norwegian switch to the North East in return for £1.3 million.

The supporters were enraged. Here was a man who had won their hearts after a bad start to his Town career, who was under contract and on whose head the club's directors had recently placed a £3 million price tag. This didn't look like the way to avoid relegation to the third tier of English football.

And so it proved; Town failed to score in six of the 10 games of the season remaining. One match was won from the last six, and come 7 May, Town finished the season fourth from bottom. Normally a safe position, the League's restructure dropped four out of Division One for the first time, and Town were the victims.

Amid all the gloom, there was one shining light that had given fans something to cheer. Back in September, Town had travelled to the Valley to face Charlton Athletic in the Coca-Cola Cup. The trip was made in hope rather than expectation, as Swindon had already capitulated by three goals to one in the first leg. By the end of the evening, Town had triumphed 4–1 and amazingly turned the tie around. Fjortoft had scored a first-half hat-trick but six minutes from time, Charlton made the aggregate score 4–4. Then Joey Beauchamp scored his first goal for Swindon in extra-time when his shot cannoned off the post and into the net via 'keeper Andy Petterson.

A 4–1 home replay win over Brighton followed, before victories over Derby County and Millwall brought a semi-final with Bolton Wanderers. A Wembley Final awaited the victors. Town took a 2–1 lead courtesy of a Peter Thorne brace in the first leg, and with an hour gone in the second at Burnden Park, Fjortoft had increased Town's lead to a two-goal margin. Then back came

Taylor shows his predatory instincts in Southampton's penalty box in February 1996.

Bolton with three goals in the last half hour to earn a place in the Final, which was lost to Liverpool.

The Cup run regularly punctuated the season and brought a break from the depressing plunge to inevitable relegation, but in October the importance of football had been thrown into stark relief when popular physiotherapist Kevin Morris tragically and unexpectedly passed away.

Once more, Shaun Taylor had tried to show his strikers how to set about winning matches. Goals in an October defeat at Barnsley, a draw at Port Vale just before Christmas, one that claimed a point at Grimsby and a strike in a 3–1 home win over Oldham in April meant that by the end of the season, the centre-back had outscored all bar three of his remaining teammates. As the season had kicked off, Taylor had been locked in a contractual dispute with Swindon Town, one that had threatened his Town career. 'Discussions over a new contract have been going on between me and the manager since the start of our Premier League campaign, but it has reached the stage where Swindon do not seem able to secure my future,' Shaun told the *Advertiser*. 'Initially I was told there would be no money available until players were sold, but despite the departures of Nicky Summerbee and John Moncur I've still had no joy. It seems to me the board do not think I'm part of their plans for the future and if I'm not wanted I don't want to stay.'

The big defender relinquished the role of club captain to Paul Bodin but stopped short of handing in a transfer request. By the end of the season he had made 37 League appearances, rebuilt his bridges with the club and taken his second Player of the Year award in four seasons.

Now to 1995–96 and towards the end of the previous season, manager McMahon had transfer listed Brian Kilcline, Andy Mutch and record-signing Joey Beauchamp. Now, relegation to Division Two compounded the financial consequences brought by the drop from the Premiership 12 months earlier. Difficult decisions were necessary, and this was a time of great change. Goalkeeper and fans' favourite Fraser Digby was one of those consigned to the transfer list as McMahon looked to trim the wage bill and shape his squad to his own liking. Fraser's friend and rival for the number-one shirt, Nicky Hammond, moved on to Plymouth, and after much badly-disguised pleading, Oxford-born winger Joey Beauchamp engineered a cut-price £300,000 move back to his old bedroom with a return to Oxford United.

In July £475,000 had been invested to bring Bristol City striker Wayne Allison to Swindon and in contrast, a free transfer brought fellow striker Steve Finney from Manchester City. Blackburn Rovers' goalkeeper Shay Given started the season in goal as Digby looked to try and get back into McMahon's good books, but when Given's month-long loan spell was up, in came Frank Talia from the same club for a similar spell.

It was 11 games into the season before Digby got a game.

Three straight wins immediately took Town to the top of the table. Shaun Taylor scored his first of the season in a 4–1 win at Twerton Park, Bath over Bristol Rovers in the middle of September. But that was overshadowed by a Kevin Horlock hat-trick, and it was almost October before McMahon's team tasted defeat, by four goals to three at Wrexham. That was the 10th game of the season and Swindon had won seven of them.

Town responded to the loss by winning four on the trot, the last of which saw a brace for Shaun Taylor at Notts County. His seventh-minute opener was an archetypal header from a Kevin Horlock corner. 'A few years ago we put in similar corners on a regular basis and I scored 13 goals,' said the skipper, whose second of the day with 12 minutes remaining helped Town to a 3–1 victory at Meadow Lane. 'If the balls keep on being delivered like that then I'll get more than a few more chances.' After a run like that it was almost a shock to draw three consecutive matches and then lose at home to Shrewsbury as November drew to a close.

December brought similar results, and the solitary win and three draws would have done more damage to Swindon's League position had the season's start not been so good. The slip allowed Crewe Alexandra to overtake Town at the top of the table, but the shape of Swindon's season's outcome was about to be defined as 1996 began. A 3–0 home win over Swansea City was followed by a defeat at York City, and that was just about that. There were 22 Division Two matches still to play, but most teams could forget about competing for the Championship from that moment onwards.

The next nine Swindon matches brought six wins and a hat-trick of draws, and the run coincided with McMahon's decision to hang up his boots and concentrate on off-field matters. Town travelled to Swansea on 10 February and Taylor scored what was rather a collector's item to win the match. A Ty Gooden corner was flicked on at the near post by Kevin Horlock, and left-footed Taylor thundered home a right-footed volley from 12 yards. 'It's rare for me to score with my feet – and even rarer with my right foot!' proclaimed the centre-back. His fourth of the season left Swindon six points clear at the top of the table. Behind them came Crewe, and languishing in 13th place and 12 points behind an automatic promotion place came Oxford United. More of them later.

Shaun Taylor was on the score sheet again with an 84th-minute opener at Walsall on 9 March, but the strike failed to grab all the points on offer. The match was into injury time when the Saddlers claimed a share of the points. But in the third week of March, Town travelled to the Manor Ground, Oxford, to face a team who had by then charged up the table to occupy a Play-off place. No doubt Joey Beauchamp and his fellow Oxford United supporters took enormous pleasure in the 3–0 win the U's claimed, not least because Beauchamp himself scored the third, but the disappointment felt by travelling Town supporters would be inconsequential by the end of the campaign.

Briefly overtaken once more, this time by Blackpool, Swindon regrouped and launched into another unbeaten run. There were a dozen games to play and they would be won and drawn in equal measure. With five matches to go, Swindon visited Bloomfield Road, Blackpool. Their hosts had just three games to play and sat second in the table behind Town. A Kevin Horlock goal with quarter of an hour gone gave Swindon the lead for over an hour of the match. Then an Andy Barlow equaliser levelled the score. With neither team able to break the deadlock, the final whistle saw celebrations, the point ensuring Town promotion and taking the club back to Division One – 12 months after their place had been relinquished.

Three days later and the news was even better. Goals from transfer deadline day signing Steve Cowe, Peter Thorne and Wayne 'The Chief' Allison gave Swindon a 3–1 win at Chesterfield and the Division Two Championship was in the bag. The end of season had brought four consecutive away matches in the last five fixtures but Swindon planned a big day for 4 May with the final game of the season bringing the visit of Stockport County. The County Ground was filled with 14,697 to see a 0–0 draw, but spirits were not to be dampened by a goalless scoreline.

Shaun Taylor was predictably named the *Adver*'s Man of the Match and, perhaps understandably, it was the picture of the skipper holding the Division Two Championship trophy that gained greater exposure than the bestowal of his record third Player of the Year award.

The early season goalscoring sensation had been free-transfer signing Steve Finney. Starting 19 of the first 20 games, Finney scored 11 times in that period including three times in the first two

February 1996. A man on the floor, an astonished goalkeeper and Taylor scores the only goal of the game against Swansea City.

matches of the season. In contrast, highly-priced fellow front man Wayne Allison had hit eight before New Year's Day. Finney then saw his chances limited as Peter Thorne, who attracted a £1 million bid from Bolton in October, partnered Allison up front. Allison took the honours of top scorer with 20 in all competitions but all three strikers reached double figures, with midfielder Kevin Horlock also striking 15. That's the sort of goalscoring combination that is needed to win honours. Shaun Taylor hit a creditable seven.

The icing on the cake for Swindon supporters may have been that Town pipped rivals Oxford United to the trophy, and not just by a slim margin but with eight points to spare. Promotion back to the division from which they had been relegated 12 months earlier encouraged fans to hope that Town were on the way back to the top flight. But after such celebrated achievement, in September of the following season manager Steve McMahon dispensed with his skipper's services, and it tested supporters' understanding that their Player of the Year was allowed to move to near rivals Bristol City. The fee of just £50,000 did little to justify his departure to supporters.

It had been reported during the season that Town's wage bill was around £3.4 million, still a consequence of the Premiership sojourn of two years earlier. Many had already been sacrificed in an effort to slash expenditure, including the controversial axing of John Trollope from his position of youth-team manager after a 37-year association with Swindon. Perhaps Shaun Taylor was another one of those to be reluctantly sacrificed.

But as Town fans saw their heroes depart, even as freshly polished silverware was finding its way into the boardroom, some wondered whether personality clashes with the manager were the greatest factor in the continued clearout. Taylor had played almost 260 matches for Swindon.

He went on to make over 100 appearances for Bristol City over the next three seasons, seasons that saw promotion to, and relegation from, Division One. But his first appearance of 1998–99 at Ashton Gate was delayed until a month from the end of the campaign by injury, and the defender faced the imminent end of his playing career.

At the end of 1999–2000, and after around 600 professional appearances, Taylor was enrolled on the coaching staff at City under the new managerial stewardship of Danny Wilson. Then he became assistant manager at Forest Green Rovers in June 2006, when he was unsuccessfully connected with the managerial vacancy at his first club, Exeter City. Coming from the heart of West Country rugby territory, there was something about Shaun's build and style that suggested he would have been equally at home playing the sport with the oval ball.

An honest, no-nonsense centre-back, Shaun had built a reputation as a reliable defender who knew his limitations, but played to his enormous strengths. At the time of his third Player of the Year award, Shaun had been a Swindon player for five seasons, four of which had seen either promotion or relegation. Sometime during this spell, a chant was first heard that became synonymous with the big man. The net would bulge from a bullet header, or an opposing striker would feel the full force of a hard but fair challenge from the Town captain, and the terraces would let loose with the simple but effective refrain of 'Ooooh, Shaun Taylor'.

The 1996 Division Two Championship trophy is held aloft by Town's skipper.

The mantra summed up the breath-stealing clattering that one of the opposing side would have just suffered, or the mental wincing that fans would have experienced as their man put his head where it would almost inevitably hurt. It was a chant that hadn't been stolen from elsewhere. It hadn't been heard in connection with a Gary Pallister or a Martin Keown, with just a change of name. The chant, like the man it heralded, was unique.

There have been many great players to pull on a Town shirt, but even Taylor's most fervent admirer would concede that he wasn't the most gifted of footballing craftsmen. Not for him the cultured ball out of defence of an Alan Hansen or the speedy interception of a Des Walker. Yet the centre-back became the first man in the history of the Swindon Town Player of the Year award to be so appreciated by supporters that he was voted their best player three times. And when he spent just over five seasons at the County Ground, that's some record.

The three seasons of Taylor's reign as Player of the Year brought huge contrast and some strange similarities. The first saw a flirtation with a Play-off spot, the second ended in relegation and the third brought the second Championship in the club's history. Then there was an assault on Wembley in the Coca-Cola Cup, the venue of perhaps Taylor's greatest day with a goal in the Play-off Final of 1993.

A crowd of 32,000 Town supporters will never forget the brave, lunging, neck-straining header that brought a 3–0 lead at Wembley against Leicester City in the Division One Play-off Final of 1993. Best brought to mind with a bloodied bandage around his head, Taylor was the strong, whole-hearted central defender that every manager values.

What Taylor had was determination. Leading by example and by sheer guts and a prepared-to-die-in-the-cause attitude, he made the most of his abilities. Ready to try until he dropped, he won the respect of every Town supporter and many an opposing striker.

Parallels are often drawn between the competition of sport and the trauma of war. As misguided as that often seems, there is no doubt that Shaun Taylor fits the bill as one of those men you would want beside you in the trenches. No other Town player has captained the club to a Championship trophy, as well as scoring at Wembley.

Making Shaun Taylor a three-time Player of the Year winner seems a fitting way to recognise those achievements.

Fraser Digby
(1986–87, 1996–97 and 1997–98) ~ Eleven seasons and three trophies

Swindon Town's Player of the Year award was first bestowed in 1964, when striker turned central defender Ken McPherson was the man who took the honour.

In the ensuing 32 years to the summer of 1996, each season brought a fresh campaign to elect the man most worthy of special recognition during the efforts of the previous 10 months, and while Joe Butler and John Trollope both collected the trophy twice, it is ironic that the year after Shaun Taylor became the first player to win the silverware three times, that record came under immediate threat.

Like buses, you wait for ages for one triple winner to come along, and then two come along at once. And unlike the lightning success of Taylor with his three trophies in five seasons, Fraser Digby had to wait 10 years between his first accolade and his second.

The season of 1996–97 began with Swindon safely back in the division they had vacated in May 1995, and with the Second Division Championship trophy to polish in the boardroom. Steve McMahon had continued a clearout of the successful team of earlier in the decade, with the release in the summer of Paul Bodin to Reading and Martin Ling to Leyton Orient. Midfielder Kevin Watson had arrived on a free transfer from Tottenham, aptly named Scot, Scott Leitch made his loan deal of the previous March permanent when he signed from Hearts, but the signing that captured the imagination most was that of ex-England, Liverpool and Aston Villa star Mark Walters.

Fraser Digby. Three times Swindon Town Player of the Year.

McMahon persuaded his former colleague to make a free-transfer move from Premiership side Southampton, and all three new men made the pitch in an opening-day defeat at Norwich City.

One man who was absent that day was goalkeeper Fraser Digby, who found himself excluded once more in favour of Frank Talia. It seemed Steve McMahon rated his own signing more highly than the stalwart Town stopper, and Fraser's days at the club continued to be considered numbered.

The opening two months of the season saw a mixed bag of results as Town sought to reestablish themselves in Division One. The usual flurry of early fixtures meant that by the time 1996–97 was into October, a dozen games had already been contested and Town lay in a mid-table position. Draws had been recorded in the opening home fixture with Port Vale and against Queen's Park Rangers at Loftus Road in the third week of September, and the remaining 10 matches had been lost and won in equal measure. But it was the 12th match of the season, at home to Huddersfield Town, that brought the most notable result of the campaign. A hat-trick from Peter Thorne and strikes from Wayne Allison, Mark Walters and Kevin Horlock gave Swindon a 6–0 win over the Terriers, who were, at the time, challenging for a Play-off position.

Impressive as that was up front, it was only Talia's third clean sheet. Starring in a narrow 2–1 loss at Manchester United in the third round of the Coca-Cola Cup, the Aussie 'keeper had generally acquitted himself well during the opening games of the season, but after blundering in a 3–2 home defeat by West Bromwich Albion and gifting the away side an equaliser, McMahon decided to make a change between the posts.

On 2 November Fraser Digby returned to first-team action for his first outing since the previous May. Successive clean sheets followed as Town recorded consecutive home wins over Manchester City and Barnsley, by the scores of 2–0 and 3–0 respectively. Diggers had waited his chance and both his patience and his manager's confidence were paying off.

It was then that now second-choice 'keeper Frank Talia did something that was never going to go down well with boss McMahon. With his contract due to expire the following summer, the Aussie rejected the offer of an extension, and in doing so handed the first-team number-one shirt to Digby for the rest of the season. Such actions were unlikely to convince the manager to play Talia ahead of Digby, although neither 'keeper seemed particularly highly regarded by the manager. Doing the same was striker and joint top-scorer Peter Thorne, who had been the subject of a £1 million bid by Bolton Wanderers the previous season. McMahon placed that figure on his head once more, and while injury played a part, a lengthy spell without first-team action was to follow for Thorne as well.

It seems unlikely that Digby would have kept his place ahead of Talia for any reason other than Talia's contract rejection. After the double victory that heralded Digby's return, between then and Boxing Day, Town would lose five matches from six. Performances up front, though, might have said more about the sudden lack of firepower and fall from grace of striker Peter Thorne, than defensive frailties. A 3–1 home win over Reading on 30 November brought a return to the County Ground for Paul Bodin, but four of the other five matches failed to see a Town player find the net.

When the season had begun after a period of many ups and downs, most fans would have been content with a season of consolidation. On the fringe of the Play-off zone as December started, perhaps Swindon were punching above their weight, but that wouldn't have prevented supporters raising their expectations to higher levels than they had dared in the summer. Now Town's results were about to justify the previous caution and the County Ground crowd would need to readopt the mantle of realism.

A 2–0 defeat at Charlton saw Digby upend Carl Leaburn. Fraser stayed on the pitch and could justifiably lay claim to Swindon's Man of the Match award, but no points were scored. A Steve Cowe goal that grabbed Town a 1–0 win at Portsmouth on Boxing Day rescued McMahon's side from a month without a victory, and by the middle of January 1997 Town had dropped as low as 18th in the table.

Also in January came an FA Cup match at Everton that was to produce a tournament record. The game was just 52 seconds old when centre-back Ian Culverhouse handled on the line from an Andrei Kanchelskis shot and received a red card, the quickest in FA Cup history. By the end, left-back Gary Elkins had also received his marching orders and nine-man Town were beaten by three goals to nil. Digby wasn't impressed by referee Neale Barry's performance. 'Once the ref had given the penalty and sent Cully off, the match had effectively ended. The ball was hit from close range and travelled at such a speed that Cully would have had a job getting his hands out of the way. Even if it did hit his hands, and I don't think it did, it was always more of a case of ball to hand.'

The game was painful for Fraser as well. Taking a set of Nicky Barmby's studs in the chest, the 'keeper added a first-minute knee injury and a pulled calf muscle 20 minutes later. Still making several outstanding saves including two brilliant stops from Kanchelskis in the closing minutes, Digby commented 'I was restricted for most of the game but hopefully with intensive treatment I'll be OK.' Sure enough, Fraser was back between the sticks for the following match, which was probably just as well. In between, four players were placed on the transfer list by Steve McMahon. Midfielder Wayne O'Sullivan was made available, and more surprisingly, Northern Ireland international Kevin Horlock had a £2 million price tag placed on his head. Less astonishingly, the names of contract rebels Thorne and Talia were circulated to interested parties.

By the end of the month, Manchester City had spent £1.5 million to make Horlock a City player and Diggers was back to his best. Recovering from a flu bug, Fraser pulled off a series of outstanding stops to help Town to a 2–1 win over Sheffield United, a match that brought Jan Aage Fjortoft back to the County Ground. Fjortoft didn't make the score sheet that day, but February brought a trip to Maine Road where new signing Horlock and another Town old boy Nicky Summerbee scored two of the three that Manchester City claimed without reply. The game also witnessed the dismissal of young midfielder Peter Holcroft, who had staked a strong claim to the shirt recently vacated by Horlock, and also the return to first-team action of Peter Thorne.

Home wins over Birmingham City and Charlton Athletic gave Fraser some food for thought. Having collected several Man of the Match accolades, the in-form 'keeper was asked whether the Play-offs were out of the question. 'If we keep playing as we have been you never know. It would be the ideal way to round off my testimonial season.' With Town back to 10th, the chance was there for the taking. There were 11 games of the season left and four points separated Swindon from Crystal Palace lying sixth. With the right application, McMahon's team could complete the return to the Premiership in two seasons.

A Peter Thorne goal helped Town to a 1–1 draw at Barnsley, but then came a result that dented any confidence they may have had in claiming a Play-off place. Travelling to Burnden Park, Town faced Bolton Wanderers, who had led the table for almost the entire season. What better opposition to measure Swindon's promotion aspirations against?

September 1997 and Fraser commands his box against Huddersfield Town.

Wanderers were two goals to the good by half-time, and with eight minutes to go had added a third. An incredible four further home goals then brought the score to 7–0, rattling any confidence that Town had gained in February and inflicting huge damage on hopes that supporters may have harboured of enjoying their football until the end of May. Stoke City visited the County Ground next, with Peter Thorne again responsible for supplying three points from the game's solitary strike, but two minutes later Town were consigned to play a whole hour with 10 men after Thorne's fellow striker Wayne Allison was sent off for the use of an elbow. Digby again excelled with some crucial stops in the second half as the superior numbers of the visitors started to tell.

The Potters' manager Lou Macari paid tribute to the contribution of the 'keeper. 'I thought we were never going to score. I think it was going to take a deflection or something for us to get a goal. Had Fraser not stayed so cool and calm then I think we would have won. He's worth his weight in gold.'

That left eight games to go and the season rapidly slipped through the fingers of Steve McMahon and his players. In the remaining 720 minutes of football just one goal was scored, an 87th-minute effort from Steve Cowe at Oldham at the end of March. By that stage of the game, Town had already conceded five. Three were shipped for no reply at home to Norwich City, and then, perhaps inspired by their near neighbours' performance, Ipswich Town came to the County Ground in April and went one better.

By the time the final whistle was blown in 1996–97, those last eight matches had seen Swindon concede 17 goals and reply just once. A finish of 19th was far removed from the hoped-for return to the Premiership, and too close to a plunge back to Division Two than anyone liked to acknowledge. One particularly painful defeat, a 2–0 loss at the Manor Ground against Oxford

Diggers at full stretch turns a Sunderland shot past the post in May 1998.

United, brought an admission from Digby. 'We're letting ourselves, the fans and the club down. Everybody's got to take responsibility for their own position and we've all got to take responsibility of what's going on out there.'

A week later, at the end of April, Crystal Palace were the opposition for the last home game of the season. Town lost 2–0. McMahon had made wholesale changes, but one man to keep his place was Digby, who polled over two thirds of the votes cast in the Player of the Year competition and who was presented with the silverware before the match.

The award represented a big turnaround for the 'keeper, who had begun the season clearly second choice in the mind of his manager and who had needed to wait until three months into the campaign to get his first League start.

A trip to Huddersfield ended the season and the game finished 0–0, leaving both clubs safe from the drop. The goalless scoreline was a stark indicator of Swindon's increasing problems up front, particularly when compared with the 6–0 drubbing they had handed out to the Terriers back in the autumn. Wayne Allison was the season's top scorer with just 11. Midfielder Kevin Horlock, who had left the club with three months of the season to run, and Peter Thorne, himself absent for two and a half months, were next with eight. Fraser Digby's performances between the posts were probably the greatest contributor to preventing the season ending much moe badly than it did.

But the story linking Fraser Digby with Swindon Town's Player of the Year award had started in 1986.

Initially signed on loan by Lou Macari in March of that year, the ex-Manchester United apprentice was called on to understudy Town's regular goalkeeper Kenny Allen. Fraser was behind Gary Bailey, Chris Turner and Gary Walsh in the Old Trafford goalkeeping pecking order and failed to make a League appearance while on United's books. Diggers didn't take to the County Ground pitch before the season concluded, but with Town storming to the Fourth Division Championship with a record 102 points, the young goalkeeper had been part of a big success in Wiltshire.

The following campaign he was back. An unconvincing start to the season brought the visit of Blackpool to the County Ground in the middle of September, and when Town trooped off on the receiving end of a 6–2 drubbing, Allen's days were numbered. He had been ever present since arriving six matches into the previous season. Now, six matches into 1986–87, Allen was out. On 25 September Macari contacted his old club again and Sheffield-born Fraser arrived from Old Trafford on a temporary deal once more. He was 19 years of age. Two days later, Swindon's new number one stepped out to face Rotherham, kept a clean sheet and Town had claimed their second win of the season. The match was Digby's League debut, since he had previously had only an unconsummated loan spell at Oldham Athletic.

Digby never looked back. The sum of £32,500 was invested in Fraser's permanent signature two days before Christmas 1986, a deal that was the first one conducted by new United manager Alex Ferguson, by which time Fraser had kept his place for 15 consecutive games. It was to be towards the end of March before he was forced to step down, due to a ban after being sent off in a Freight Rover Trophy area semi-final defeat by Aldershot. By then Allen was long gone back to Torquay, and the man considered best qualified to step into Fraser's boots was England Under-21 man Tim Flowers, who made two appearances on loan from Southampton. But as Fraser had already claimed the first of his own England Under-21 honours on 18 February against Spain, it seems apt that it was his fellow England rival who stood in for him.

Not only that, but Swindon had laid a consistent claim to a top-five place in Division Three. In the first season in modern history that a Play-off place was at stake, the format involved the third-bottom placed team in Division Two in a four-team tournament with those finishing third, fourth and fifth in the Third Division. Diggers was reinstated to the first team as soon as his ban was completed, and with a dozen matches remaining the 2–0 loss at Chester City was to be the last game surrendered before the end of the campaign.

The last game of the regular season took place at Ashton Gate, where a 1–1 draw claimed third place for Town but left Bristol City a point and a place away from the new end-of-season promotion fiesta. Fraser had kept 16 clean sheets over 39 League appearances. The Play-offs paired Swindon with Wigan Athletic, and just three minutes into the away leg the home side took the lead. By half-time, Athletic had added a second and appeared to have complete control of the tie.

As the second half progressed, though, Town became the stronger of the two teams, but it took until 18 minutes from time for Dave Bamber to pull a goal back. Wigan's first-half superiority had been such that at half-time, a 2–1 defeat would have been gratefully accepted, but eight minutes after the first Swindon goal a Jimmy Quinn effort brought the sides level. Then, with two minutes to spare, Peter Coyne gave Town what had looked an unlikely 3–2 victory. A 0–0 draw was played out at the County Ground to take Swindon through to the Play-off Final against Gillingham, victors over Division Two Sunderland.

At Priestfield, Town succumbed to a 1–0 defeat, then in the return leg, Carl Elsey crashed home a stunning 25-yard drive to leave Swindon two goals down on aggregate with 17 minutes played. Peter Coyne and Charlie Henry fought back for the home side and a replay was required at neutral Selhurst Park. Three minutes into the third match with the Gills, Steve White gave Town the start they so wanted, and then repeated the feat with minutes of the match left to play to hoist Town into Division Two for the first time since 1974.

What a year for Fraser Digby. He had recorded his League debut, international honours, a promotion campaign and won the supporters' Player of the Year. Diggers had arrived.

In 1997–98, by the time the Division One season kicked off, one of the contract rebels had flown the Robins nest. Peter Thorne moved on to Stoke City in return for £350,000 in July, but, perhaps surprisingly, fellow procrastinator Frank Talia remained at the County Ground, and this time he started the season playing second fiddle to Digby. Also competing for the number-one shirt was a new kid on the block in the shape of Swindon-born Steve Mildenhall.

As a replacement for Thorne, Chris Hay came in from Celtic for £330,000, but it was the old guard of Wayne Allison and Steve Finney who scored the goals that gave Town a 2–0 win at home to Crewe Alexandra to commence the 1997–98 programme. Dropping just two points from the first 12, Town remained undefeated through August and sat fourth in the table as September started. These were times that Town supporters were not sure what to hope for. Was it realistic to hope to challenge for promotion, when relegation had been avoided by just three places the previous season? Or had 1996–97 been the season of consolidation after the previous year's Division Two Championship, that could provide the springboard to a successful campaign challenging the top of the table?

There were, perhaps, signs of an identity crisis at the County Ground. Just where did Town sit in the pecking order of football?

The answer seemed to be closer to the top of the table than the bottom. 20 September brought the eighth game of the campaign and a 0–0 draw away at West Bromwich Albion left McMahon's team second in the table. If a trip to 20th-placed Manchester City might have looked routine,

September 1993 and Digby foils a West Ham United raid at Upton Park.

defeat by six goals to nil proved it was anything but. Kevin Horlock was again among the goalscorers for the Maine Road outfit, but to Town's credit they bounced back.

Six wins from the next eight matches took Swindon to the very top of the table, although a 3–1 defeat at Wolves saw midfielder Lee Collins receive his third red card of the season and a huge but justifiable seven-match ban. New striker Chris Hay was on fire. A hat-trick in a 4–2 win over Port Vale was followed by a brace in a 3–1 victory over Bury. A further five strikes in the next seven League matches and fans had completely forgotten the name of Peter Thorne – the man Hay had replaced in the summer.

A battling 0–0 draw at the brand new Stadium of Light was achieved most notably by the performance of Fraser Digby. Saving a penalty from Sunderland's Kevin Phillips in the 15th minute, Fraser collected the Man of the Match award and told the *Adver* afterwards 'The lads defended well and it was a good defensive performance.' The spot-kick save was the modest 'keeper's first since rule changes allowed goalkeepers to move along their line before the kick was taken. 'You just dance around and do your best to put the striker off, and maybe I did that.'

On a Friday Halloween night Digby was suffering from a chest injury, but his understudy Steve Mildenhall made his full League debut as a replacement and played a courageous game at Portsmouth to keep the run going with a 1–0 win. The three points took Town to the top of Division One overnight. Then, with Mildenhall himself injured and Frank Talia suffering a knee injury, a far from fit Fraser was forced back between the posts in a home match with Queen's Park Rangers. Painkillers got Diggers through the 90 minutes and Swindon claimed a 3–1 win to regain the top of the table, but the County Ground crowd came in for particular recognition from Town's

Reading are foiled by goalkeeper Digby in April 1995.

stopper. 'I can't thank the crowd enough. They were brilliant. I've got such a great rapport with them and I'd love to stay here for the rest of my career. I don't think I could go anywhere else and feel the same warmth and kindness.'

Little doubt, then, that Digby intended to stick around for a while longer.

McMahon secured the signature of Liverpool goalkeeper Tony Warner on loan for a couple of matches while his regular number ones regrouped, but by the end of November Fraser was back between the posts.

But an event which would prove a major influence on the season was about to take place.

A sum of £800,000 was paid by Huddersfield Town and striker Wayne Allison, known wherever he went as the Chief, stopped being a Robin and became a Terrier. Ever present for the first 16 games of the League programme, Allison had scored three times in the first five games and then not at all since the first match of September. Having just passed his 30th birthday he would still be knocking in goals in the Football League a full eight seasons later, but at the time the deal could have been considered good business.

With Chris Hay suspended, McMahon recalled Steve Finney from a loan spell at Cambridge United. Ten days later on 21 November, it was announced that striker George Ndah had been signed from Crystal Palace for £500,000, and three days after that, the new boy struck his first goal at home to Middlesbrough. By the end of the season, Ndah had hit just one more. Both matches were lost.

In contrast, Allison took two weeks to get his first goal for Huddersfield, but when the season ended he had hit six. All but one of the matches in which he scored witnessed a Terriers win. Had the deal that had replaced Allison with Ndah been a good one after all?

Four goals in a win over Oxford United at the beginning of December masked further problems, and it was to be the end of January and eight matches later before Town won again. Worryingly, the four matches between Boxing Day and 17 January yielded not only no points, but also no goals. By then, Swindon were down to 10th in the table. One particular match, a 1–1 home draw with Birmingham City, saw manager McMahon, recently linked with a return to Liverpool to replace under-pressure manager Roy Evans, outraged by the performance of referee Rob Styles, who had sent off midfielder Darren Bullock. Digby was named Man of the Match by the Swindon *Advertiser* and said afterwards 'It was as if we were playing 12 men at times. There's a great spirit. It was always going to be difficult with 10 men.'

Also, as December started, came news that the club had made 'a substantial' offer to buy the freehold of the County Ground from Swindon Borough Council, a move that chairman Rikki Hunt saw as instrumental in taking the club forward. The issue wouldn't be resolved until April, when the council rejected what was revealed as a £1.5 million bid. As 1998 began, Giuliano Grazioli, a man who would one day wear the shirt of Swindon Town, heaped shame on the Robins as he scored a 66th-minute winner for Conference part-timers Stevenage Borough to dump Town out of the FA Cup. The embarrassment was palpable and the game was indicative of Town's loss of momentum.

League form continued to reflect the Cup upset. A 1–0 home win over Stoke three days before the end of January was the first victory since the beginning of the previous month, and it did not signal a turnaround. On 7 February a home match with West Bromwich Albion saw Fraser Digby return after a bout of flu, but the 2–0 defeat witnessed scenes which saw Town defender Mark Robinson squaring up to midfielder and teammate Scott Leitch as the ball flew in for Albion's second goal. Referee Mark Halsey booked them both as Town supporters looked on through their fingers. How could the season be slipping away so badly?

Some members of the County Ground crowd seemed in no doubt. Chants of 'Macca Out' were heard as Swindon stumbled to further defeat at Tranmere Rovers four days later. McMahon had recently placed eight players on the transfer list, including costly signing Jason Drysdale, who had failed to complete six consecutive matches since the boss had invested the cash from the sale of Jan Aage Fjortoft two years earlier. At last a 1–0 win at Port Vale brought three points but at a cost. Knocked unconscious for five minutes after a last-minute goalmouth scramble, Digby was stretchered off wearing an oxygen mask and hospitalised in Newcastle-under-Lyme, leaving striker Steve Finney to deputise between the posts.

Thankfully, while the incident left the Town 'keeper out for three weeks, no greater damage had been done. During Fraser's absence Steve Mildenhall again stepped up to the plate before being replaced by Frank Talia. Three matches later and Town had shipped another five goals and surrendered all nine points. Calls for McMahon's head continued as banners were displayed urging his dismissal, but chairman Hunt insisted his man was here to stay. 'I will never sack Macca' shouted the *Adver* headline, but a day later the same man was back in the headlines as he apologised to supporters for calling them 'mindless morons'. Town were in crisis and supporters demanded that someone's head should roll.

The publication of the club's accounts, showing a £600,000 loss over the 13 months prior to June 1997, did little to help the mood or the club's public relations, and supporters would have been more surprised when Hunt announced the return of ex-favourite David Kerslake as 'a natural left-footer, and Steve has been wanting a good left-sided player for some time'.

Kerslake had previously played over 140 games for Town at right-back.

Now recovered from concussion and back for the trip to Middlesbrough as March reached its midpoint, Fraser Digby was unable to prove the saviour at the back that Town desperately needed. Six goals were conceded without reply. Three days later, referee Alan Butler decided Diggers had deliberately handled outside his penalty box and the 'keeper was shown a red card at Queen's Park Rangers after just 21 minutes. With the game already at 1–1, ex-QPR man Alan McDonald took over in goal and new signing Iffy Onuora, a £120,000 capture from Gillingham two days earlier, grabbed the goal that gave Town an incredible victory.

There were eight matches to play and Town sat 12th in the table. Successfully appealing against the red card and avoiding suspension, Fraser was to play in every one, but they were not to be particularly happy experiences. Hopes would have been focused on the three consecutive home games to come, but draws with Wolves and Stockport, followed by defeat by Charlton, produced just two points. Then a loss at Oxford United rubbed Town's noses in it.

Back at the County Ground, the point from a draw with Sheffield United was the last of the season. Pressure on McMahon and his supportive chairman continued. 'McMahon and Hunt Must Go' banners became a regular sight and the beginning of May saw McMahon proclaiming 'I will NOT walk away.'

Three straight defeats heralded the end of the campaign. Ten more goals were conceded and an 18th-place finish was the end result. From a season that had once promised much more and had seen Town sit at the very top of the table, relegation had been avoided by just four points. Starting on Boxing Day, Town had failed to score in 14 of the remaining 23 games.

And for Fraser the writing was on the wall.

Towards the end of March, Digby had been transfer listed after refusing a new three-year deal. 'Digby can go,' proclaimed the Swindon *Adver*, while McMahon said 'I'm the last person who wants to see Fraser go. He's one of the best 'keepers in the division. It's a long-term deal and includes a substantial rise but he's turned it down. It was his decision.'

A day later, and another side to the story.

'I don't want to quit Town,' Fraser told the newspaper. 'It's been quoted that I was offered a substantial rise when in fact it is still quite a bit less than three years ago.' He felt there was still a chance that he could start 1998–99 in Swindon, but chairman Rikki Hunt said 'We need a replacement, so the worry for Fraser is if we sign someone else then he could end up being unemployed.' Ahead of the last game of the season, a 2–1 home loss to Sunderland, Fraser's longstanding supporters, perhaps mindful that this could be their last chance to raise the 'keeper to an exclusive group, voted him Player of the Year for the third time. No fewer than 50 percent of voters considered him their most worthy winner, and few questioned that the figurine was safe in the hands of the person who had kept goal so effectively over 11 seasons. 'I'm very honoured to have won the trophy again,' Digby told fans, but remained tight-lipped about his future. Hunt was less so. 'If it's time to move on for Fraser, it's time to move on,' he said helpfully.

In the summer and as predicted by his chairman, Fraser left the County Ground. Joining Division One rivals Crystal Palace on a Marc Bosman free transfer due to being out of contract, he was to understudy Kevin Miller. When Miller started 1998–99 at less than his best, Digby made his Eagles debut against Oxford United, keeping a clean sheet in a 2–0 victory. Then injury struck at Christmas, allowing Miller to reclaim the first-team shirt. Over 60 appearances were made at Selhurst Park before Diggers requested that his contract be paid up at the end of October 2000. A shoulder injury looked like impeding any further footballing action, but the help of Town physio Dick Mackey led to another chance with Bristol Rovers.

How frustrating it must have been, then, that on his first day with the Pirates, a ruptured cruciate ligament stole another four months of his career and cost him the chance of taking to the pitch as a Rover.

Then Peter Nicholas, an old acquaintance from Fraser's Palace days and then manager of Barry Town, made a call that brought Digby back to the pitch. Two successful months between the posts helped Barry to the title of the Welsh League and the Welsh FA Cup, but defeat in the Final of the principality's League Cup denied a treble. His rehabilitation complete, a spell back in the Football League with Huddersfield Town from the summer of 2001 proved there was still football to be played for Fraser Digby. Quickly moving on to Queen's Park Rangers with one eye on the future, a return to the County Ground to take a part-time role in the marketing department was soon combined with a two-month playing stint at Division Three Kidderminster, then, with the arrival of Rhys Evans at Swindon, Andy King invited Fraser back in a coaching capacity.

Now with sporting consultancy Sports Solutions GB Ltd, Fraser is helping clubs relocate, redevelop and reinvest in their facilities. That seems like another skill that could be useful to Town.

There are Swindon Town Player of the Year winners, and then there's Fraser Digby – one of just two players to have won the fans' ultimate award three times. To achieve such a feat, it's useful for your Town career to demonstrate longevity, and the fact that goalkeeper Fraser's winning streak spanned 11 seasons certainly fits the bill. And if those trophy wins came in some of the most successful seasons in the club's history, you can be sure there will have been stiff competition for the fans' votes for the end-of-season award. Diggers had a long and distinguished career with Town and built up a loyal band of supporters, who appreciated his assured handling, agility and consistency.

His three wins spanned the managerial reigns of Lou Macari, Ossie Ardiles, Glenn Hoddle, Steve McMahon and John Gorman. Fraser was a Swindon Town player when the club were in Divisions Three, Two, One, the Premiership, back down to One, Two and back to Division One again. And he had to overcome some suspicion from bosses Hoddle and McMahon, who dropped Fraser in favour of Nicky Hammond and Frank Talia respectively. But each time, Diggers dug in, turned the situation around and reestablished himself as first-choice goalkeeper once more.

A total of five England Under-21 caps were claimed between 1987 and 1990, but his continued stay at Swindon had not always been guaranteed. In November 1990 Fraser had attracted attention from Aberdeen and West Ham United, and he was pondering a new contract offer to replace that which was due to expire the following summer. 'My future at the moment is with Swindon Town.

Ossie has been to me with a new contract, but the details are not sorted yet. Apart from our League position everything at Swindon is OK,' the then 23-year-old said.

Five years later and the picture was very similar. 2 November 1995 was announced as the deadline for the 'keeper to sign a further deal, his procrastination hastening the arrival of Blackburn Rovers goalie Frank Talia on a permanent deal.

In between, Fraser had spent a month at the tail end of 1992 back at Old Trafford, where he covered Peter Schmeichel without taking to the pitch. He kept some auspicious company through his career but after 500 appearances for Town over 11 seasons, he will always be considered a son of Swindon.

An armful of trophies in the safe hands of Fraser Digby in 1997.

George Ndah

(1998–99) ~ Fit for purpose

Town manager Steve McMahon spent the summer of 1998 preparing for a campaign that he hoped would buck the trend of the previous two. So far, the boss had presided over relegation to Division Two and then a triumphant return with the Championship trophy 12 months later. But then things had stagnated and successive 19th and 18th-place finishes in Division One had supporters wondering whether McMahon had achieved as much as he could with Swindon Town.

With gaps to fill in his squad after the release of some key players, Wimbledon centre-back Alan Reeves arrived to take the shirt vacated by Ian Culverhouse. Joining him at the back was ex-Coventry City man Adam Willis, while left-back Gareth Hall came in from Sunderland after making over 130 appearances for Chelsea and Jimmy Glass was recruited from Bournemouth in an attempt to fill the goalkeeping gloves of Fraser Digby.

George Ndah hurdles a challenge in September 1999 against Crewe Alexandra.

Perhaps surprisingly, bearing in mind the goal shortage of the previous season, all the new signings had defensive duties to perform as McMahon pinned his hopes on an injury-free campaign for Iffy Onuora and George Ndah. Any assistance would have been welcome, so a 60th-minute own-goal from David Holdsworth at Sheffield United in the opening fixture helped, but that was the last goal of the afternoon and the Blades were already two to the good, so the season started with defeat.

The partnership of Ndah and Onuora didn't immediately spark into life. In the first five League games of the season just one goal had been claimed between them, but a goal from both contributed to a 3–2 win at home to Bristol City in the first game of September, bringing some local pride to the County Ground as well as the first three-point haul. Commenting afterward, goalscorer George said 'This was probably one of the most exciting matches I have ever played in. We had a dream start with both Iffy and myself on the score sheet but they certainly gave us a bit of a pushing in the second half.'

The goal was only George's third since joining Town for £500,000 the previous November from Crystal Palace. A knee tendonitis problem had interrupted his first 10 months at the County Ground and the Dulwich-born striker had taken to the pitch in only 14 matches by the time 1997–98 had finished. The former England Youth international was 22 years old when he signed for Swindon and had started as a trainee at Selhurst Park, signing his first professional contract in time to start the 1992–93 season. Born of Nigerian descent a day before Christmas Eve 1974, George gloried in the magnificent middle name of Ehialimolisa, enough to endear him to anyone.

He didn't have to wait long to make his League debut, but the experience would have been both bitter and sweet. Coming on as a Palace substitute at Anfield, his team were annihilated by Liverpool by five goals to nil in Division One, but he kept his place and played his part in successive wins over Sheffield United and Queen's Park Rangers as the Eagles launched into a run of five straight wins.

By the end of his first season George had made 13 League appearances and scored his first senior goal in a Coca-Cola Cup fifth-round win over Chelsea, a run that took Palace to a semi-final defeat at the hands of Arsenal. But already it could be seen that the hallmark of Ndah's game was his electric pace, and it was seen as an ideal attribute to bring off the bench when a match needed changing. Only four of the 13 games saw George on the pitch at the kick-off.

Competing for a place in the starting line up with established wide man John Salako, George found his opportunities limited to occasions when the England international was unavailable. With chances still at a premium as 1995–96 commenced, George went out on loan to Bournemouth in October before returning when Dave Bassett arrived at Selhurst as manager. The new boss seemed prepared to offer a career lifeline. Four goals in March helped Palace to a Division One Play-off place and an appearance at Wembley, but defeat by Leicester City added to his experience.

Injury, though, had already started to blight the burgeoning Ndah's career, and despite signing a new three-year deal with Palace in November, he came on as a substitute 22 times during 1996–97 to take his total appearance tally to more than 100. A four-match loan spell at Gillingham in August 1997 gave way to just two starts and a further substitute appearance, then it was back to Selhurst Park in October, but before November was out, George was a Swindon player.

Ndah was called on to prove his ability from the off. The fee to capture his signature had come from the £800,000 generated through the sale of Wayne Allison to Huddersfield, and with fellow striker Chris Hay starting a three-match suspension, George was handed his Town debut in a home match with Middlesbrough just 48 hours after signing. It took just 12 minutes for the 6ft 1in, now ex-Crystal Palace man to register his first goal for Swindon. 'I couldn't believe it', was George's reaction in the after-match interview. 'It's such a great feeling to come to a new club and then to score on your debut. The fans were brilliant and that goes for everyone. They've made me feel so welcome. If we carry on playing like that I'm sure we'll be up there at the end of the season.' But a flare up of an old knee tendonitis problem soon damaged his season. A lengthy lay-off meant that by the time George was back to fitness in the spring, his penalty strike against Oxford United in April in a 2–1 defeat at the Manor Ground was only his second and also his last of the campaign. By the last match of the season, Ndah was once more unavailable due to his ongoing knee injury.

Back to 1998–99, and in light of the striker's fitness record, the decision of McMahon to pin his hopes on an injury-free season for his half-a-million-pound signing looked to have been built on fragile foundations. The partnership of George and Iffy Onuora continued to develop, however. When both hit a brace in a 4–1 County Ground victory over Oxford United on 9 September, the season looked significantly brighter after seven games than it had seemed after five, when Town had already occupied 21st in the table. Obviously on a roll, both found the net at Portsmouth on 12 September, but this time Pompey scored five. McMahon's gamble on last season's strike force appeared to be paying off, but his newly-constructed rear-guard was struggling to find cohesion.

Frank Talia had retained his place in goal ahead of the newly-arrived Glass, but Reeves and Hall, accompanied by Brian Borrows and either David Kerslake or Mark Robinson at right-back, were shipping goals at an alarming rate. Another four were claimed by Watford immediately after the loss at Fratton Park, and this time the defeat took place at the County Ground.

McMahon was under pressure again. At an away defeat at Bury supporters had already restarted their public campaign showing their lack of confidence in the manager. The wins over Bristol City and Oxford brought a reprieve and instead, reserve-team coach Ross MacLaren, chief scout Les O'Neill and youth co-ordinator Tommy Wheeldon were all axed to save money. It was revealed that Town had a break-even crowd figure of an incredible 13,500, while just 8,537 had witnessed the local derby with Bristol City. It was difficult to see how on earth Town's fans could possibly cover the finances required of them.

Another goalkeeper is left on the floor.

And there were many questioning whether the money had been saved in the right place. 'I'm no quitter' was the *Adver* headline attributed to Steve McMahon on 10 September, even as his team basked in the convincing win over local rivals Oxford, so if the strain was telling after a victory over the local rivals, it increased significantly after the 5–2 loss at Portsmouth was followed by a 4–1 home defeat at the hands of Watford a week later.

A pitch invasion at the final whistle left little doubt of the lack of faith that many fans had in the continued leadership of McMahon, and four days later the boss was gone. Citing the pressure that members of his family were under, McMahon announced his resignation at lunchtime on 23 September and pleaded with supporters to get behind the team he was leaving behind. Rikki Hunt, always loyal to the team manager, was plainly upset and announced that he would do what he could to identify those who demonstrated against the boss and ban them from attending the County Ground. A week later, Hunt retracted his threat.

McMahon's assistant, Mike Walsh, was placed in temporary charge of the side while a replacement was sought. Lou Macari's name quickly surfaced among the gossip but was immediately dismissed at boardroom level, and it was another man with a long-term Swindon connection who returned to take the reins of a club who took just one point from the two games under Walsh.

Jim Quinn had spent two spells as a striker with Town, starting in December 1981 before moving to Blackburn Rovers three years later. December 1986 saw him return to the County Ground for another two seasons, then £210,000 took him to Leicester City. The Belfast-born man claimed almost 50 caps for his country and included West Ham United among his clubs before he joined Reading, where he teamed up with Mike Gooding as a joint managerial team and led the Royals to within a whisker of the Premiership with a 4–3 Play-off Final defeat by Bolton Wanderers in 1995.

Quinn arrived back in Swindon on 2 October from Peterborough, where he had been Barry Fry's assistant while continuing to knock in goals for Posh on the pitch. He inherited a team that sat dangerously close to the bottom of Division One and when his first match in charge ended in a 3–2 home defeat against Stockport County, he was immediately given a glimpse of the magnitude of the task he faced. The defeat left Swindon 22nd in the table.

A convincing 3–0 win over League leaders Huddersfield Town a week later was only the third victory in 13 League matches and signalled the start of an upturn in fortunes. Defeat by a single goal at Ipswich was the only loss in the next six matches and Town made slow but crucial

Ndah shows a Crystal Palace man a clean pair of heels in April 1999.

movement up the table through October. A 2–0 win at Crewe as November began left Town five places above a relegation place and suggested that the arrival of Quinn, or perhaps the departure of McMahon, was having the desired effect on the team.

George Ndah missed the trip to Gresty Road after suffering internal bruising to the knee in a 3–1 win over Queen's Park Rangers in the previous game, a knock that kept him out of the following 3–0 defeat at Bradford City. But the injury had cleared up sufficiently for George to take his place on the bench for a match that he would have looked forward to from the moment the fixture list had been published. On 21 November the Eagles visited the nest of the Robins as Ndah's new team faced his old club, Crystal Palace.

After just 15 minutes Ty Gooden pulled up with a hamstring problem and George was on the pitch as his replacement. Six minutes later a Mark Walters free-kick found Ndah, who narrowly headed wide of Fraser Digby's goal between the posts for the away side. With Palace apparently not learning from that, a minute later the pair repeated the act and this time Ndah guided the ball past the ex-Town custodian to open the scoring. It was George's first League goal since mid-September and understandably, the striker was pleased.

'We knew it would be a tough game because Palace have got quality players but the boys produced a great result today,' he said after Mark Walters had produced some breathing space with a second-half penalty. 'I did not think I'd come on so early and I did not think I'd score, so today has been a dream come true. Today was very special because I've got a lot of friends at Palace and to score was a special moment personally. I don't score many headers but as soon as it hit my head I knew it was going in. I met it with a lot of power and Fraser really didn't have a chance with it. I am a Swindon player now and I am 100 percent committed.'

The result lifted Town to 15th in the table, as high as had been achieved all season, and a slip that produced just two points from three matches as the festive season approached was corrected with two wins either side of Christmas Day, to bring Town back to the same position for the new year. The brightest star in Jim Quinn's pre-Christmas side was winger Mark Walters, who was clearly benefiting from the change in management. Scoring in Quinn's first game in charge, the man many knew as Wally netted in all of the first six home matches under his new boss, with a brace against Queen's Park Rangers bringing his total to seven in two months.

When his run came to an end, Iffy Onuora chipped in with four goals in three games, the last coming three minutes into added time to give Town a single goal victory over Wolves on Boxing Day. Then George Ndah rediscovered his shooting boots with three in consecutive matches and Swindon's strike force seemed capable of getting the goals necessary to climb the table from the position of 15th, which was beginning to seem increasingly difficult. George's effort in a 2–1 loss at Ashton Gate, though, failed to gain points. His next, at home to Sheffield United, helped towards a 2–2 draw and came from a spectacular scissor-kick after 11 minutes. 'As soon as the ball left my foot I knew it was going into the back of the net. I think that is easily the best goal of my career,' the goalscorer commented.

The boss was also impressed, but with reservations. 'George was tremendous. If he could use his right foot he would be top notch. At the moment everything he does is on his left peg. He needs to spend an hour each day slamming the ball against the wall with his right.' But Quinn recognised that Ndah was rapidly turning himself into a crowd favourite. 'He is very exciting, crowds love him and when he comes deep to pick that ball up there is a buzz.'

The major factor helping George establish himself was his fitness. 'Last season I was not 100 percent fit and that was showing in my performances. This season I have been playing regularly, I have been enjoying my football and that has made a lot of difference to my form. I now feel that I have settled down well. I love it at Swindon. I love the club, I love the players and I am really happy here.' All these were comments likely to endear him to Swindon Town supporters, but Sheffield United rained on the parade when David Holdsworth netted a last-minute equaliser for the visitors.

A week later Ndah hit his 10th goal of the season, and this time it claimed all three points in a 1–0 win at Port Vale. It was the middle of January, there were 18 games to play and Town's season could go either way. Still sitting 15th in the table, Town were the same distance from a Play-off place as from the last place in Division One. George also wondered which way the season would swing. 'Who knows what we can achieve? If we keep on winning then a top-10 place or the Play-offs is not out of our reach.' And on his goal, he said 'Ty Gooden pulled wide and I knew he was going to have a hard job getting a decent cross into the far post, so I went to the near post and fortunately got a good connection and it went in.'

While the goals had flowed relatively well up front, the defence had continued to show its weaknesses. The win at Vale had produced what was only the sixth clean sheet of the League season. Town had shipped three goals in a match on four occasions and twice the defence had been bypassed four times. Then there were the five conceded against Portsmouth at Fratton Park back in September, and it was plain that far too often it was left to Onuora, Ndah and Walters to tip the goal balance in Town's favour while the defence seemed intent in doing the opposite. If Quinn's strikers hit a barren patch it could be an uncomfortable last three months to the season, and at the end of January the boss made the short trip to Chippenham to snap up Bluebirds' teenage front man Charlie Griffin, for £10,000 as cover.

A 1–1 home draw with Bury came courtesy of an own goal, then successive 2–0 defeats, first at Sunderland and then, to the supporters' horror, Oxford, demonstrated that reliance on your strike force risked uncomfortable consequences. The visit of Portsmouth on 20 February brought the chance to try to avenge that 5–2 embarrassment at Fratton Park earlier in the season and, after half an hour, Chris Hay produced the opener for Swindon. Then a horrendous collision between Iffy Onuora and Pompey 'keeper Aaron Flahavan left the latter with six broken teeth, a broken nose, a fractured cheek bone and a cracked shoulder blade. Iffy, with his eyes firmly on the ball, was deemed innocent of intent and a foul was not even given, but the incident completed an unfortunate double for the visiting goalkeeper, who had mysteriously collapsed during the away fixture in September.

Defender Russell Perrett donned the green shirt to replace Flahavan and Hay stuck his second past the new 'keeper with four minutes of the half remaining. A breathless end to the half saw Steve Claridge capitalise on a bad Bobby Howe back-pass to reduce the arrears, before Onuora headed past the stand-in goalie to restore Town's two-goal lead. But Pompey staged a dramatic fight back in the second 45 minutes and pulled the deficit back through sustained pressure, another goal from Claridge and a Jean-François Peron effort in a six-minute spell. Town rallied to try to grab a winner, but two efforts were cleared off the Pompey line in the last three minutes of the match.

The visitors' number included ex-Swindon men Alan McLoughlin, Fitzroy Simpson and Adrian Whitbread, and future Town midfielder Sammy Igoe also featured in the dramatic encounter.

George was named as Town's Man of the Match and said 'To be honest it feels like we've been beaten. We were thinking how many could we score when the goalkeeper went off, but it never went for us. To be fair Portsmouth really came back at us after the break. We tried to get crosses in to test the 'keeper but we didn't do it enough.' That was a setback and an eye opener to ideas of climbing the table, but a 1–0 win at Play-off chasing Watford through a Bobby Howe goal the following Friday night in front of the TV cameras restored hope.

Bolton Wanderers do not know which way to turn to block Ndah.

The midweek visit of Tranmere followed and twice Town took the lead. What was perhaps more surprising was that central defender Alan Reeves hit both goals, his only two of the campaign. By the end of the evening, though, Rovers had struck three times and while no one knew it at the time, Swindon had begun a six-match run without a win. Another home match three days later, this time against Bolton Wanderers, produced the second 3–3 draw in three home matches and a worrying trend had started. Despite scoring eight goals over the three games, Town conceded nine and collected just two points. The best efforts of the strike force were being negated by the flimsiness of the defence, which was proving unable to stem the flow of goals against them.

In typical Swindon tradition, if there seemed trouble on the pitch, it must be time for bad news off it. A £1.5 million loss for the year ending June 1998 was announced on 8 March, and the reasons didn't make for pleasant reading. Gate receipts had fallen, the overdraft had increased and compensation paid to the departing manager Steve McMahon had all contributed to the bottom line. The previous July had seen chairman Rikki Hunt declare his admiration for Pride Park, the new home of Derby County, and he chose the occasion of the release of the financial books to confirm his commitment to move the club from the County Ground.

There could be little doubt that the effect of the Bosman ruling, which allowed players to leave for nothing at the end of their contracts, was beginning to bite. The financial year had produced a transfer income of £400,000, while the 12-month period of the previous year had brought in £4 million.

And there was no chance of that position being reversed.

Then came a four-match losing run that first saw Swindon surrender all the points in successive 2–1 defeats at Stockport County and at home to Crewe Alexandra. Goalkeeper Frank Talia had missed just one League match all season, but boss Quinn felt he needed to give his reserve 'keeper a chance. For the trip to Queen's Park Rangers in the last match of March, boss Jimmy Quinn decided to give reserve 'keeper Jimmy Glass his first outing since conceding four against Oxford back in September.

At half-time the score stood at 0–0, but 45 minutes later Town trooped off the Loftus Road pitch on the back of a 4–0 hiding and Mark Walters had seen an 85th-minute penalty saved. Ndah had this to say. 'We let ourselves down with some sloppy goals. We want to play again straight away but we've got a two-week break now. We will have to train well and hope that we can put things right in our next match.' The problem was, the next match was against Ipswich Town, who were sitting second in the table and nicely placed for automatic promotion.

Glass was again between the posts when the Blues made the trip to Swindon and he must have been hoping for a more flattering scoreline than that produced at QPR in the previous match. By the end of the afternoon, boss Quinn was describing the experience as 'probably one of the worst results of my career in football', and Glass had picked the ball from his net half a dozen times.

The 6–0 battering was Town's worst-ever home defeat and meant that Jimmy Glass, having waited patiently to be given his chance, had conceded 10 in two matches. There were seven games to go and, only three months earlier, George Ndah had been entertaining thoughts of a Play-off place. Instead, the losing run had dropped Town to 19th in the table and a real threat of relegation had materialised.

At last, a midweek 2–1 win at Huddersfield through goals from Bobby Howe and Chris Hay reversed the trend and saw Talia returned to the first team. George admitted 'The last week has been difficult and getting beaten 6–0 at home has been difficult to take. We knew that if we didn't play to the best of our ability Huddersfield would have beaten us. Hopefully now we will be able to build on this result.'

George's hopes were not completely fulfilled, although the worst-case scenario of relegation was to be avoided. A 1–0 defeat at home to Play-off bound Birmingham City saw all three points head off to the Midlands. George felt 'It was a dramatic improvement from last week and it was against one of the top teams.' The conditions had been a factor and the striker's assessment was that 'against the wind you could play the longer ball, but with it, you would find it would run out of play.' The only goal of the match came in the 83rd minute and George's view was 'I think we will definitely get a result at Albion', referring to the trip to the Hawthorns to face West Bromwich Albion three days later.

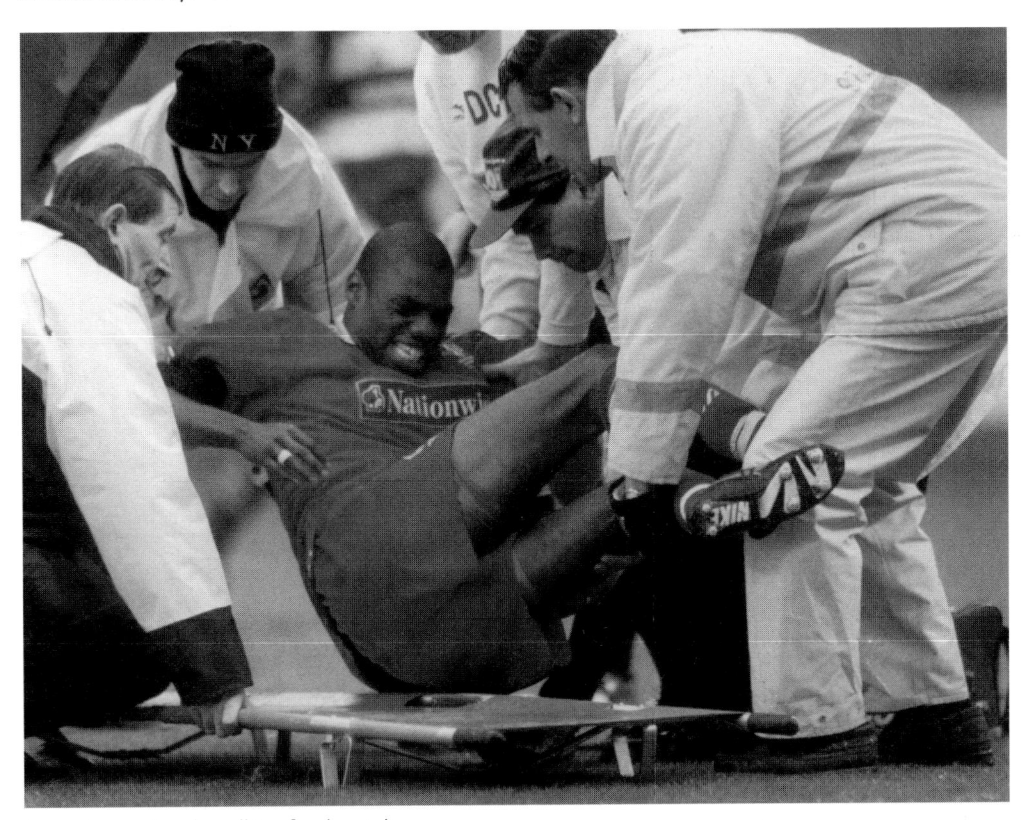

November 1998 and an all too familiar sight.

Town lay four places and four points off a relegation place with five matches to play, and three of them were to be away from home. A 1–1 draw at West Brom made Ndah's prediction come true, and it was George himself who was instrumental in bringing it about. After half an hour, and one minute after conceding, he collected the ball wide on the left, cruised past three tackles and fired a left-footed shot past the despairing dive of Phil Whitehead from 25 yards to square things up. Manager Quinn described it as 'A truly great goal from George,' but the goalscorer himself was more concerned about the League position. 'We have thrown two points away. They have lost their last five. We should have won.' But he did confess a contribution from his boss. 'The Gaffer has emphasised that we need to take any opportunity to shoot, so I had a dig and it went in, so I'm very pleased.'

He would have been just as pleased the following weekend when Town travelled to Selhurst Park and George made his first return to Crystal Palace since leaving for Swindon the previous season. An Iffy Onuora goal clinched the game in the 51st minute, and the chance came after George had sprinted down the left wing past three defenders and squared the ball for Onuora to tap in from six yards. 'It's been great and a very nice day coming back,' said the ex-Palace man. 'There were a few shouts of "Palace reject", but when you get that it means you are doing something right.'

The result did a lot to reinforce the belief that Town had what it took to avoid the drop, and when both Iffy and George were on the score sheet in a 2–0 win over Grimsby in the last game of April, Town had grabbed six points from six and kept two successive clean sheets to boot. Frank Talia was back between the posts and Jimmy Glass was soon on his way to Carlisle United, where his injury-time goal in the last game of the season after he had come up for a corner was to keep the Cumbrians in the Football League.

Incredibly, Swindon's victory over Grimsby was the first at home since Boxing Day, but the win secured Town's place in Division One for another season. George was named the *Adver's* Man of the Match, having supplemented Onuora's third-minute strike with his 12th of the season as the pair hit their 31st and 32nd goals as a partnership during 1998–99.

Ndah's goal came at the start of the second half and was from an uncharacteristic scramble.

More familiarly, now safe from relegation, Swindon took their foot off the gas. Defeats at Norwich and at home to Barnsley brought down the curtain on the campaign and gave the impression that Quinn was using the games to help formulate his plans for the next season. Even with one match to play, Quinn announced that a push for the Play-offs must be the aim for 1999–2000. A brave new world was expected to accompany the new millennium and the first full season of a new managerial reign. So with all attention focussed on the summer break, Town succumbed to Barnsley by 3–1, a game that brought ex-Chippenham man Charlie Griffin's first League goal to open the scoring but culminated in a 17th-place finish in Division One.

That day, George Ndah collected the Player of the Year award ahead of his strike partner Iffy

Thanks for the accolade. Ndah accepts the Player of the Year trophy 1999.

Onuora. With the performance of the defence throughout 1998–99, it was unlikely that a defender was going to catch the eye of the supporters sufficiently that he would be nominated Town's Player of the Year, but there was stiff competition up front for Ndah to overcome before he could be crowned the fans' favourite. Fellow striker Iffy Onuora struck 20 goals to finish top scorer and the wing play of Mark Walters, himself with 10 strikes to his name, offered an alternative for votes cast by supporters who felt speed and wing play were the most important factors.

George made 41 League appearances in 1998–99 and it was a sad reflection that his career never featured such a high number of outings in a single campaign either before or after. After rejecting a £1 million move to Queen's Park Rangers in October 1999, he made the trip to fellow Division One club Wolverhampton Wanderers for the same fee later in the month. Surprisingly, and costly for Town, Londoner George chose the Black Country in preference to a move back towards the capital to join Premiership club Watford, who had offered £500,000 more for his services.

He would again be hugely popular, but he made just 87 League appearances over seven seasons. A broken leg in only his third game after joining the Molineux club limited him to only four outings that season, returning in 2000, but almost an entire season would pass after another injury sidelined the man who had endeared himself to Wanderers' supporters in the same way that he had won over Swindon fans.

Just as it looked as though his career might be resuscitated, a knee injury suffered at Reading requiring surgery meant that he missed the entire campaign that Wolves spent in the Premiership after promotion in 2003, and after being granted a 12-month contract extension, George suffered further muscle damage to prevent a League appearance throughout the following season as well.

Ndah had signed for Wolves under Colin Lee, but by 2005 and with the club now managed by Glenn Hoddle, the ex-Swindon boss declared that even an 80 percent fit George was sufficient to terrify defenders. It would seem almost inevitable, then, that having fought back to first-team fitness, his last League appearance would see him leave the pitch on a stretcher, having suffered knee-ligament damage in a 52nd-minute challenge by Peter Gilbert at Sheffield Wednesday just after Christmas 2006.

At the age of 31, George announced his retirement from the game on 28 April, finally thwarted by the series of injuries that had punctuated his career. He had taken to the pitch 14 times in his last season, scoring his last League goal of a career total of 39 at Derby County the previous November. He had made just 248 appearances throughout his playing career.

Steve McMahon took much criticism during his reign as Swindon's manager, but the outlay that brought Ndah to the County Ground was recouped twice over when he left for Wolverhampton Wanderers, and McMahon's confidence that George could last the full season of 1998–99 was fully justified.

When looked at from a mercenary point of view, it seems George was bought and sold by Town at just the right time in his career.

Frank Talia

(1999–2000) ~ Aussie Rules

Back in July 1972, Swindon supporters were able to look back at a season that had seen the club establish itself in Division Two. An 11th-place finish had been one place higher than 12 months earlier, centre-back Frank Burrows had been crowned Player of the Year and with new manager Les Allen replacing Dave Mackay during the season, hopes were high that Town could build on the stability achieved since promotion in 1969 and mount a push for the top flight of the Football League.

Meanwhile, half a world away and taking his first breath of Melbourne air was someone who would one day pull on the green shirt of Swindon Town, at that time usually occupied by Peter Downsborough. 20 July 1972 saw the introduction of Frank Talia to the world, someone who would grow into the man who would one day be called on to replace the legendary Fraser Digby between the posts at the County Ground and to live up to the standards set by such respected custodians as Downsborough, Sam Burton and Jimmy Allan.

Frank Talia tips a Bolton shot around the post in September 1998.

Born Francesco Talia, Frank's decision to leave Australia to try his glove-encased hand in England saw him join Blackburn Rovers as a trainee. Rovers' regular between the posts at the time was Bobby Mimms, who played every one of the 42 Premier League matches that Rovers contested in 1992–93. With two other 'keepers ahead of him should Mimms's form fail, Talia moved out on loan to Hartlepool in Division Two. That brought a League debut in a 0–0 draw with Leyton Orient on 9 January 1993, and with it the experience of an extended run of first-team football, but it was an experience that would have done as much to blanch an Aussie's tan as the North East's winter weather.

A desperate looking lunge ends with the ball in Talia's hands.

A second goalless draw followed at home to Preston, but then eight consecutive defeats plummeted Pools down the table and in every one, Frank's new teammates failed to find the net. Apart from doing what he could to keep a clean sheet, he might have wondered whether he should try to bolster what appeared to be a non-existent forward line.

Faced with that introduction to English football, things really could only get better. A clean sheet for the loan 'keeper at home to Wigan at the beginning of March gained a point, and after 11 games without a goal Hartlepool finally made the score sheet at Blackpool a week later to claim another. Frank must have thought he was on a bit of a roll when another goalless match, this one at Burnley, was rewarded with the third point in as many matches, but his last match after a long haul down to Exeter brought a 3–1 loss and his tenure at Victoria Park came to an end.

When Frank had joined Hartlepool, his new team lay fourth in the table. By the time he returned to Ewood Park, Pools were down to 16th. It was hardly an inspiring introduction to an English footballing career or a record that would see a young Talia travel back south to Blackburn with his head held high, even if the greatest failing of his temporary employers had been up front.

So when England Under-21 international Tim Flowers arrived in Blackburn in November 1993, the odds of a first-team outing for Frank seemed to be getting longer, a feeling that was reinforced when Flowers made the transition to the full England side before the season was out.

Things got better for Rovers, but perversely worse for Talia, when Flowers played all but three Premiership matches in 1994–95 and Blackburn claimed the title of the top division in English football. Mimms filled in when called upon, and Frank must have felt he was as far away from making it at Rovers and in England as ever. When Town manager Steve McMahon made an approach for his services in the early stages of 1995–96, a loan spell at Swindon may have appeared ideal. Talia's Rovers teammate Shay Given had just completed his own month in Wiltshire, suggesting that McMahon was likely to give another loan signing first-team chances ahead of permanent signing Fraser Digby.

Frank got just that, and after five League matches throughout September he returned to Ewood Park, having made a good impression in the mind of manager McMahon. At the beginning of November Fraser Digby was under pressure to sign a new contract and the Town boss felt compelled to move to protect himself against the loss of the man who had been at the club for a decade. Even as Digby's contract signing deadline passed, McMahon splashed out £150,000 to bring the 23-year-old Australian to Wiltshire.

Frank had to be patient until March to get his next first-team outing, when a run of 11 matches made the new 'keeper a big contributor to the success that brought the Second Division title. After 15 League games at the start of the following year he was replaced by Digby until the end of the campaign. Then came the complication of a cartilage problem that required surgery, and Frank found he could look back at 1997–98 with just two more League outings under his belt. Of the two, he played through the pain barrier in a 1–0 defeat at Bury after Digby was injured, emerging as Town's Man of the Match.

By the time 1998–99 began, Frank had enjoyed an injury-free preseason, Digby had moved on to Crystal Palace and Frank could finally look ahead to a new campaign safe in the knowledge that he was considered his club's senior goalkeeper. All but three League matches of the season saw Talia don the gloves at the kick-off, and he could be confident that he had made good progress establishing himself in England as his Football League career reached the 90-appearance mark.

The summer of 1999 offered the promise of continued success and professional progress for Frank Talia. Arriving in Swindon to supplement the strike force was old Stevenage Borough foe Giuliano Grazioli, who signed on a free transfer from manager Jim Quinn's previous club Peterborough United, but there was a net reduction in the squad headcount as Kevin Watson, David Kerslake, Peter Holcroft and Phil King were all released from their contracts.

As 1999–2000 kicked off, manager Jimmy Quinn seemed happy to retain confidence in the goalkeeping duo brought in by his predecessor Steve McMahon. Frank Talia started the first eight games before being replaced by Jimmy Glass for a similar spell. When assessed over those first 16 games, the opening third of Swindon's Division Two season could not be considered a success.

A goalless away draw at Walsall might have seemed respectable enough, but eight days later came a Sunday 4–1 home defeat by Ipswich Town. The match went out live on Sky TV and while it may have been well received in Suffolk, the viewers in Wiltshire would have been less than satisfied. With Swindon going 1–0 ahead through a Grazioli goal that crashed in off the underside of the crossbar, Ipswich stormed back with braces from David Johnson and Richard Naylor.

A respectable 2–1 win over Crystal Palace after going a goal behind the following weekend restored some hope, but, in truth, hope throughout 1999–2000 was to be in short supply. A two-legged defeat by Third Division Leyton Orient in the first round of the Worthington Cup perhaps gave a warning of what was to come. Talia was nominated as Town's Man of the Match in the home leg that was lost 1–0, but he was outshone by the performance of one of the opposition, ex-Swindon midfielder and future Orient boss Martin Ling, who ran the match from the centre of the visitors' half. Despite being sent off in the second leg, Ling's team still claimed a draw and progressed at Town's expense.

Back in Division One, defeats at home to West Bromwich Albion and away at Blundell Park, Grimsby, meant that August concluded with three defeats from five, leaving Town 22nd in the early table. A Perry Groves penalty was fired past Talia's left hand after half an hour to earn Grimsby all three points.

Any manager would say it was far too early to judge their team at that stage of the season. A goalless draw at home to Nottingham Forest, relegated from the Premiership seven League matches earlier, was a boost, then successive away defeats at Crewe and Port Vale destroyed the feel-good factor and Town slipped another place.

In a bizarre incident in the 72nd minute of the match at Vale, Talia blocked a shot from Tony Rougier but when teammate Gareth Hall kicked for safety, his clearance struck Talia in the head and rebounded to give Vale a 2–0 lead. If that was any indication, luck was going to be in short supply over the next nine months. Only goal difference now kept Swindon off the foot of Division One.

By the time September ended, a 2–1 win over Blackburn Rovers brought Swindon's second win in nine matches but made little impact on their League position. Jimmy Glass had taken his place for his first start of the season and the change gave the impression that a corner may have been turned. Seven games came throughout October, but just one returned maximum points. The first, a 4–0 home humiliation by Bolton Wanderers, ended with the Town manager relieved that his side hadn't conceded six, as in the match with Ipswich towards the end of the previous season.

That period had seen goalkeeper Glass dropped as a result, but Quinn seemed ready to show further faith in his newly-returned 'keeper. Glass said afterwards 'I was annoyed at conceding four goals but I would be disappointed if I was dropped.' Quinn concurred and picked Glass ahead of Talia for a home draw with Stockport County a week later. Eight minutes into the match, Glass tried to kick a long ball to George Ndah, misplaced his pass and was powerless to stop Tony Dinning open the scoring from 35 yards. Glass was again upset with himself and manager Quinn, while declaring his continued faith in the man who had started the season as second-choice 'keeper, knew his number one had to cut out the slip-ups. 'Jimmy made a mistake in the Stockport game but it cost us the win and I would not like him to make any more. I think he deserves a little run in the side. If he cuts out making those silly mistakes then he will keep his place in the side. If he does struggle, he has Frank Talia breathing down his neck.' Continuing, Quinn elaborated 'Frank had a great game in the reserves the other day. What I want is players going out there fighting to keep hold of their shirts. It is down to Jimmy to do that.'

Next came a trip to Fulham and an 84th-minute goal from Geoff Horsfield deprived the visitors of any points, dropping Town to the very bottom of the table. The goal came after Glass had parried but failed to hold a Steve Hayward free-kick. Another 1–0 defeat came at Barnsley the following Wednesday, when Geoff Thomas scored with his first touch after coming on as a 70th-minute substitute. Glass couldn't be faulted, but the game was the 13th of the season and just two had ended in clean sheets.

So in light of the under-performing defence, it might have appeared a risky piece of business when, ahead of a home game with Sheffield United, Town accepted a bid from Wolves for the signature of striker George Ndah. But the player had scored just one goal all season and, with a seven-figure cheque being dangled, there was little chance that Town would be in a position to refuse the approach.

If the departure of last season's favourite Ndah produced mixed feelings among supporters, many of the same group offered a different reaction when faced with the news of 25 October that chairman Rikki Hunt was also leaving the County Ground. It is important for any club manager to know that he has the full support of his chairman, but a large proportion of fans felt that the unswerving and perhaps unjustified faith that Hunt had demonstrated in previous manager Steve McMahon had been misplaced. Vice-chairman and long-standing servant to the club Cliff Puffett, who had fostered an affection for the club while assisting his uncle as groundsman at the County Ground in the 1940s, stepped up to hold the fort as Hunt made it plain that it was 'other interests' rather than the pressure exerted by his critics that had resulted in his resignation.

In between the two departures, a two-goal, first-half brace from Chris Hay was surrendered in the match with Sheffield United and another chance to make progress away from the foot of the table was lost. Again, Glass emerged with credit as Talia watched from the bench. At last, a win over Port Vale temporarily lifted Town above their visitors to join a group of four teams on 13 points.

Full stretch.

The contest was decided in the first and last minutes of the game, an Iffy Onuora strike inside 60 seconds opening the scoring and then a Giuliano Grazioli injury-time winner cancelling out a 22nd-minute goal for the away side. After a third of the season it was just the third League win of Town's campaign.

Finally off the bottom of the table, any thoughts of further progression evaporated quickly. With three minutes of the game at Bolton Wanderers remaining and the score goalless, a brilliant save from Glass from Eidur Gudjohnsen in the first half was rendered meaningless when the Town 'keeper allowed a Bob Taylor toe-poke to squeeze under his body. Two minutes later Bo Hansen crashed home from close range and a morale-boosting draw had slipped through Town's, and Jimmy Glass's, fingers.

Town manager Jim Quinn decided action was required. Pointing the finger of blame firmly in the direction of Glass, Quinn announced that he was in the market for another 'keeper. 'You can't win games making mistakes like that,' the boss had to say. 'I have seen it on the replay and I don't know what Jimmy is trying to do. I am embarrassed about it. Jimmy made one or two good saves but I pay him to do that. What about the one he has let in that has cost us the game? Good goalkeepers don't let in goals like that, full stop. Me saying I'm looking for a goalkeeper may shake them up a bit.'

With a judgement like that, it was inconceivable that Glass would start the next game between the posts. After six games of first-team action, every one had seen at least one ball enter the net he defended and when the first week of November passed without any incoming staff, it was inevitable that Frank Talia was given a recall to face Huddersfield Town at the Alfred McAlpine Stadium. Ninety minutes later and Town trooped off the pitch, having been given a 4–0 hiding. It was hardly the instant response Quinn would have hoped for after his rocket of the week before.

Now it was Talia's turn to defend his performance. Having suffered with the sun in his eyes for the first half, Frank said 'It's possibly the worst conditions I've played in as far as the sun is concerned.' That offered an explanation for the two goals conceded in the first half, but did little to justify the two in the second with the sun behind him. Looking to the future Frank continued 'I'm sure we can survive. We've got the spirit and determination and we're not going to chuck the towel in.'

A Friday night game at home against Norwich City clawed back some credibility for the 'keeper, who had started the first eight matches of the League season. A 0–0 draw on 12 November was the first clean sheet in over two months of action, but by now Quinn had identified a problem at the other end of the pitch. The game was the second in which Town had failed to score.

The manager announced his readiness to step back into the fray to try to bring new firepower up front and named himself among the substitutes for the match that paired the Robins with the Canaries. A week before his 40th birthday, Quinn stepped off the bench with six minutes to go and came close to breaking the deadlock in the last minute with a shot that was deflected onto the bar by Norwich 'keeper Andy Marshall.

Quinn was to take to the field in each of the next four games, and while everyone willed the manager to make the difference up front, there was an air of desperation surrounding the way in which the boss was trying to solve the problems himself. No one, however, could deny that he was prepared to lead by example when it came to fending off relegation to Division Two.

The Norwich game saw the introduction of future Manchester United and England midfielder Michael Carrick, who had signed on loan from West Ham United the week before, and after an Iffy Onuora penalty secured a 1–1 draw at Wolves – a game that George Ndah missed through injury having played just three games since his transfer – Carrick made his mark in Swindon with a 43rd-minute goal against Charlton Athletic on 23 November. But Carrick's first goal for Town was to be in vain. Already two goals up, soon-to-be-crowned champions Athletic held the lead to travel the M4 with the points at the end of the evening. Swindon had gone six games without a win and there was little indication that the trend was going to be turned around. The defeat left Town five points adrift of Sheffield United at the bottom of Division One.

A day later, it was made public that the now second-choice 'keeper Jimmy Glass wanted away. Quinn had told Glass of his intention to place his faith in Frank Talia and to rotate the role of back up between Glass and up-and-coming Swindon-born 'keeper Steve Mildenhall. The news left a less than happy Glass deciding his future lay elsewhere, and his decision to look for a regular game with another club was to have a big influence on the next 18 months for both Talia and Mildenhall. He remained with Swindon until January when he made a free-transfer switch to Cambridge United, but it looked as though the effect on Talia might start as soon as the last match of November.

An Onuora goal in the last minute of the match secured a 1–1 draw at St Andrews, as Play-off-bound Birmingham City were denied a victory. Frank Talia gained good reviews despite being unable to keep out Martin Grainger's 26th-minute opener and said afterwards 'We ground out a good result in front of a very big crowd. They dropped off a bit in the second half and we were able to finish them.'

But Town remained bottom, and new Town chairman Puffett pleaded with his club's supporters to come out of the woodwork. Writing to the *Adver,* he emphasised the financial plight that Town still suffered. If the attendance for the upcoming fixture with Walsall dropped below 8,000, Puffett warned, the board would need to 'face up to reality and admit defeat in our battle to ensure the survival of the club in its current form.' 'It's Town's last chance,' screamed the headline. 'If support is not forthcoming, we will have some difficult decisions to make over the coming months. It would be personally heartbreaking to me and all associated with the club', continued Puffett. 'It really is a case of use it or lose it. I hope and pray you will react in a way that all Swindonians and Wiltshire folk alike would want to react, one that says this club is too much part of our heritage to let die.'

Sobering stuff indeed and a plea that seemed to strike a chord with some fans, but not enough to satisfy their chairman's prayers. When Walsall visited the County Ground at the beginning of December, and despite the offer of free half-time soup in the reopened Stratton Bank, 7,186 attended the fixture – an increase of less than 700 on the previous home match.

An advertisement was placed in *The Times* appealing for anyone ready to invest £900,000 in return for a 10 percent stake in Swindon Town to come forward. Town were being touted around like a product on a TV shopping channel but the stakes looked high enough to justify the indignity. The club had faced many financial challenges in the past, but this looked like being the greatest so far.

The game brought a 1–1 draw, a result that helped neither Town nor second-from-bottom Walsall. Third-choice 'keeper Steve Mildenhall replaced Frank Talia, who was unable to overcome a groin strain, for his 10th professional appearance and his only League start of 1999–2000. He kept his place as Town were eliminated from the FA Cup at Charlton, but when Talia was restored to first-team action for a trip to Manchester City a week before Christmas, most fans probably have thought that the team would have been brought back to full strength. Three goals from the home team at Maine Road were more than enough to see off Town, and Talia looked to be suffering from his two-match absence.

Refreshingly honest about his own performance, Frank said 'I think the rest of the lads can hold their heads high but I was ridiculously bad. I take pretty much full responsibility for the defeat. I made a couple of errors that I just should not have done. It was one of those games where you wish the earth would swallow you up. I apologise to the manager and all of the lads. I've let them down badly.' It was a fulsome apology that would have been acknowledged by his teammates and fans, and just may have saved the goalkeeper from the sort of hairdryer treatment that Glass experienced from his manager back in October.

Talia can not prevent a controversial Wolves penalty entering the net in August 1998.

The Christmas period saw just one point gained from a 1–1 Boxing Day draw at home to Portsmouth, before a 3–1 capitulation at Tranmere brought the curtain down on a year and a millennium. Town's League record over the previous 12 months stood at played 45, won 8, drew 14, lost 23. In total, 76 goals had been conceded and just 39 scored.

It was not a set of figures to be proud of, and proof, if any was needed, that the bottom of Division One was exactly where Town deserved to be. In the aftermath of the statements by Cliff Puffett towards the end of the previous century, the County Ground staff faced the new year with news that matched the chilling winter weather. Budget cuts brought a 30 percent reduction in the office staff in January as the club set about trying to make a million pounds worth of savings, and the arrival of a new chief executive with the brief of formulating a rescue plan brought the former CEO of the *Daily Mirror*, Bob Holt, to Swindon.

Puffett was plainly hurting. 'I want these staff to know from the bottom of my heart I will be eternally grateful for their services and support. We have tried in vain to live with a plan to achieve a Play-off position in Division One. In hindsight it appears a foolish gamble. It has been a painful process but this is the start of a new beginning for Swindon Town.'

But not on the pitch. The game at Loftus Road was in added time when Richard Langley struck the only goal past Man of the Match Frank Talia to give Queen's Park Rangers a win. 'It looked like we were going to get a point then bang, 93rd minute, they score and it's all over,' said the 'keeper, 'but we can still turn things around.' The week before, though, had seen both Iffy Onuora and Ty Gooden leave for Gillingham, while £200,000 eased the fiscal perils. Mark McCammon had arrived on loan from Charlton Athletic, but the Town debutant had limped off the pitch at QPR with an ankle injury.

Town were in the midst of a four-match losing run and, in Onuora, they had sold their second top goalscorer. Although the sale had been forced, the importance of the decision would be seen as the season entered a critical phase.

The headline that former Town favourite and now Eintracht Frankfurt striker Jan Aage Fjortoft would 'love to play for Town again' was the sort of story that allowed Town supporters to clutch at straws. What chance did Town have to find the cash to bring back a Norwegian international,

Talia bowls out.

albeit a 33-year-old one, to try to solve the problems up front and help the club avoid the drop to Division Two?

The answer to that question was none at all.

The new century continued with defeat at Ipswich followed by a 4–2 reverse at home to Crystal Palace. Visiting goalkeeper Fraser Digby maintained his disappointment in the position his former club found themselves and the match with Palace was preceded by a minute's silence for Town president Cecil Green, who had passed away the week before. The descent through the trapdoor leading out of Division One was beginning to look inevitable and the two games saw seven goals enter the Town net. January ended in a 1–1 draw at West Bromwich Albion, during which Frank Talia was replaced by Steve Mildenhall a minute into the second half after the former sustained an ankle injury, then chairman Cliff Puffett delivered perhaps the worst news for supporters in the history of the club. Swindon Town was in administration.

Calling in the administrators gave Swindon Town 90 days to save the club. 'We are looking over the precipice and no one can over-estimate the seriousness of the situation,' said the man who had first watched Swindon over 50 years ago. Puffett declared that he had offered his resignation at an emergency board meeting.

Still reeling from the recent funeral of Swindon stalwart Cecil Green, Puffett compared the decision that he had been forced to make on behalf of the club he loved to another bereavement. In the light of such bleakness, relegation seemed the least of Town's worries. The very survival of Swindon Town Football Club hung in the balance.

Such off the field developments were never likely to make concentrating on football easy, and February passed with just one point claimed. Ahead of a home match with Grimsby Town and after injuries to both Talia and Mildenhall, Quinn moved to secure the loan services of Bart Griemink, a Dutch goalkeeper with Peterborough United. Griemink gained the appreciation of the pundits, but couldn't prevent yet another home defeat. Town were now a huge nine points adrift at the foot of League One and two more points than that from safety. Having played two more games than closest rivals Port Vale, the chances of Division One survival were thrown into sharp relief.

Back behind the scenes came the news that the Professional Footballers' Association was to step in and pay Town's players' wages, although manager Jim Quinn, not a member of the PFA, would still go without.

A point at Blackburn came courtesy of the first clean sheet for three months as Griemink earned his corn, but the remaining two matches of the 6ft 3in 'keeper's spell in Swindon showed more like the form suffered by the previous incumbents between the posts.

Birmingham City and Crewe Alexandra came to Swindon before the end of February and each left with maximum points. Trevor Francis's City stuffed four past Bart and by the time Alex returned north with their spoils, Town's winless run had stretched to 18 games. Swindon Town were still nine points off 23rd place and 11 from the safety of 21st. A 3–1 defeat at Nottingham Forest brought a disappointing return for Talia but only compounded the problem as Town edged ever closer to Division Two. The reinstated 'keeper was implicated in what manager Quinn described as schoolboy errors. With just over half an hour gone, Talia flapped at a speculative cross and the ball dropped over the goalline off a post.

It was March, there were a dozen games to go and Swindon hadn't won since October. That run was finally ended when a 90th-minute Chris Hay penalty supplemented a first-half goal from midfielder Lee Collins to conquer Play-off chasing Huddersfield Town at the County Ground, but it was clear that time was running out on Town's Division One survival. Four days later and, incredibly, Town had won consecutive matches for the first time during 1999–2000. This time it was the turn of Athletic 'keeper Dean Kiely to fumble a hopeful stab into the net when a fifth-minute Steve Cowe goal at Charlton secured the second, three-point haul.

Frustrating as ever, Town, entrenched at the foot of Division One, had contrived to win at Charlton, who, even after surrendering the points on offer, remained 11 points clear at the top. With wonderful understanding of Swindon's plight, perhaps born of the experience of their own past problems, Charlton donated £2,000 to Swindon's coffers, a sum that helped secure the very existence of the Under-14 set up. Sometimes the family of football can act in a manner that restores faith in a sport that is increasingly mercenary.

With huge irony, the last time Cowe had scored, the resultant win at Bradford City in November 1997 had taken Swindon to the very top of Division One.

No one who had travelled to the Valley was fooled. The task facing their team looked insurmountable. Talia had made some outstanding saves during 85 minutes of rearguard action and the following week, at home to Wolves, he was named the *Adver's* star man. Annoyingly, the game still ended in defeat, the winner coming for the away team in the 86th minute.

George Ndah missed the match for Wolves as he was injured. Whether the pressure was lifted off the shoulders of Quinn's team with relegation all but confirmed, with eight games to go Town actually began to achieve some results that had been conspicuous by their absence for the majority of the season.

Consistency, however, was not one of the new attributes. A Chris Hay double brought a win at Norwich City, then three consecutive defeats did far greater damage than the win had achieved. Straight home wins over Tranmere Rovers and Fulham gave a glimpse of what might have been if Town had shown such application from the start. At Queen's Park Rangers, the first of the three losses, ex-Portsmouth director Terry Brady was seen in discussion with chairman Cliff Puffett as it was revealed that Brady was looking at the potential of reinvesting in football once more. With Town still in administration, the thought of the man who was among the country's top 1,000 on the rich list joining Town's boardroom would have been more than welcome.

'Let's talk,' proclaimed the *Adver* headline, as the club indicated that a favourable response from the local council regarding a ground development was crucial in persuading Brady to come on board. Brady was later spotted at the County Ground but beforehand a constructive meeting was held with the council. One problem remained. Barring a remarkable combination of results, Swindon were doomed to a spell in Division Two and any possibility that Town might be saved disappeared at Stockport County. A 3–0 reverse consigned Town to the drop on Easter Monday. Talia felt he was unlucky to be shown a red card for handling outside the box after 68 minutes. 'The ball struck me on the shoulder. It certainly wasn't deliberate.' Anything that happened on the pitch now would be incidental and most talk was of the prospective £3 million takeover by Terry Brady, about which further talks had continued with the board. A fresh offer to creditors was tabled in the hope that the club could move out of administration.

As is the nature of football, Quinn had suffered speculation about his future as boss, then, at the beginning of May and with Town still one game to play, it was announced that former Bolton Wanderers manager Colin Todd would take charge of the team with immediate effect. Quinn was appreciative of the support that his fans had offered. 'I just can not thank the Swindon supporters enough for the support they have shown me over the last 18 months. I can assure you that Swindon supporters are second to none. They understand football and have stuck with me through some tough times.'

Now it was Todd's turn to discuss the future for Town. 'I know this club can go forward. It is a new regime and hopefully everyone will get behind the team. There is a lot of work to be done.' Words like that suggested Todd might be in it for the long haul, as he unveiled his backroom team of Andy King and Malcolm Crosby.

Swindon finished a horrifying 13 points away from safety and there was every indication that Todd would have his work cut out to turn things around at Swindon Town. Nine players were out of contract in the summer, with Frank Talia one of them. After 31 games of the League season, during which he had surrendered his place to no fewer than three other 'keepers, Frank was named the Player of the Year for 1999–2000.

But the fans' favourite of 1999–2000 was one of those the new boss would not be depending on. In August Frank was released from Swindon Town, signing for Wolverhampton Wanderers of Division One. That seemed an interesting move for a player whose team had just taken the drop, but his stay in the Black Country was short-lived. After a little over a month and without making an appearance at Molineux, the 'keeper moved on to Sheffield United on a free transfer. Six League appearances came at Bramall Lane, where he filled in for Simon Tracey for the last half dozen matches of the season.

Frank had long demonstrated his wanderlust, so a move to Royal Antwerp in Belgium was taken in the Aussie's stride and then Reading came in for him in March 2002. It was plain that

Franks seems happy with his award.

Talia was generally being signed to cover an established 'keeper, but when in August 2002 Lawrie Sanchez took Frank to Buckinghamshire and Wycombe Wanderers, there followed a spell of stability after some uncertain times.

Over the next four seasons, Frank vied for the first-team goalkeeping shirt and made over 140 League and Cup appearances for the Chairboys. Initially brought in to pressurise Martin Taylor, Frank forced his way into first-team contention and earned a longer deal before being dropped by newly-incoming boss Tony Adams.

Under John Gorman, Talia reclaimed the first-team shirt despite a bizarre incident when he lost part of a toe while cutting the lawn. In 2005–06 his place was threatened by a succession of loan signings, and Steve Williams grabbed the number-one shirt ahead of Talia in the Play-off campaign at the end of the season.

Then, as pre-season training kicked in before the start of 2006–07, a knee injury wrecked Frank's campaign, leaving the Aussie on the sidelines. Unable to take to the field for the entire season, he was released by the Chairboys after almost 150 appearances over a five-season spell.

Before arriving in Britain, Talia had played for a team known as Sunshine George Cross in Australia, the sort of name that conjures up images of clear blue skies, lush green grass and the sound of crashing surf somewhere in the distance. As Frank made his debut at Hartlepool in January 1993, who would not have forgiven him a longing thought of home?

Steve Mildenhall
(2000–01) ~ Local boy made good

As the saying goes, a new broom sweeps clean. Colin Todd spent the summer of 2000 preparing to lead his new team in a fight to return directly to Division One. From a distance, now departed manager Jim Quinn might have had a frustrated grimace at the funds that Todd had at his disposal compared to the cash that had been available to Quinn the previous season. Apart from the £65,000 that Quinn had been granted to capture Southampton midfielder Andy Williams, he had been forced to rely on a succession of wheelings and dealings in the loan market as he battled the drop. In contrast, while fees were rarely spent, it looked as though Town's salary ceiling might be taking a battering as Todd made big changes.

Along with Talia, among those out of contract were midfielder Scott Leitch, defenders Adam Willis, Sol Davis and Mark Robinson, and striker Steve Cowe. All remained to start 2000–2001, but Frenchman Philippe Cuervo and midfielder Lee Collins trod the same path out of the County Ground as Talia. Todd was prepared to cast his net far and wide in a search for new troops. A former Boca Juniors teammate of Diego Maradona was brought in when Argentinian full-back Juan Cobian arrived from Sheffield Wednesday. Goalkeeper Bart Griemink made his move from Peterborough permanent, and midfield pair Matt Hewlett and Keith O'Halloran arrived from Bristol City and Scottish Premier League side St Johnstone respectively. Then there were the arrivals

Fifteen-year-old Steve Mildenhall signs for Swindon accompanied by proud parents Ralph and Teresa.

of strikers Gary Alexander, a £300,000 capture from West Ham United, and ex-Marconi Stallion, Australian Danny Invincibile, who had been spotted while on trial with the Hammers and persuaded to join Swindon instead.

Continuing to use his apparent world football knowledge, Todd carried on shopping.

Kim Heiselberg, a Danish Under-21 international left-back, was signed from FC Midtjyllan after previously having a spell at Sunderland, and Dutch centre-back Antoine Van der Linden signed from Sparta Rotterdam. Town's Aussie count was increased once more when another ex-Marconi Stallions man, Under-23 international midfielder Mark Robertson, was signed initially on loan from Burnley, followed by Todd deciding on a Scotsman when he went to Sunderland to sign defender David Duke.

The 51-year-old boss had returned to the game after a six-month absence. Speaking after his appointment, he had said, 'This is a daunting task and there is a lot of work to be done. Division Two will be tough. Everyone will be trying to achieve promotion, that has got to be every manager's objective.' Now on the eve of a new season, everyone with an interest in events at the County Ground looked to the future with renewed optimism.

By 11 August, and a day before the big kick-off, Cliff Puffett announced that he expected to stand down as chairman at an imminent emergency board meeting. The move would see Terry Brady take the mantle while two other names were heard for the first time. Danny Donegan and Ian Blatchley would join Brady to make up Swindon Town Properties Limited and the search for funding for a new £35-million stadium would be pursued. More good news came when the club's creditors voted overwhelmingly to accept a new CVA, allowing the club to move out of administration after a 28-day cooling-off period.

With the club trumpeting the fact that nine new players had been signed and that the atmosphere at the club was fantastic, who could fail to be upbeat ahead of Town's first match of the season at home to Colchester United? Supporters were being promised that the problems of previous financial management had been dealt with, that new cash was about to be injected and told to prepare for moving house to a new stadium. Couple that with a new manager and a completely revamped squad, and the future looked bright. A return to Division One was surely just a matter of waiting the 12 months necessary to play sufficient matches.

The reading of the first Football League results of 2000–01 came 24 hours later. Swindon Town 0, Colchester United 0. Not the start supporters had prepared themselves for. A week later and fans could admire the new surroundings of Reading's Madejski Stadium as they watched their side go down by two goals to nil against a side which included both past and future Town players in Adi Viveash, Sammy Igoe and Andy Gurney. In each game Town had had an early 'goal' disallowed, but a goal that counted in each half for the Royals of Reading meant Town had claimed only one point from the first six.

Terry Brady had been at Reading to cast his eye over their recently-opened home. He seemed to like what he saw, as well as what he heard from a meeting with the company who had developed the Chelsea Village. A visit to Bolton's Reebok Stadium was being planned, as a change of environment for Swindon Town seemed to roll purposefully forward. Brady had this to say about the Madejski. 'It's another council-aided development and I would like the Swindon council to take a look at what's been done there.'

Back to the pitch, and a goal nine minutes from time gave Third Division Exeter City a 1–1, first-leg Worthington Cup draw at the County Ground, Kwame Ampadu equalising Bobby Howe's first-half strike ahead of the third League match of the season. Walsall had joined Town in the drop from Division One the previous May and the Saddlers visited the County Ground in the last week in August. Both fixtures between the two clubs the season before had ended in draws. Here was a team against whom Town could measure their progress since the arrival of the new manager.

Danny Invincibile's 18th-minute goal after a Bobby Howe corner was his first for the club but the second of the game, Bart Griemink's net having already been sullied as early as the fifth minute. By half-time the visitors had regained the lead, and after 90 minutes they had added two more. 'What's it like to be outclassed?' sang the Walsall supporters. Todd said 'It was very disappointing. The one thing I said to the people of Swindon when I came here was that they would get a bit of passion, commitment and desire from the players. That was not evident. I am not making any excuses. I have brought nine of the players here to take this club forward and at the moment they are letting everyone down. Not just those players, even those that were here last season.'

Two days later, on August Bank Holiday Monday, came a trip to the Potteries to face Port Vale. The Valiants had been another team to be relegated with Town the season before, when the teams had shared the League points from their matches equally. As one of just eight clubs over whom Town had claimed a victory, both teams finished on 36 points and there had been little argument that the pair had been far and away the worst teams in Division One during 1999–2000.

Another opportunity, then, to test Todd's team against a known quantity.

The holiday, and the opening month's worth of fixtures, concluded with a 3–0 defeat, the third successive reverse. After the first four League games of the season, Town had failed to score in three and were unable to keep a clean sheet in the same number. One goal had been scored and nine conceded. Todd responded by signing a new player. Striker Martin Williams joined on a three-month deal to prove his fitness after being released by Reading. The deal had been agreed in principle in the summer but placed on hold after Williams had picked up a knee injury. Now the manager completed the formalities and his new man scored on his reserve-team debut.

The trip to Exeter City saw Williams's partner Invincibile up front and Swindon completed a victory for the first time in 2000–01. Goals from the Aussie and defender Alan Reeves put Swindon through to round two of the Worthington Cup, but it was the following result that finally gave

Steve Mildenhall.

supporters something to cheer. Alan Reeves made it two goals in four days and this time his 81st-minute strike claimed a victory over close neighbours Bristol City at Ashton Gate. At last, not only had Todd's side gained three League points from a match, they had done so at the home of a local rival.

The season was still young and there was still much to believe in. Or at least to wish for. September did bring improved results, but a very mixed bag of them. Another away win at Luton was the third travelling fixture on the trot, and sandwiched between had been a 3–0 defeat at Bournemouth. Defeat over two legs to Tranmere Rovers ended interest in the Worthington Cup and the month ended with a 2–2 home draw with Wigan Athletic. Eight games into the season and pessimists would be quick to point out the contrast between results and the expectations of two months earlier, while optimists could possibly claim that a corner was being turned. One truth that could not be overlooked was that Swindon ended the month in a relegation place, enough for many to fear for the future once more and a statistic that just had to be improved upon.

Continued improvement came with a 2–1 home win over another, perhaps the greatest, local rival, Oxford United. Defender Reeves was once more on the goal sheet, with Giuliano Grazioli claiming all three points for Town.

Retrospectively there may already have been indications that Todd's team had ability, but that the manager himself was unable to raise their game. Of the three wins of the season so far, two had been claimed against local rivals and the third against Luton Town, the team for whom new Swindon signing Martin Williams had once played and against whom his brace of goals made the difference between a 2–1 loss and a 3–2 win.

The Town side that took to the pitch seemed to be looking to the crowd or their own sense of pride to inspire them. If that reasoning rang true, away games at Oldham and Swansea were almost destined to disappoint. One point from a 0–0 draw at the Vetch followed a single goal defeat at Boundary Park, but when a 3–1 home defeat to Bristol Rovers came on 21 October, even the hope of local bragging rights could not seem to motivate Swindon.

Three days later on 24 October, and with Millwall travelling for an evening fixture at Swindon, few Town fans entering the County Ground would be wise enough to keep a special eye on their manager's movements in the 52nd minute. The visitors had taken the lead two minutes before half-time and with seven minutes of the second half gone, Andy Williams fell to the ground in the Millwall penalty box under a challenge from the goalkeeper, ex-Swindon loan player Tony Warner.

Referee Keith Hill responded by firstly deciding that a penalty was not appropriate, then that Williams had dived and deserved a yellow card. Already booked for a foul halfway through the first half, the next card that Hill waved was red. Todd was incensed and protested vehemently from his place on the bench, so much so that he was told by the referee to accompany his player from the playing surrounds and take a place in the stand. By the end of the match, 10-man Town had leaked a second goal and Todd told the press afterwards 'Once again we are talking about a scoreline that hurts people. It hurts us. We just have to keep pushing forward and hope that we get that little break somewhere. I must have killed a black cat somewhere.'

The events at the start of the second half would take on a new meaning within hours. The 52nd minute had seen Todd leave his place on the bench for the very last time as the manager got just the break he might have been looking for.

The following day it was announced that Todd had quit as boss at the County Ground and that Puffett and Brady were aware of Todd's decision before the Millwall game had even kicked off. Then came news that Todd was in discussion with Derby County, the club that he had served for eight seasons as a player and where he intended to act as assistant to boss Jim Smith. The Town boardroom immediately gave notice that they expected a full compensation package from the Rams, a subject that would need some time to sort out, but the events threw the whole season into further dramatic confusion.

Having led the club for just 18 competitive matches, Todd was off to what some might consider his spiritual home, but doing so under what many others would have viewed as less than honourable circumstances. Brady was later to say, after an appearance at a Magistrates Court as a deal was being sought, 'Derby may say their prodigal son has returned, but where were they when he was unemployed?'. But, after such a disappointing start, there were some who were secretly heaving a sigh of relief. If change was looking necessary, how could Town have either justified or afforded to axe their manager after such a short spell, during which he was allowed to make such huge and far-reaching changes?

Thrust straight into the still-warm manager's seat in a caretaker capacity was assistant Andy King. Acknowledging the frustration of the season so far, King urged 'Let's bring back that sense of anticipation and create a really positive atmosphere. I'll do things my own way. I am my own man.' The man who had led Mansfield Town to an unsuccessful Division Three Play-off campaign in 1994–95 during a three-year stint as manager at Field Mill started doing things his own way by signing midfielder and free agent Ian Woan.

Officially, Todd was still the Town boss but on 'garden leave' while terms were agreed with Derby, yet King wanted the full-time position and had some time to prove his worthiness for the role. A loss at Notts County didn't get the new boss off to a good start, but a 3–1 home win over Cambridge United on the last day of September brought the fourth win in 15 matches.

November came and went with just two points claimed from four matches. A 4–0 defeat at Peterborough was followed by a 3–0 home loss to Stoke and everyone's patience was close to breaking point. Brady proclaimed that Town's players were 'a disgrace' and sympathised with the man currently in charge. 'I feel sorry for Andy King, we have inherited this squad and they are not good enough. He is a hard working man who I have complete faith in. I will not let these players cost him his job. It's not the manager's fault. Most of these players have had three managers now and have proved to be no good. Others have earned big contracts then failed to deliver the goods.' Continuing, he said 'I nearly walked out at half-time I was so disgusted. I didn't leave for Andy's sake. I wanted to give him my support.'

If that rasping from the chairman looked to have done some good with successive wins at the beginning of December, either side of the festive period there were four defeats on the trot and Town were still rooted in the relegation zone.

Patiently sitting on the bench and watching all of the season's preceding League action take place had been reserve-team 'keeper Steve Mildenhall. Having already made the starting line up in a 4–1 first-round win over Ilkeston in the FA Cup, then a win on penalties over Millwall in the LDV Vans Trophy, Mildenhall's first League chance of the season was about to come when King named him between the posts for the visit of Port Vale a week after the trip to the New Den. It would be the young 'keeper's 11th senior start of his career and whatever was to happen, it was unlikely to be as bizarre as his first appearances in a Town shirt back in January 1997, when he came on not as a goalkeeper, but as a striker!

Town were chasing a game at Tranmere Rovers when manager Steve McMahon decided what his team really needed was a 6ft 4in man up front. Mildenhall fitted the bill, and the boss threw him on for his first game in the familiar shirt of Swindon Town, but in the unfamiliar colour of red. McMahon was already attracting some quizzically-raised eyebrows regarding some of his decisions, and moving his second-string goalkeeper on to the pitch as an outfield player made some question why McMahon had named himself among the subs. If the boss was a worse bet to have on the pitch than Mildenhall, then why had he bothered to put himself on the bench?

Goalkeeper Mildenhall makes his debut in bizarre circumstances, replacing midfielder Kevin Watson at Tranmere.

Mildenhall might have been a local lad, but that did not stop him looking elsewhere for the experience that his early career was lacking. Behind Digby, then Talia and Glass in the fight for a first-team shirt, Mildy took to the road. Loan spells at the cities of Gloucester, Worcester and several at Salisbury made more productive use of his skills than hoping to be selected ahead of the men in his way. A couple of Coca-Cola Cup outings for Swindon were forthcoming, but it was his four Town appearances in 1997–98 that brought Mildenhall's first League starts in his preferred role between the posts. Once again the first was unforgettable, although Steve may have tried many times to cast it from his memory since.

It was an injury to regular 'keeper Fraser Digby on Friday 31 October 1997, with Talia also unavailable through a knee injury, which handed Steve his full League debut in a Division One fixture at Portsmouth. The evening was to bring a Halloween trick that no one would have wished for. 'I only found out in the morning that I would be playing. I was a bit nervous to say the least,' Steve commented afterwards.

Town were riding high near the top of the table and a Chris Hay goal gave Town a 1–0 Fratton Park victory, but no matter how long Steve's career proves, the game will always be etched in the

Steve writhes in agony having collided with Portsmouth's Robbie Pethick at Portsmouth in October 1997.

memory of the 'keeper for one particular reason. Six minutes before half-time, and with Town one goal to the good, Mildy dived at the feet of Pompey defender Robbie Pethick and suffered an injury that would make any man's eyes water. Referee Paul Danson refused to stop the match as Steve lay on the ground, but eventually Town physio Jonathan Trigg ran on to the pitch with play still going on to minister to Town's debutant custodian.

After lengthy treatment Mildenhall continued, but twice fell to the floor in pain as the game progressed. Picking himself up to continue, Town's defence dropped deep to protect their last line of defence, but Steve was still equal to a Russell Perrott header which he pushed away superbly, and a one-on-one with future Swindon man Sammy Igoe just before the hour mark saw the Town 'keeper emerge victorious once more. By the end of the night Town had grabbed top spot in Division One for the first time in six years, Steve had been named Man of the Match by the *Adver*, who gave the 19-year-old 10 out of 10 on his full debut, and six stitches had been inserted in the young man's testicles.

Smiling through the ignominy and pain, he said afterwards 'I haven't got a girlfriend at the moment which is probably quite lucky! Their lad went in and got me with his studs. It was very painful and it wasn't very nice to look at either. I was never going to come off. I've waited a long time for this chance so a little cut was not going to stop me. It was sore after the game and I think I'll be walking like John Wayne for a few weeks.'

Not surprisingly, Steve was out of first-team contention for a little while, but towards the end of January 1998 he again understudied Digby, first at home to Stoke City and then away at Huddersfield Town. Four points were claimed and two clean sheets were kept. The young Mildenhall had announced his arrival and demonstrated his credentials. And it was another horrendous injury, this time to Fraser Digby, that gave Mildenhall a further chance the following month. Digby suffered a head injury at Port Vale and ended up in hospital. This time Steve could only watch as three goals rained in from Manchester City.

But now Town were fighting to stay in Division Two and Andy King was fighting to rally his new troops to the cause. Replacing Bart Griemink between the posts for the visit of Port Vale to the County Ground, after 83 minutes of the match Town had held their own. Then Tommy Widdrington hit a stunning 25-yard effort for the only goal of the match and Mildenhall's line was breached for the only, but decisive, occasion. Having already made two excellent stops, Steve was considered the man most worthy of Town's best-match rating. 'Steve was the only plus on the pitch,' said boss Andy King. But the result brought the third of three successive League defeats – Town were 22nd in the table and, midway through January, there was little reason to look to the coming three months with any optimism. Consecutive relegations (again) looked a real likelihood.

Then, at the end of the month, Town scored three and for the first time that season they also kept a clean sheet. A three-goal margin of victory over Bury was the first of such magnitude in a

League match since 19 October 1998. Loan signing Michael Reddy, captured from Sunderland through Andy King's friendship with Black Cats manager Peter Reid, scored after four minutes, then Keith O'Halloran added a penalty inside the first 15 minutes of the match. Steve Cowe wrapped things up three minutes from the end and Town had produced their most comfortable victory of 2000–01.

If anyone knew then that a five-match unbeaten run had begun, spirits would have been raised. If they had also known that the spell would drop Town to the foot of the table, that mood would have been tempered.

Through February, Town gained draws at home to Bristol City and Bournemouth, and another Michael Reddy strike, his third in four games, won the match at Cambridge, but when Luton travelled to Swindon and left with all the points in the last game of the month, Town were still deeply entrenched in the Division Two relegation zone despite the apparent improvement in results. Reddy was proving to be a big hit, and answering questions regarding his long-term availability King joked it would take £5 million and a good bottle of wine to coax his friend Reid to part with him.

After the Bournemouth draw Swindon had hit the very foot of the table and when Oldham came to Wiltshire in the first week of March, King didn't allow the 3–0 win to cloud the reality of Town's position. 'Make no mistake', he proclaimed, 'Swindon Town will not be out of the relegation zone until the last two games of the season.'

This remark proved prophetic in the extreme.

A brace of volleys by midfielder Steve Robinson that earned Town a 2–0 win at Oxford meant that whatever else he might do in a Swindon shirt, he would be remembered with warm affection and brought successive League wins for only the second time in the season. Then a point in a 1–1 draw at home to Swansea City kept the good run going. Steve Mildenhall reckoned 'That's the sort

Steve Mildenhall makes a penalty save against Millwall in January 2001.

of match we would have lost two or three nil, three months ago. It could prove to be a valuable point.' Indeed, but after another win at Colchester United and a point at Bristol Rovers, with nine matches to go Swindon had clawed themselves up to 18th in the table – the highest place occupied all season.

Some breathing space had been opened up at the bottom of the table. Then came the headline 'Back us or we'll pull out.' Terry Brady and his fellow investors Donegan and Blatchley were losing patience with the council regarding support for a new stadium plan near junction 16 of the M4. A winding up order for the sum of £500,000 had been issued and a High Court appearance threatened, and while the three businessmen assured the funds were available, a stand off was developing between the boardroom and the local authority.

Things looked fragile on the pitch and now financial clouds were gathering once more. Extinction for the club was a real possibility. Two days later, Brady announced 'I'll leave', warning he would walk away if planning permission for the new ground wasn't forthcoming. 'We are filling up a black hole with money. I have to admit this is looking very bad. When we came in this club was a very sick patient that was going to die. We have prolonged its life for 12 months and now it needs a bypass that it can get with the support of Swindon Borough Council. If we do not get that support, I do not even want to think about what might happen. We do not want to walk away.'

With things like that going on behind the scenes, the goalless draw at Bristol Rovers had been achieved through great concentration and the scoreless outcome was the fifth consecutive clean sheet that 'keeper Steve Mildenhall had been responsible for. With King publicly calling for the club's directors to 'sort it out,' a home defeat to Reading in front of almost 10,000 was narrow, but unwelcome all the same. Royal's striker Jamie Cureton scored the only goal in the 52nd minute and belief continued to be battered.

But if you score three times away from home, surely there should be the reward of some points. A Gary Alexander double and Ian Woan's first for the club at Rotherham gave Town a lead they held as late as the 67th minute, before Mark Robins completed his hat-trick six minutes from the end to deny Town any points. The season entered April with Swindon staring at the possibility of falling straight through the division they had plunged into just 12 months previously, and the results gave little hope for salvation. A win at Brentford came after Matt Heywood scored his first goal for the club, but when his second came two matches later it couldn't offset a 2–1 loss at Notts County and time was running out rapidly.

Three games to go and Town sat 20th, just one place off the drop. Then a 0–0 draw at Wycombe looked too little to make a significant difference. Oxford United, Swansea City and Luton Town were already cast well adrift, but below Swindon, Bristol Rovers and Cambridge United were looking to overhaul Town in the fight to retain Division Two status.

On the evening of Saturday 21 April, Swindon lay sixth from bottom of the table on 49 points.

Bristol Rovers and Cambridge United were both one point behind and both had two games in hand. With four teams going down and three spaces looking booked already, should both teams overhaul Swindon, Town would be facing Division Three football. A week later Town's last home match saw them entertain Peterborough United, and with 15 minutes to go Town held the lead from a Gary Alexander seventh-minute strike. Then Alan Reeves got on the score sheet, but his own goal counted for the visitors and Town supporters' hearts were in their mouths.

With the match deep into injury time, Danny Invincibile latched onto a through ball down the left, cantered forward and lashed the ball past Posh 'keeper Mark Tyler. Pandemonium ensued, but the suspicion around the County Ground was that it would be too little, too late. On the same day, Walsall claimed a 2–1 win over Bristol Rovers. That left Rovers with three home matches to play and Town with just a trip to Stoke City to come.

But by the season's last Saturday, it didn't matter. Rovers beat Wrexham 4–0 and Town lost 4–1 at the Britannia Stadium, but Rovers' inability to take anything from the previous two matches had left a four-point gap. Town had been overhauled by Cambridge, who had managed four points from the last six, but King's men were saved from the drop by a point, thanks to Bristol Rovers' help. Ahead of that dramatic win over Peterborough, Steve Mildenhall was christened the season's Player of the Year and said 'I'm delighted to have won because all players really appreciate awards that are voted for by the fans.'

After the huge optimism that accompanied the start of the season, Town supporters had watched the campaign unfold into a damp squib. Mildenhall's honour of claiming the Player of the Year award was a little unexpected but, looking back, it was perhaps entirely understandable.

Almost without exception, the huge influx of Todd-inspired signings during the summer had failed to perform. All optimism for the campaign quickly evaporated as the season progressed, and when the usual focus of the fans' frustration, the manager, left without a word of apology or explanation, it seemed that everyone associated with the task that he had first started, looked to be failing dismally with and then walked away from, had to accept their own share of the blame.

Just 23 League appearances for Mildenhall represented only half of a regular season – an astonishingly low figure to claim the votes of the Swindon Town electorate.

When Steve took to the field for his first start in the middle of January, Town were 20th in the table and when the whistle was blown on the season, they lay in exactly the same place. While Griemink was in goal, Town had kept just four clean sheets, yet following the turn of the new year and the appearance of Mildenhall, more than twice that number were achieved in the second half of the season – a statistic suggesting that of the two craftsmen, it was Steve who could lay claim to be the better. But the continued advancement of Mildenhall's career produced a home-grown talent, someone who was young enough to help supporters look once more to the future and, perhaps as important as any, someone who was untainted by the mistakes of a previous regime.

Of Todd's signings, Heiselberg left soon after the departure of the boss who brought him to Swindon, and 6ft 4in Finnish international defender Marko Tuomela from Tromso, whom Todd had offered a loan chance to in September, was shipped out by King after just two outings. Van der Linden lasted until the summer and retained the confidence of Andy King, but there was some scratching of heads when King consistently thrust his central defender up front towards the closing stages of a match, insisting that his man could play anywhere 'because he was Dutch'.

Mildenhall arranges his defensive wall at Rotherham in March 2001.

The winner of the Player of the Year trophy the year before had travelled almost 11,000 miles to claim it, making the trip from Melbourne, Australia, via Blackburn Rovers. When Steve Mildenhall became the fourth goalkeeper in five years to raise the silverware, he had made an altogether less challenging journey. Making the daunting trip from St Joseph's school, in the shadow of the Shrivenham Road stand, Swindon-born Steve put pen to paper on a contract in November 1993, watched proudly by parents Teresa and Ralph. The 'keeper was 15 years old and dreaming of donning the gloves occupied by the already veteran custodian Fraser Digby.

Steve Mildenhall did just that, replicating Digby's feat of being voted the fans' most-valued player at the first time of asking. After such a meteoric six months there was a shock in store in the summer of 2001. Initially refusing to sign a new contract with Town, there was a feeling that the young 'keeper was holding out for a better deal from Andy King, so when the news came in June that Mildenhall's signature was drying on the fresh paperwork, there was relief but little surprise. That was to come 24 hours later, with the announcement that Mildenhall had left Swindon for Notts County in return for £150,000. The sequence of events ensured a fee for Town and secured a sell on clause. Three seasons followed at Meadow Lane for the player before a move on to Oldham Athletic in December 2004 after almost 90 appearances, but with the deal involving no exchange of funds the move failed to generate extra cash for Swindon's coffers.

Boundary Park was hardly the venue for an unmitigated success for Steve's career, a transfer to Grimsby only six months and six appearances later brought a complete season's worth of outings at Blundell Park and a Play-off Final appearance at the Millennium Stadium. Then, just as Swindon were on the look-out for a replacement 'keeper in the summer of 2006, Steve moved back west once more, but this time to join Yeovil Town in League One.

Steve grabbed the first-team shirt at the beginning of the campaign and hung on to become a mainstay of the Somerset side's fight for their highest-ever League position. Fifty-one appearances followed as Mildenhall again helped his employers to a Play-off place.

After going down 2–0 at Huish Park in the first leg against Nottingham Forest, Yeovil astonishingly turned the tie around at the City Ground. Still trailing by two goals with less than 10 minutes remaining, Yeovil struck twice to take the match to extra-time, then triumphed by an aggregate score of five goals to four.

The fairy tale came to an end at Wembley when Blackpool took the third promotion spot to go up to the Championship with a 2–0 win, but Yeovil and Mildenhall could reflect on an excellent campaign.

Matt Heywood
(2001–02) ~ Concentrated effort

For the third summer on the trot, Swindon Town's pre-season preparations were led by a manager starting his first full season in the job, and just like each before him, now-permanent manager Andy King wanted to change his team to his own liking.

Versatile defender Andy Gurney joined the squad from Reading in June and pacy French striker Eric Sabin made the switch from Wasquehal soon after, but before the month was out, supporters' attentions were focused on matters off the pitch once more.

Ex-chairman and shareholder Cliff Puffett ruffled feathers by publicly questioning the foundation of the investment that board members Terry Brady, Danny Donegan and Ian Blatchley were said to have brought to the club. Having already put together a consortium which included Sir Seton Wills and Willie Carson, aimed at regaining control of the club, a bid to wrest power from the current board was rejected and Puffett called for the annual general meeting to approve the accounts for 1999 that were long overdue. Less than a week later and the confusion increased when printing tycoon Brady announced his departure from the club. Amid rumours that Puffett's questions may have caused a boardroom bust-up, Brady said 'I'd dreamed of an exciting future with Swindon but now it's all gone. I'm feeling really bad about it.'

Matt Heywood.

Danny Donegan was announced as the next chairman and indicated his intention to stay at the County Ground, but manager Andy King found the financial uncertainty had hampered his team building.

But this was about to become the least of King's worries.

On 31 July 2001 Town impressed in a 1–1 pre-season draw with Premiership Derby County. Twenty-four hours later, King was asked to take training, but in between Donegan had issued a statement saying that King had been axed as Swindon manager. Astonishingly, the chairman seemed to expect the sacked man to steady the ship until his replacement was found, but King walked away with dignity as a termination package was still being agreed. Ex-Player of the Year Shaun Taylor, now coaching at Bristol City, was among the names mentioned in connection with the new vacancy, as was another Town favourite, Paul Bodin. King, though, claimed that ex-Liverpool centre-back Neil Ruddock had been behind leaked stories that his position was under threat, and Ruddock's name, along with that of previous Anfield boss Roy Evans, was also in the frame.

Three days later and the speculation was over. Evans was the new boss at the County Ground, and a day after that Ruddock was his second in command.

The turmoil was hardly ideal preparation for a new season and it wasn't over yet. Swindon owed £87,000 to the council for unpaid rent on the County Ground, the departure of Brady meant that the club was no longer considered the preferred developer for the area known as the Front Garden near junction 16 of the M4 and the £35 million stadium project looked as far away as ever.

On the cusp of a new season, Town supporters were getting yet another crash course in what it was like to support their club. The optimism of 12 months earlier had proved as ill founded as the millennium bug that had threatened disaster at the turn of the century. Now another season was dawning and in the light of the unconsummated hope of the year before, fans were growing sceptical that this year's changes would bring better results than last. And if evidence was needed to substantiate their suspicions, it arrived on the opening day of the season.

Heywood powers his way to an aerial ball against Doncaster in February 2005.

The occasion brought the return of Peterborough, who had conceded the last gasp goal in May that had ultimately kept Swindon in Division Two, but the result had more in common with the first game of 2000–01 than the last. Just as in the initial game of the previous campaign, Swindon's fixtures started with a 0–0 home draw. A first-half penalty miss by Keith O'Halloran and the dismissal of Giuliano Grazioli after an hour for clattering into visiting 'keeper Mark Tyler completed a disappointing start to the campaign. If Roy Evans, who was officially described as director of football, had wondered how tough his introduction to the third tier of football would be, he had been given his first lesson.

Lesson two came the following Monday, and this time it was a lesson in Swindon Town the company, rather than Swindon Town the football club. Two leased mini-buses used to ferry players to and from the training ground were repossessed, the council gave the club four weeks to pay its outstanding rent and it was revealed that Donegan, acting in the role of chairman, was not registered at Companies House as a director. 'What is going on?' screamed the *Adver* headline, echoing the question on every Swindon supporter's lips.

Back to the football field and a trip to Ashton Gate. Skipper and central defender Alan Reeves became the second Town player to receive a red card in the two matches of 2001–02 played so far, and the remaining 10 players trooped off the pitch half an hour later on the end of a 3–1 defeat at the hands of Bristol City. The game had stood at 1–1 until the dismissal of Reeves.

There was little to be cheerful about at the County Ground, as things on the pitch offered nothing to ease the minds of fans troubled by things that were occurring off it. Matt Heywood had been named Swindon's Man of the Match in the battle at Ashton Gate and he brought a rare ray of light for the embryonic campaign. While it was difficult to find a Colin Todd signing still on Town's books, never mind shining, a year after the curtailed reign of the boss of 12 months before, Heywood was proof of Andy King's knowledge in the transfer market.

The ex-Burnley man was building a reputation as a defender who was solid and dependable, and whose performances were often only acknowledged after the final whistle. After 90 minutes, and after it was noticed that the opposition's danger man had been shackled effectively, leaving most of the danger emanating from a part of the pitch not under Heywood's jurisdiction, the young defender's contribution was often recognised as the best of Swindon's game.

Born in Chatham in August 1979, Matt had come through the trainee ranks at Burnley and signed professional terms in July 1998. Early season injuries gave the Clarets manager Stan Ternent problems at the beginning of Matt's first season as a full-timer, and the departure of the boss in favour of Steve Cotterill brought Heywood's debut against Wigan in September. Matt started to form a good partnership with Brian Reid, but then the up-and-coming defender lost his place with the arrival of Steve Davis from Luton. No doubt the justification of the £800,000 fee that the boss had invested in Davis was part of the reason he was selected ahead of the young Matt.

After just 15 first-team appearances, Heywood agreed an 18-month deal and a move from Lancashire to Wiltshire was completed on 23 January 2001. He said after signing 'I knew Mark Robertson (who had spent a loan spell at the County Ground) from his days with Burnley and he was quite positive about the club. Things had gone a bit stale for me at Burnley and I wasn't really getting a sniff of the first team. Hopefully I can add something to Swindon. I'm strong in the air and I like to play football.' King said 'He's a young boy who will give us something different in defence. We don't have anyone else on our books with a 6ft 4in presence.'

Whether King was mastering a Shanklyesque description of his new signing or whether 5ft 9in King had been over-impressed by the towering play of his new man, it was a fact that his signing was a full two inches shorter than his new boss's estimate. Then, in a 1–0 win at Cambridge in Matt's fourth match, he was the *Adver's* Man of the Match. He said 'It was good to be alongside Alan Reeves. We are both strong in the air. There is nothing fancy. We just aim to win the ball and take it from there', the new centre-back explained.

Before the end of his first season as a Robin, Heywood had won a succession of Man of the Match awards, scored two goals as he settled in and looked a good acquisition. And it was the Man of the Match accolade that Heywood gained after the defeat at Ashton Gate in the second game of 2001–02. An unfussy and hard-working performance in the centre of defence couldn't rescue anything from defeat, but it did indicate that the young defender could be relied on in a battle.

Forty-eight hours later and the front page of the *Adver* screamed 'Showdown'. A consortium comprising Willie Carson, James Wills, Cliff Puffett and Newbury businessman Mike Diamandis was preparing a takeover bid for the club, as it was announced that a meeting with creditors was to take place following the club's inability to meet its debts. In breach of its payments to settle the previously agreed creditors voluntary agreement, Swindon Town faced the possibility of closure or being placed in liquidation.

Again, whatever was happening on the pitch seemed inconsequential compared to what was happening off it. Donegan announced his intention to sort the problems out, but the council unveiled its own probe into its tenant's affairs regarding the continued unpaid rent bill. As further information became evident, it was revealed that Southampton were still owed the fee that had brought Andy Williams to Swindon under Jimmy Quinn, and the supervisor of the CVA stated that he was calling a creditor's meeting at which the Inland Revenue, owed over £470,000, might decide to 'pull the plug'. Then, the four-man rival consortium announced that it was taking the club to the High Court to force the board to call an AGM. Supporting Swindon Town was giving all fans a lesson in company law.

The season was just a fortnight old and a home defeat at the hands of Oldham seemed to pale into insignificance when compared to the very real possibility that the club could soon be no more. So what concentration it must have taken for Town to travel to Bury and return with not only

A neck straining header from Matt Heywood.

three points, but also three goals to the good and a clean sheet to boot. Five days later and on the same day that a Michael Owen hat-trick inspired England to a 5–1 World Cup qualifying win over Germany in Munich, Evans' men had claimed another win. This time it was a 1–0 victory over Colchester at the County Ground, which came from a 25-yard pile driver of a free-kick from player-coach Neil Ruddock on his Swindon Town debut. To their huge credit, the playing staff were doing all they could to counter the turmoil in the boardroom. Swindon Council responded by considering repossessing the County Ground.

By the end of September Town had coped well with the off-field events, distractions that looked likely to undermine anything that boss Roy Evans might be able to conjure. Two draws and a win gave way to a reality check 4–0 defeat at Chesterfield, before another four points from six closed the month. What right did anyone have to expect a team of players who were living in fear of their wages not being paid, to produce results that left their team 10th in the table? An 87th-minute goal from Andy Gurney earned Town a draw at home to Tranmere Rovers, but it was Matt Heywood who took the acclaim of the pundits. Always looking dangerous in the opposition's penalty area, Matt was still looking for his first goal of the season, but it was his assured performance at the back that continued to attract the greatest praise.

When October started with a 3–1 win at Reading, not only was local pride satisfied but there might have been the temptation to ignore the behind the scenes rumblings. Roy Evans had rested Matt Heywood, but he came off the bench to replace recently-signed and new star Paul Edwards with seven minutes to go, and a strike from Grazioli was the striker's third in three games. Even a televised 3–0 home defeat at the hands of Cardiff City was quickly corrected with four points from matches with Cambridge United and Wycombe Wanderers. Grazioli was on fire with five goals in as many matches and Town still had a Play-off place in their sights.

November broke with the High Court appointment called by the four-man consortium looking to oust the current board. Donegan was facing accusations that he was unable to claim the post of chairman without an AGM to ratify his place, and the man himself indicated that he would walk away if the ruling went against him. It had already been suggested that if Donegan went, Roy Evans, the man he had brought in as director of football, would go as well.

Matt Heywood dominates the defence again.

The players were in no doubt about the effect the boss had had on the side. 'The gaffer has had a big impact and the place is buzzing again. How important is it that he stays? Look at the transformation this season,' said in-form Grazioli on the eve of the court case. 'This club deserves stability. There are more plot twists here than an episode of *Neighbours*.' David Duke agreed. 'I'd be gutted to see him go,' was the defender's assessment, while 'keeper Griemink said 'It's crucial he stays. Look at the impact he's made in just a couple of months.' The signatures of 1,500 Town supporters echoed the views of their players ahead of a 3–0 home defeat by Stoke City. So when the courts ruled in favour of an enforced EGM in December and announced that Donegan couldn't continue as chairman of Swindon Town, Evans refused to comment.

Finally, the goings-on at the County Ground distracted the efforts of the players on the pitch. A Danny Invincibile penalty was saved at the Bloomfield Road home of Steve McMahon's Blackpool, Town went down by a goal to nil and 11 days later it was four goals for no reply at Queen's Park Rangers. A home win over Hartlepool in the FA Cup brought a goal for Ruddock and passage into round two, but there was consternation about how easily the visitors had been able to breach Town's defence in the 38th minute, immediately after Swindon had taken a two-goal lead.

Matt Heywood was back in the centre of defence and had made it apparent that he had not felt a break in first-team action necessary. Striking Town's third goal with a quarter of an hour to go, Heywood had given his team some breathing space to finish the match and claimed his first goal of the season. Man of the Match once more by the reckoning of the *Adver*, he was described as 'not blessed with pace, but not one to shirk a 50–50 ball. Heywood loves a battle and few have got the better of him in the air this season. Teams can pump as many long balls as they like but the chances are, Heywood will be on the end of 80 percent of them.'

This was ringing praise for a man who was about to confirm his status as the regular choice in the centre of Town's defence.

The headline on the back of the *Adver* on 23 November indicated yet another change was inevitable. 'Donegone!' announced the departure of the man who had acted as chairman. At a meeting of the Supporter's Trust, Donegan said any incoming consortium would need to find enough cash to plug a hole that was haemorrhaging £120,000 a month. And on top of the rent that the club still owed the council, it had been discovered that there was a bill for £92,000 worth of business rates as well.

There appeared no end to the bad news that could emanate from the SN1 postcode area of Swindon, and the man who most influenced the activities on the pitch was as confused as anyone. 'Just what on earth is going on?' asked Roy Evans. 'The people that follow this club are fantastic. I just wish we had some information to give them.' The statement showed how ill-informed Evans was and seemed to make a mockery of the term 'director' in his job title.

Again the players responded with a 3–1 home win over Wrexham, and again Heywood was on target. Shackling the up-and-coming Lee Trundle, Heywood seemed confident that he could keep the goalscoring run going. 'I keep saying that my goals come in twos and threes. I got in a header, the ball's rebounded off someone and come back to me, and fortunately I was able to stick it in the net. Winning against Wrexham was very important. We didn't want to get sucked into trouble.'

The players seemed intent in keeping the trouble off the pitch and in the boardroom.

Ominously, in a public meeting with the Supporter's Trust in which Donegan and Puffett were among those giving their views, Puffett said 'This club can not survive on the income from football alone. It needs to be part of other income streams. We have to work with the council to see how this is achievable and I think that it has to be in place in blueprint within a two-year period. Any longer than that and I don't think we'll survive.' Donegan suggested, 'Aim for the Second Division and you end up in the Conference.'

Things didn't look like getting any easier behind the scenes, and December began with a single-goal defeat at Wigan followed by a slender 3–2 win over Hereford, taking Town to the third round of the FA Cup. Four days before Christmas came a loss at Notts County, but in truth, while the players were doing all they could to focus the fans' attention on the pitch, it was the action off it that was causing the most headlines. An EGM at the beginning of the month gave control of the club to the consortium headed by Willie Carson, but with the majority shareholder Sir Seton Wills lending his support, the rest gathered at the meeting had little power to influence a different outcome anyway.

The new chairman indicated that he'd like Roy Evans to stay at the club, but just before Christmas the director of football announced his departure after less than five months. 'It's been a difficult decision for me,' said the ex-Liverpool boss. 'The fans, players and staff at Swindon Town have made me feel very welcome.' But it was the financial instability that had led to the likeable Evans concluding that Swindon wasn't the place to continue his managerial career.

Neil Ruddock immediately threw his hat in the ring as the successor to his old boss, but Malcolm Crosby was asked to lead the team in the defeat at Notts County. Even as the temporary boss watched his charges capitulate at Meadow Lane, he may have been aware of a familiar face being entertained by the new boardroom members. Before the end of the evening and four days before Christmas, the new board appointed their 'new' manager. In the season of the three kings, Andy King was given the keys to the Swindon Town manager's office, just 141 days after being ousted.

It took all of three days before the new board were denying that the reinstatement of King was purely commercial. It was said that he had still been seeking a compensation settlement from the club after his removal from office in the summer and, while he appeared to have been patient, the conclusion that to reappoint the man removed the need to pay him off was an easy one to reach.

Boxing Day came and a 0–0 County Ground draw with Bournemouth brought the first point of the month, but also a frosty reception from the home crowd for the return of the once ex-manager. With sections of the crowd calling for the elevation of Ruddock to the managership, King suffered chants of 'get back on the dole.' Andy Gurney, back after suspension, received two yellow cards inside a minute and Grazioli was dismissed in injury time as the performance of referee Paul Taylor, who also sent off Bournemouth's Eddie Howe, took some of the attention away from the boss. Rarely could a manager have felt under so much pressure in his 'first' match in charge.

The result left Town 15th in the table, neither threatening the Play-offs nor overly worried about the relegation places, and 2001 wound down with a comfortable 3–1 home win over Bury. Matt Heywood remained upbeat. 'Psychologically it would be a real boost to see our name in the top half. You just want to see the gap between you and the bottom four sides growing bigger.'

January 2002. A new year, a new board, a 'new' manager.

Same old bad news.

On 4 January, Town's bankers Natwest asked the club to take its business elsewhere. Revealing that if its creditors called in all their debts it would leave the club needing to find £10 million, Town were left looking for another bank to handle the accounts. With postponements affecting the winter fixture and with a £15,000 bill from the local constabulary needing to be settled before policing at matches would be resumed, the financial situation looked as bleak as ever. The finger-pointing continued between the board and the departed Donegan and Blatchley, the former alleging huge excesses incurred by the latter had exacerbated the problems.

Any glimmer of a lengthy Cup run to boost the coffers was extinguished when Kevin Horlock inspired Manchester City to a third-round win over Town at Maine Road. Heywood had a tough day. 'Every time the ball was pushed forward to one of their men, you didn't know what to do. All of a sudden these midfielders came out of nowhere to support them. Nobody likes to lose but I think 2–0 was a respectable defeat in the end.' Talking of the style he and his teammates had encountered against the Premiership opposition, Matt said 'It was always on the floor and the man on the ball had options. That's how we'd like to play every week.' Former Town midfielder Horlock had scored the killer second goal just after the hour.

A week later Bristol City were in town. Future Town man Lee Peacock struck an astonishing free-kick to win the game, but not before another player to later wear the red of Swindon had made his mark. Matt Hill headed Aaron Brown's cross home and it took an hour before Town loan signing Dominic Foley scored to reduce the arrears. It was for a kick at Brown that Town skipper Alan Reeves received a red card, his second against City that season, after 53 minutes. The team from Bristol also included Tony Thorpe and Robin Hulbert, with future and past Swindon connections respectively, but all the warm handshaking counted for little when the evening showed Swindon had dropped to 18th in the table.

Clearing the lines.

A 2–0 defeat at Oldham three days later as the middle of January passed didn't lift any spirits and had King describing his side's performance as 'awful'. 'I'm not happy at all,' said the boss. 'It's got to improve.' There would have been a few dissenting voices from the County Ground stands, so a five-match unbeaten run was just what the doctor ordered.

Draws at Peterborough and Wrexham, interspersed with wins over Notts County, Northampton and away at Colchester, meant that February started with Town back in mid-table. King might still be trying to win over his detractors, but his side sat higher up the table than they had when Roy Evans left Wiltshire. Heywood had experienced a variety of emotions through the winning spell. Admitting responsibility for a mistake at Wrexham he said 'The first goal was down to me', but after coming close to redeeming himself at the other end of the pitch as well as setting up Alan Reeves's equaliser, Matt proclaimed 'I like to get forward as a striker in training from time to time but I wouldn't fancy it on a permanent basis.'

Having already provided the ball for Eric Sabin to score at Colchester, then doing the same at Northampton for Danny Invincibile to seal a 2–1 victory over Northampton Town, the defender was considered Town's superior contributor of the afternoon at the Racecourse Ground. Swindon seemed to be reaping the rewards of the performances of Matt, whichever end of the pitch the big man found himself at. 'In the last few games there have been some quality balls put in, I've managed to get a touch and we've scored from them,' Matt said modestly. The game had seen fellow defender Sol Davis sent off, causing Matt's defensive skills to be placed under even greater pressure. 'They kept putting balls into the box, but even after they'd got one back, I felt we did okay. We kept doing the right things, concentrating on winning our headers and tackles. In the end I thought we deserved the points.'

Two thirds of the season were over and Swindon's campaign could swing either way, but such was the advanced stage of the proceedings that even after just two points in four games through February, and despite failing to hit the net in any of them, Town retained their mid-table status. King again assessed his side as 'awful all over the pitch' after a 3–0 defeat at Cardiff City, but a Football League-imposed transfer embargo while an agreed payment plan to the Inland Revenue was actioned tied the bosses hands.

The goal drought was overcome as February turned into March when consecutive home games brought victories over Chesterfield and Port Vale. The latter included a 45th-minute strike from Heywood that gave Town the comfort of a two-goal cushion and Matt his third of the season. The result took Town's points haul to 50 for the season, traditionally seen as the mark where relegation thoughts can be banished, and with nine games still to play most clubs would expect to heave a sigh of relief that minimum expectations had been achieved.

But Swindon Town are not like most clubs. Off the field, the situation was about to reach crisis point.

Talks with ex-chairman Donegan about settlement of a £1.2 million debenture owed to Swindon Town Properties failed, forcing the club to plead with the Inland Revenue for more time to resolve a £300,000 tax bill, and the players' wages for February remained unpaid. A 2–0 loss at Brentford was the least of the club's worries. The very future of Swindon Town Football Club hung in the balance. Director Bob Holt explained, 'The club needs just over a million pounds to satisfy its creditors. If (benefactor) Sir Seton Wills puts in £1.2 million to satisfy the bills as they fall due to bring some sort of financial stability, it still doesn't deal with the problem of the debenture.' The fear was that if Sir Seton injected the cash to solve the cash flow problem, Donegan and Blatchley would immediately claim the money by calling in the debenture.

The players left Griffin Park having been told there was no likelihood of being paid in the immediate future, and Andy King announced 'Our club is in grave danger of no longer existing.' The PFA were approached to see if they could help with players' wages, while discussions continued to try to form a plan that could allow Sir Seton to add money into the club without the risk of it being taken straight back out again. Defeat at Lou Macari's Huddersfield Town hardly registered on the scale of concerns.

Matt Heywood's performance at the McAlpine Stadium was typical, producing the usual reliable showing that helped keep the score down to 2–0. 'We played some decent stuff in the middle third, but we lacked the final ball', was the assessment of Swindon's Man of the Match. The game was the third that Matt and his playing colleagues were asked to play for nothing, and two days later Holt travelled to Football League headquarters to plead for approval of a financial rescue plan. Breath was held as the news of Monday 11 March was carefully monitored. Three hours after entering the offices of football's authorities, Holt emerged a relieved man. The League had accepted Town's financial strategy, and the director admitted 'If the Football League had said no, then it would have probably finished us.'

There were meetings still to take place with the Inland Revenue, Swindon Borough Council and the PFA (who had been persuaded to cover the players' wages), but for now there were sighs of relief all over town. But when details emerged of how the rescue was to be achieved, those sighs of relief turned into sharp intakes of breath. Swindon Town were to be placed into administration once again, with the board insisting it would allow the club breathing space by eliminating the possibility of it being wound up by its creditors. The collapse of ITV Digital and the loss of the revenue of its broadcasting deal with the Football League was particularly bad timing.

The High Court's agreement set a precedent. Never before had a club been placed into administration twice and it was made plain that there would be no third chance. It was time for supporters to place all their trust in the business acumen of the club's leaders.

Not surprisingly, Town's players had struggled to keep their concentration throughout the ordeal. Just two goals were scored in four games to the end of March, but Eric Sabin's effort claimed a home point against Wigan, and 18-year-old Swindonian Alan Young's strike against a Steve McMahon-led Blackpool was the youngster's first ever, and also the only goal of the game.

The season was running to its conclusion with Swindon guaranteed a mid-table finish, but most fans were just relieved that they still had a club to support. A win at Cambridge United three matches from the end was to be the last of the season, but a point from each of the last two games left Swindon 13th in Division Two, a huge triumph against monumental adversity. The last game of the season brought the arrival of Wycombe Wanderers at the County Ground and Matt Heywood set about making the day his own.

Collecting almost twice as many votes as second-placed goalkeeper Bart Griemink, Matt was voted Player of the Year for 2001–02 and presented with the award ahead of the match with the Chairboys. Not content with the one trophy, Heywood was then presented with enough silverware to fill a sizeable mantelpiece as he was acclaimed the star performer of the season from all interested parties who had watched the big defender's performances all over the country. 'I am very happy that the *Adver* readers have voted for me. I have been quite pleased with my form and I like to think I have been pretty consistent. Hopefully we can make further progress as a team next year.' Andy King was also appreciative. 'Our main strength has been our defence and Matty Heywood has done tremendously well. I have seen improvement in him this year and I think there is more to come.'

Then, taking to the pitch, it was Heywood who grabbed a 56th-minute equaliser that ensured Town's campaign avoided ending in defeat and left the 22-year-old with yet another Man of the Match accolade. The goal was his fourth of the season.

One story that had rumbled on throughout the campaign had been the relationship between coach Neil Ruddock and the club. Reported to be costing Town in excess of £200,000 a year in wages, King had dropped the man who had proclaimed his readiness to step into the manager's office before his return. Not selected for action since before Christmas, Ruddock refused to take the heavy hint that he should walk away. It made for an awkward atmosphere, but, after all, who would quickly and easily abandon a salary of such proportion? Contracts had been signed and they needed to be honoured.

With the bestowal of the Player of the Year award on Heywood, it was Ruddock who typically stole the *Adver's* photo call.

In July 2005 Matt made the move west to Bristol City on a free transfer. He had made over 200 first-team appearances for Town over his four-and-a-half-year stay and signed for City under manager Brian Tinnion. He took a little while to capture his best form at Ashton Gate, and then, having established himself as a regular, injury meant he missed the last third of the season. With the arrival of new boss Gary Johnson from Yeovil Town, he seemed to struggle to make a good impression on his new boss and a loan spell with Brentford, where he began 2006–07, was made permanent in August.

Heywood holds up the Player of the Year award, as well as Neil Ruddock, in April 2002.

His first season as a Bee was not an easy one. Although a fixture in Brentford's defence up until the new year, as the campaign entered its closing stages only Rotherham, who had been docked 10 points for going into administration, kept the team off the foot of the League One table.

By the end of the season, even that luxury had slipped through Brentford's fingers. Just 37 points were claimed over the 46 matches played in League One and the Bees found themselves heading towards League Two as the division's bottom club.

After 30 appearances and with a year of his contract still to run, Matt looked assured of a squad place for 2007–08 as Brentford looked to climb back to League One.

But back to 2001–02, and if teams had suffered a points deduction for entering administration then, Town's campaign would have been even more fraught.

The season had been a triumph of the players' concentration over all that had happened off the pitch. Two changes of manager, two changes of chairman and a complete boardroom clearout had all combined to overshadow Matt's elevation to Swindon Town's Player of the Year. No one had epitomised the strength that it had taken to get through the season more than Matt Heywood. The mental strength to keep focused while everything around you was threatening to undermine your efforts, and the physical power to dominate proceedings at both ends of the football field, brought exactly the sort of stability that was in desperate need behind the scenes.

Sam Parkin
(2002–03 and 2004–05) ~ Super Sammy Parkin

Town manager Andy King had his critics, but almost everyone agreed he possessed one particular attribute. His eye for a player was responsible for bringing in many a man at a bargain price and, on 8 August 2002, King made what was perhaps his most significant signing for the club.

Just £50,000 was spent to secure the signature of a 21-year-old striker who was to go on to win Swindon's Player of the Year award twice in three years. Sam Parkin had been an England Schoolboy International and was lured west from Chelsea in pursuit of greater first-team opportunities.

Born in Roehampton on 14 March 1981, Parkin had failed to make a first-team appearance at Stamford Bridge and had already spent loan spells at Millwall, Wycombe Wanderers and Oldham Athletic. Each of Sam's temporary employers reaped the reward of goals for taking a chance on the self-confessed Queen's Park Rangers fan. Four came in seven games at the New Den, and it took

Sam Parkin on his Swindon debut against Barnsley. He scored a hat-trick.

just two minutes of his League debut on 23 September 2000 to make his mark. The opening strike in a home game with Oxford United was supplemented by another an hour later. Sam Parkin had announced his arrival on the goalscoring scene. His brace consigned Oxford to a 5–0 defeat and contributed to the U's eventual 24th-place finish and relegation to Division Three.

Just one strike was forthcoming from an eight-match run at Wycombe, before three in two games were produced over seven matches at Oldham. Then, a season-long stint at Northampton in 2001–02 gave the youngster the chance to experience a prolonged introduction to League football, so it would have been a disappointment to both Sam and Northampton Town manager Kevan Broadhurst when the 6ft 2in striker could manage just four goals in 40 appearances at the Sixfields Stadium. One more came in a 3–1 defeat at Middlesbrough in the Worthington Cup, but the tally hardly indicated a prolific goalscorer in the making.

Not so, though, for Swindon manager Andy King.

As Town prepared for another season of Division Two football, the County Ground boss was pondering how to solve a problem that had seen just 47 League goals struck the previous season. What was needed was that much-coveted, 20-goals-a-season striker that every manager announces they are looking for, and King had seen enough to suggest that Parkin was the man for the job.

Signing a two-year deal after a week's training with Swindon in Southport, Sam said 'The advice I was given was never to leave a big club unless you have to. I had loan spells at other clubs but there comes a time when you have to move on to help your career and to improve yourself.' Significantly, Sam finished by saying 'I haven't signed here as a quick stepping-stone to go somewhere else.'

Initially King had tried to capture the Chelsea man on loan, and when the opportunity arose to prise his man away from London on a permanent basis, it was too tempting to ignore. Even at just £50,000, though, Sam's fee had been difficult to raise.

The summer had seen many headlines about financial goings-on. The collapse of the Football League's deal with ITV Digital had whipped the fiscal carpet from under the feet of all 72 clubs. The acceptance of the club's creditors of a Creditors Voluntary Agreement in May paved the way for better times, but Town's position as a club in administration (for the second time) would not be corrected until 20 August. All signings had to undergo League agreement, delaying the completion of close season deals, and various embargoes were placed on Town to further complicate Andy King's team restructuring.

Further concern was caused when previous directors Danny Donegan and Ian Blatchley took an interest in reclaiming their £1.2 million debenture and Town appeared to be in the sort of financial mess that supporters found sadly familiar. One on-going story concerned coach Neil Ruddock, who had fallen out of favour and whom the club wanted to remove from his post. The non-payment of his salary promptly brought another signing embargo just as the previous one ended.

With all that going on off the pitch it was a relief to concentrate on football matters, and on 12 August the first match of the 2002–03 season saw Barnsley entertained at the County Ground. The match was to herald the arrival of a new hero for the supporters to laud. Parkin had struck four goals in four starts during pre-season and said 'I think you know when something feels right, and after a few days training I was convinced that this was the right place to come. I have a two-year deal, and over that time I hope to score goals for this club while improving as a player. I'm going into games believing I can get goals. One against Barnsley on Saturday would certainly be great.'

He went two better.

After falling behind to a Chris Lumsdon penalty, Town's fresh recruit helped himself to a hat-trick, completing the goalscoring from the penalty spot. The Swindon *Advertiser* promptly named the striker the 'Star Man' of the match, awarded his performance nine out of 10 and instantly dubbed him 'Super Sammy Parkin.' It was a name that Sam would do justice to for three years.

He was as pleased with his start as his manager would have been. 'I wasn't enjoying my football last season but that has completely changed since coming to Swindon', he told the *Adver*. 'I wake up in the morning now and can't wait to get to training. I suppose it was a dream start against Barnsley but it was just one game and nobody is going to get carried away. There are 45 games still to go.'

'I hope to keep scoring but I don't feel under any pressure. Swindon haven't paid a massive amount of money to bring me here and I'm really just starting out in League football. It's going well for me at the moment and I hope it continues that way.'

Describing his success in front of goal, Sam said 'For the first goal I spun round and bent it into the bottom corner. Danny (Invincibile) got a good shot in for the second and as the 'keeper pushed it out I just concentrated on hitting the target. It was quite a tight angle but I connected well and it went through Marriott's legs into the net. It was a fantastic feeling to see the ball hit the back of the net for the third. There was no doubt that I was going to take the penalty.'

Sam paid tribute to some of King's other signings, highlighting the class of one in particular – loan signing Jimmy Davis, who had arrived on a three-month deal from Manchester United and who came on for Danny Invincibile in the 84th minute.

Pre-season odds had seen the bookies name Town as one of the favourites for relegation, so a 4–2 win at Chesterfield in the second game of the season was not what they had expected. Sam was on target again, and when a trip to Steve McMahon's Blackpool produced a point from a 0–0 stalemate, Town found themselves in the lofty position of second in the embryonic Division Two table.

That, sadly, was as close as Swindon were to get to upsetting the odds. A horrendous run of six straight defeats plummeted the side down the table as all of the early optimism disappeared. After

The Notts County defence does not look happy as Parkin celebrates.

describing his squad as the best he had assembled at Swindon, the fourth of those losses, a 2–1 home defeat by Port Vale in the first week in September, brought this comment from King. 'We have lost another game of football and I just don't have a clue.'

Supporters were beginning to wonder as much!

A similar defeat by Wycombe Wanderers in the Worthington Cup the following week did nothing to lift spirits. Goalless after a dire 90 minutes, Wanderers, who included ex-Town 'keeper Frank Talia in their number, netted just one minute into extra-time. The *Adver's* Jon Ritson commented 'One fan in the Arkells Stand yelled "Why didn't you do that a minute ago? We could all be on our way home now."'

It's not often that my shouts gain such exposure.

Town were in free fall and 17 September was to be a significant date. As Town prepared for the short trip to near neighbours Cheltenham Town, Andy King made the brave decision to bring in some coaching assistance and announced that ex-England star Steve Coppell was to join the staff. King said 'I decided to take command of the situation before the situation took command of me. We needed something new to liven the place up. Steve Coppell performed miracles at Brentford last season on no money. If it makes no difference and we keep losing games, my situation will take care of itself.'

Coppell signed for a month as first-team coach, but with King retaining responsibility for team selection. His first view of his new charges would have given Coppell reason to question the wisdom of his decision. A 2–0 defeat at Whaddon Road witnessed sour scenes that will long live

Parkin lays the ball off against Cardiff City.

in the memory. With 1,700 travelling Town supporters increasingly aiming abuse at their own team, skipper Andy Gurney turned on the terraces as patience ran out on both sides of the perimeter fence. Matt Hewlett deflected a free-kick into his own net on 30 minutes, and things got worse in the second half after chants of 'What a load of rubbish' accompanied the half-time whistle.

Cheltenham 'keeper Steve Book was clobbered by Parkin as the striker challenged for the ball. A red card was waved and Swindon's task became even harder. By the end of the match, Cheltenham had netted a second and the calls for King's head were not a reference to the pub in which supporters were going to drown their sorrows later. King said afterwards, 'When your own supporters are screaming at you from the off, you've got problems. What's happening at the moment is affecting the players. They are nervous wrecks. Fans are even arguing with their own players now.'

The defeat was the sixth in the League in succession. In Jon Ritson's match report for the *Adver*, his closing comment was 'Surely this is the lowest point?' But despite a win over Northampton four days later, by Monday 30 September a 3–0 loss at Luton brought this Ritson riposte. 'Surely things can't get much worse than this?'

A stomach bug had meant that Sam had been named substitute in a 1–0 home defeat by Cardiff City during the terrible run, and his suspension meant that Town would be without his services for another three matches. On 5 October Town lost 1–0 at home to Oldham and supporters continued to call for King's sacking. Nine defeats in 10 games saw a gate of just 4,326, and they contained a high proportion of Andy King's critics. The manager said 'The directors have to make a decision. This isn't a good time at this club. I won't take this club down and neither will these players. I can't walk away and admit defeat.'

Just one point was claimed from nine during Sam's suspension, and a 2–0 defeat at Bristol City on 19 November left Swindon 22nd in the table.

It was now that the importance of Sam Parkin, the goalscorer, began to become patently clear. Returning for a home fixture with Mansfield Town, his 21st-minute strike put Town on the way to a 2–1 victory over the club that Andy King had previously managed and the forward began an extraordinary goalscoring run. Seven goals in six League matches helped Town to an unbeaten sequence. A Parkin penalty four days before Christmas was little reward in a 3–1 home defeat by Crewe, but the match was to be the only one that season in which Sam would score but Town would lose.

A goal from Parkin on Boxing Day sent the fans home happy on the back of a 2–1 win over Brentford, and after defeat at champions elect Wigan Athletic two days later 2003 started as the previous year had ended. Three Parkin goals in successive matches began a seven-match unbeaten run, taking Town to both mid-table and mid-February.

King was to comment on more than one occasion that Sam's goals had sometimes kept him in a job. That three-month span did more to prove that statement than at any other time.

The manager had suffered a serious test. On 8 October it had been announced that Steve Coppell had departed the County Ground to take the managerial post at Brighton, and 10 days later came the news that Town's board were ready to relieve King of his duties. In the 2–2 home draw with Colchester United, ex-Town captain Colin Calderwood and former England defender Stuart Pearce were pictured in the crowd, but it was former Manchester City, Barnsley and Bournemouth manager Mel Machin who was offered the role as Town boss, with Andy King expected to accept an 'upstairs' role involving scouting for new talent.

King stayed tight-lipped but was clearly unimpressed. Three days later, Machin still had not said 'yes' or 'no', and in between Town had lost at Bristol City. Then, on 22 October and with the situation still up in the air, Town faced Division Three outfit Southend United in the LDV Vans Trophy. It was a competition that few took seriously, but an incredible 6–1 home win saw six different scorers for Town, Parkin sealing the victory with a 90th-minute strike. It was a result that perhaps more than any other kept King at the County Ground helm.

Even then the club announced they had spoken to ex-Liverpool star Jan Molby with a view to appointing him boss at Swindon, but when the Dane announced his lack of interest, the tide finally started to turn in favour of King once more. The pressure on the manager had been relieved by the goals of Sam Parkin, and he had much to thank his star striker for. On 9 November Sam struck in the first two minutes to claim a 1–1 draw with Tranmere Rovers. After the game the striker said,

'It's another step in the right direction. We haven't lost for the fifth game in a row so let's look at it in a positive way. I was a bit tired at the end as I hadn't trained all week, but it's amazing how a goal can give you some extra adrenalin to keep you going. I'm happy off the pitch and hopefully that is being reflected on the pitch.'

Going on to talk about one of his colleagues Sam praised winger Jimmy Davis, whose three-month loan spell had just finished. 'Jimmy has done really well for this club but we always knew he would be going back to Manchester United at some point. If he hadn't done so well then maybe he would have been allowed to stay. He can certainly go back to Old Trafford with his head held high.' The form of young Davis had been one of the bright spots over the early season tribulations. Not to become fully significant until the following season, the *Adver's* headline on 11 November after a 1–1 draw with Tranmere Rovers, 'Loan star Davis plays last game for Town', was both accurate and tragically prophetic. The Manchester United man had played 13 times for Town, scoring twice. Those games were to comprise his entire Football League career, and Sam had been fulsome in his praise.

As always, Town's fiscal status continued to give major cause for concern.

In October, Donegan and Blatchley declared their intention to go to the High Court to call in their £1.2 million, and had the law ruled in their favour, the pair would have won the right to appoint the receivers to reclaim their money. Thankfully, the threat of closure was avoided, and when on 10 October the Football League Tribunal decreed that Luton must pay £105,000 for the signature of defender Sol Davis, who had switched clubs in the summer, there was some brighter news for a change.

Getting in where it hurts against Bournemouth.

As 2002 drew to a close, a line was drawn under a saga that had dragged on for over a year. On 12 December it was announced that Neil Ruddock had finally accepted a 'six-figure sum' to leave the club that he had joined as a player-coach 16 months previously. A contract that was not due to expire until July 2004 had been settled early and the agreement lifted a transfer embargo that had been enforced by the PFA after Ruddock's £58,000 'loyalty bonus' had remained unpaid since October. Until his acceptance, the threat of a winding-up order had hung over the County Ground.

Stripped of his coaching duties back on 17 October, the club had at last removed the man who was said to be responsible for 20 percent of the wage bill and whose fitness had been an increasing cause for concern. It lifted the cloud that hung over the payment of £140,000 of TV money, paid after Town's trip to Oxford in the FA Cup and that Ruddock's advisors had sought to freeze. That game on 7 December had resulted in a 1–0 defeat by their closest geographical rivals and also cost Town valuable local kudos.

So, a new year and a new beginning.

The first home match of 2003 brought a 3–0 win over Chesterfield with Parkin claiming his 17th goal of the season. Also on target was Australian strike partner Danny Invincibile, of whom Sam commented 'I think Danny and I worked well. He needed a goal and let's hope he adds a few more before the end of the season. I don't honestly have a preference to which system the gaffer plays, but with just the two in attack it's more tiring on the legs.' On 25 January Town faced Wigan Athletic at the County Ground, a side who were nine points clear at the top of the table and who incredibly had won their last 11 games on the trot. Time, then, for Swindon to show their infuriating side, taking the match by two goals to one.

There were no goals for Sam that day, but he was presented with the PFA Player of the Month before the match. It was typical of the modest striker that he had more praise for colleague and scorer Danny Invincibile than comment about his award. 'I didn't need to come out for the second half as Danny was that good. Having him alongside me with his attributes, makes my job a whole lot easier.'

A 1–1 draw at Barnsley on 1 February was most notable for the goal that Rory Fallon scored for the Tykes prior to his arrival in Wiltshire, but as spring arrived and with Swindon in a position of relative safety, Town once more faltered as inconsistency began to take its toll. A 3–1 County Ground win over Queen's Park Rangers on 1 March brought Sam's 20th goal of the season against his childhood heroes, but that was to be the only win in seven attempts.

Inexplicably, Town were at their most vulnerable against what, on paper, was inferior opposition. Northampton Town were to finish the season at the very foot of Division Two, but Swindon returned from Sixfields on the end of a 1–0 loss. Then Cheltenham visited the County Ground and took the points, courtesy of three goals without reply. Bobby Gould's side had begun the game in 24th place and the result added insult to the injury suffered at Whaddon Road six months earlier. Next, a trip to Mansfield yielded nil points and then, in April, Swindon lost the home game with Huddersfield.

In little over a month, King's team had contrived to lose to all four teams that would be relegated that season. The good news was that Sam was still among the goals. One at home to fifth-placed Bristol City on Wednesday 19 March saw the points shared, with future Town players Lee Peacock, Aaron Brown and Christian Roberts all featuring for City. After the game Sam said 'My goals have tended to come in bursts and I want to try and give the supporters an easier end to the season by grabbing us a few more. Obviously I'm pleased to have scored the goals I have this season, but next year, having got a little more experience under my belt, I'll be aiming to score goals more consistently. Hopefully the goals will come more regularly throughout the season next year.'

Sam already showing commitment for next season sounded like good news for the fans, and it took just three days for him to show his resolve. A hat-trick, stuck past Notts County and ex-Town goalkeeper Steve Mildenhall, helped Town to a 5–0 win and unsurprisingly won Parkin the Man of the Match award. Again, modest Sam was keen to play down his own contribution in favour of his colleagues. 'I think Junior Lewis (recently signed on loan from Leicester) added a different dimension to the midfield and Steve Robinson and Stef Miglioranzi complemented him well. Now we have to push on, finish as high as we can and hopefully I can get past the 25-goal mark.'

With a mid-table finish all but assured, three wins were produced in the last four matches. A 1–0 win at promotion-bound Crewe underlined Town's infuriating propensity for lifting their game against better opposition, while falling to the lower teams.

Sam signed off 2002–03 with the last goal of the season on 3 May, a strike that turned a draw into a 2–1 home win over Luton Town. It was the striker's 26th of the season in all competitions, a return which justified confidence in Andy King's talent-spotting ability of the previous summer. Before the game came the annual award ceremony, and it was of little surprise to anyone at the County Ground that day that the Player of the Year accolade should be bestowed on Sam Parkin.

'It's been an unbelievable first season for me', said the now 22-year-old. 'The manager showed great faith in me because I know there were a few people wondering what this young lad from Chelsea could do. I was determined to succeed this year and I will be coming back in the summer with an even greater desire to score goals for Swindon Town. I was probably a bit of an unknown quantity but I like to feel I've proved a few people wrong. If someone had told me this time last year that I'd be winning awards like this, I'm not sure I'd have believed them.'

Andy King was also pleased.

'My vote for Parkin is not based purely on goals. His contribution as a whole has been incredible. He has worked hard, shown great belief and that is why he deserves to win the award. I just hope he goes and does it all again next year.'

Two seasons later and Parkin's early resolve to remain at Swindon had been vindicated. Another

23 goals had flown in during 2003–04 and he had continued to attract admiring glances from other clubs. Coventry City had a £150,000 bid turned down, and rumours had connected Sam with Sunderland and, more worryingly, Queen's Park Rangers. It was suspected that there could be a 'special arrangement' that could allow him to move to his boyhood heroes if the price was right, but in November 2003 he penned a new contract that tied him to the County Ground until the summer of 2006.

Despite that, on 11 June 2004 it was reported that Hull City had made a £250,000 bid for Sam, but the attempt to lure the Londoner to Yorkshire never got off the ground. The man himself said 'I've signed a two-year contract which I feel demonstrates my commitment to the club. I'm not someone that's motivated by money. I think those who know me well are aware of that.'

Tigers manager Peter Taylor was reported to have turned his attention to Bristol City striker Lee Peacock. After 25 loan appearances at the County Ground, defender Jerel Ifil was persuaded to make a permanent move from Watford to Swindon, and the likelihood of another red card for Parkin was reduced when Cheltenham 'keeper Steve Book made the short trip from Gloucestershire to Wiltshire.

Sam shows his style at Elland Road, Leeds.

Behind the scenes, assistant manager Malcolm Crosby left Swindon in July, bound for Middlesbrough – a move that saw the return of Mike Walsh (who had occupied the same post under Steve McMahon and Jimmy Quinn) as Andy King's second-in-command.

Season 2004–05 started with a couple of defeats. Firstly, striker starlet Andy Caton, who had impressed during pre-season, had the honour of opening the scoring for Town. The 16-year-old's 90th-minute strike at Wrexham on the opening day of the season, though, produced no reward, coming as it did after the Red Dragons had already struck two of the own. Then Luton Town visited the County Ground and left with the points, despite Sam registering his first goal of the campaign.

Three wins on the trot, including victory over Bristol City at Ashton Gate, then restored hope to Town's season. That triumph came as a result of two goals from another new kid on the block, someone who had been brought in by Andy King to lift the responsibility off Sam Parkin's shoulders.

Darius Henderson was a 6ft 2in, 22-year-old ex-Reading striker, who joined Town on a month's loan from Gillingham and certainly made a good first impression. Darius himself was understandably pleased with how well his new partnership with Sam Parkin worked. 'He's an excellent striker who just makes it easy for you', was his assessment.

Another goal in Darius's first game at the County Ground a week later set Town on the road to a win over Hartlepool.

In a six-match spell in Wiltshire, Henderson produced five goals and overhauled Parkin's total. The run enticed Town to make an approach to the Gills in an attempt to capture his signature on a permanent basis. Over the course of a week the story changed daily, until the end of September saw Henderson back at Priestfield on his way to becoming the Gills's top scorer.

His return to Kent could hardly have been timed more badly. A week later, on 25 September, Sammy Igoe struck the only goal of the match in the 87th minute to win the home game with Bradford City, but three minutes before Igoe's winner Parkin had been shown the red card after a fracas with Darren Holloway. 'It's a massive blow to this club,' said Andy King, possibly mindful that Parkin's subsequent suspension coincided exactly with the one that had endangered King's job two seasons earlier.

It was an opportunity for Rory Fallon to grab his chance, and his brace helped Town to a 3–0 lead at Stockport before the result was extraordinarily turned round with three goals in a late, five-minute spell from the home side.

On 14 October Christian Roberts signed from Bristol City to help fill the spaces up front, and by the time Sam was back in harness Town were still on the fringes of the Play-off places.

Significantly less damage had been inflicted on King's career than déjà vu might have led him to fear.

Fortunately, Sam got straight back into the goalscoring groove with four goals in four matches up until the middle of November. December saw the emergence of a man who had so far failed to fulfil his potential in well over a year. Grant Smith had signed from Sheffield United in the summer of 2003 and, if used at all, had tended to come off the bench. Doing just that at home to Huddersfield in the first game of December, Smith scored a consolation 89th-minute goal in a 2–1 defeat, his first for the club, and by the end of the season Grant had hit another nine to finish second to Parkin in the club's scoring chart.

January brought the usual 'surprise' news from the boardroom when an 'unexpected' VAT bill landed on the mat. A 'six-figure sum', a phrase that Town supporters had become all too familiar with, was owed to the Inland Revenue and a winding up order was issued yet again. Many fans couldn't help wondering what sort of company could overlook such a figure.

The man who so often rescued Town in their hour of need, Sir Seton Wills, was believed to have come to the rescue yet again. Then, on 4 February Mike Walsh made what was described as an amicable departure from the County Ground and Mick Harford's name surfaced as a possible replacement.

Harford, who was a personal pal of King's, was trying to settle up his contract after being released as Nottingham Forest manager, but rumours that King could move upstairs for Harford to take the reins were disputed by the Town boss. It would be towards the end of the month before Harford joined Town as King's assistant, but in April the lure of Millmoor proved too great and Harford was announced as the new manager of Rotherham.

On 12 February Parkin scored both the goals that gave Town a 2–1 win over Barnsley, the club against whom he had hit a hat-trick on his Town debut. It was Town's third win on the trot and ended a 13-match unbeaten run for the Tykes. Parkin's 16th and 17th goals of the season lifted Town to seventh in the table and stirred hopes of a top-six finish. Parkin said 'Scoring goals is my job. It doesn't mean anything if we don't get into the Play-offs. We're two points off sixth place now.' Two more for Sam came in the 2–2 draw at Torquay a week later.

He then found himself teamed with yet another striking partner when supporters' group the Red Army Fund financed the loan arrival of Rotherham man Michael Proctor, and the faith of the fans was repaid when Proctor struck the only goal against Port Vale in his debut on 23 February. On 19 March Sam was elevated to an exclusive group of just four other players: those who have hit 20 or more goals in three consecutive Town seasons. A hat-trick against Wrexham in a 4–2 win included a 90th-minute penalty and took his haul to 22. Town had been 2–0 down at half-time and were booed off at the interval. The *Adver's* assessment was 'What can you say that hasn't already been said about Super Sammy? A class act.' There would be just two more goals for Sam in a Town shirt.

On 19 April Parkin made what, for an ex-England Youth player, was an unusual appearance.

Called into the future's squad by Walter Smith, he played 23 minutes in the blue of Scotland in a 2–1 defeat by Austria in Mattersburg, qualifying for Scotland through his Scottish mother. Sadly, a collision with the opposing goalkeeper after just 10 minutes curtailed his international debut with an injured hip and Sam was forced to limp off. 'I'm obviously bitterly disappointed and maybe I was a touch over eager going for the ball. I was feeling full of confidence as I'd worked hard and trained well. You have to accept that injuries are part of football. If I had tried to carry on then I clearly wouldn't have done myself any justice.'

More worryingly for Swindon fans, the injury left Town without their main striker as the last three matches of the season approached.

On 7 May Chesterfield visited the County Ground for the last game of the season. Swindon were already 12th and out of the Play-off scene. Determined to take to the field, Sam shrugged off

Goal celebrations at Torquay.

his injury and typically scored the opening goal in the 13th minute. But before that, the man who had joined from Chelsea three seasons beforehand was reunited with a piece of silverware.

For the second time in three seasons, Sam Parkin collected the Player of the Year award. He said 'It means the world to me. I've had a great relationship with the supporters since I came here and to win this award is a great feeling. I think this has been my best year personally in terms of my all round game. I love it down here, it is a great club.' Talking of speculation about his future he said, 'I have another year left and for the time being I am still a Swindon player. I'm sure there's going to be some column inches filled over the summer.'

Town supporters were already reading between those lines.

Watford manager Adrian Boothroyd had been at the match, and after mid-season interest from Fulham and Sheffield United, Boothroyd was next to make an approach. A deal worth around £550,000 was tabled. But as the summer progressed, the Hornets manager seemed genuinely surprised that Town weren't ready to snatch his hand off for the cash, and towards the end of May, Crewe Alexandra had an undisclosed bid knocked back. Then Brighton and the cities of Norwich and Stoke made offers, but when Ipswich Town manager Joe Royle made his interest known, Sam Parkin's Swindon Town career was reaching its conclusion.

In June Royle made his move, and once a figure of £450,000 was mentioned there seemed little chance that cash-strapped Town would be in a position to turn it down. The deal was completed on the 23rd of the month.

The move to a club in a rural location like Swindon, accessible to London and playing in a higher division seemed more suited to Sam's ambitions than any other. Some time after the deal was done it became clear that Chelsea had insisted on a sell-on clause when Sam had left Stamford Bridge, and suddenly the transfer windfall didn't seem as attractive as first thought. As much as 40 percent was rumoured to be earmarked for the London club, but after some lobbying by supporters it seems billionaire Roman Abramovich looked compassionately at Town's financial dilemmas and agreed to waive the fee.

This was a very welcome gesture if true, and one that the Chelsea supremo, perhaps fearing setting a precedent, would understandably prefer to keep quiet.

Sadly, though, Sam's career as a Tractor Boy would be short-lived. A broken ankle forced his omission for much of Ipswich's season, although five goals were forthcoming from 17 Championship matches, and then when Jim Magilton replaced Royle as boss in June 2006, Parkin was on the move again. A sum of £340,000 took him off to Luton Town in August, but in November and after just one goal in eight appearances as a Hatter, an operation to cure the troublesome ankle laid the striker off once more. With his new side spending much of the season in the Championship relegation zone, it was not what Luton or Parkin would have wished for.

A disastrous campaign at Kenilworth Road saw Luton finish on 40 points, a haul that would have left them bottom had Dennis Wise's Leeds United not chosen the route of administration in the final week of the season and suffered a 10-point deduction. That spared Luton the ignominy of finishing bottom, but could not prevent both clubs dropping into League One.

But back to the summer of 2005. It was inevitable that Sam Parkin would move on from Swindon, and everyone connected with the club recognised that now was the time. There was an air of resignation at the final fixture with Chesterfield when Sam finished his Town career as it had started: with a goal.

The signing of a contract extension 12 months earlier had simultaneously ensured one more season at the County Ground for Sam and guaranteed a fee for his signature when he moved before the deal expired.

Retrospectively, there seems an eerie similarity between the two seasons in which Sam collected his Player of the Year awards. A 10th-place finish in 2003–04 was followed by 12th two years later, and each season contained the usual stories of financial doom and gloom. Perhaps the difference was that in the second there was expectation rather than hope on the young striker's shoulders.

Both seasons saw Sam paired up with a succession of partners up front, and each October brought suspension. One saw the arrival and departure of Steve Coppell as Andy King's assistant, the other saw Mike Walsh and then Mick Harford through the same revolving door. Both seasons were also true reflections of Town's ability and ambitions at the time. To keep the club's head above choppy financial waters and to live to fight another day was an achievement in itself.

After three seasons, 126 League appearances and an average of a goal in every other match, it was time for pastures new for the player.

Tommy Mooney (2003–04) ~ He came, he conquered, he left

It pushes fans' understanding to the limit when the player they vote their number one jumps ship in favour of their most bitter rivals just weeks after having an honour bestowed upon him. In the summer of 2004 Tommy Mooney did just that, accepting the club's Player of the Year award in May and then opting to join local opposition Oxford United in July.

To be introduced to, court and win the devotion of the home supporters and then throw that love back in their faces, all in the space of just 12 months, divided the very people who voted Mooney their 'main man', and that his very last kick in a Swindon shirt contributed to costing his club promotion added drama to the controversy.

After first taking the Town helm in October 2000 when he replaced Colin Todd, Town manager Andy King was looking to build on the previous season's 10th-place finish and Tommy Mooney was one of many summer acquisitions during the close season that was the summer of 2003.

Nineteen-year-old left-sided defender Andy Nicholas was signed from Liverpool on 3 June on

Tommy Mooney takes in water .

a 12-month deal, Leicester City forward Jon Stevenson followed on 18 June and the squad restructuring was under way. 24 June saw the announcement that former Reading midfielder Sammy Igoe had joined Town after Luton had tried to get him following a successful loan spell at Kenilworth Road the previous season. With over 150 starts under his belt, his signing captured the imagination of Town supporters and lent anticipation to the start of the coming campaign.

Swindon-born Adi Viveash had started with his local club and moved on to Walsall in 1996. Now aged 33, he had the strange ignominy of being substituted both on and off the field of play by Town boss Ossie Ardiles in September 1990. He rejoined Town on 27 June on the same day that Grant Smith, 10 years his junior, came in from Sheffield United.

Another local boy, but at the other end of the experience spectrum, was 21-year-old goalkeeper Rhys Evans. He had departed Wiltshire for Chelsea but hardly found it easy to displace Carlo Cudicini in the Chelsea goal, despite claiming the England Under-21 shirt. Evans considered his future long and hard. With a desire for first-team football, he rejected an approach from Southend and insisted that money was not to be the greatest consideration for him. Then, after thanking managers Glenn Roeder and Sam Allardyce of West Ham United and Bolton Wanderers respectively for their interest, he put pen to paper on 16 July. The day before, ex-Southampton midfielder 20-year-old Brian Howard had joined the County Ground staff.

The dealings looked a good mix of exciting prospects and seasoned campaigners, with Tommy Mooney perhaps the jewel in Andy King's transfer treasure chest. He signed on a free transfer from Birmingham City on 9 July, on a one-year deal with an option of a second. His job was to augment

Mooney encourages the Town end to offer some support.

the goals of star striker and bargain find Sam Parkin, who had joined Swindon for £50,000 from Chelsea a year earlier. The youth of 22-year-old Parkin was to benefit from playing alongside the experienced Mooney, as Tommy took some of the weight of expectation off the young striker's shoulders.

There was some surprise in football's lower League circles that King had persuaded Mooney to sign on at the County Ground at all. The general consensus of opinion suggested he was capable of continuing at a higher level than the Division Two stage that Town were performing on. Mooney himself, though, had indicated his readiness to retire from football, having grown disillusioned by his treatment at St Andrews, so King's persuasive tongue had paid dividends in his chase for the striker.

Always a handful for opposing defences, Mooney's 13 years in the professional game had taught him every trick in the book. Beginning as a trainee at Aston Villa in Division One, Tommy needed to move to gain first-team football – an early lesson that the strongly-built striker was never to forget. After leaving Villa Park in August 1990 without making a first-team appearance, Mooney, who was born on 11 August 1971, had signed for Fourth Division Scarborough, then managed by former Swindon midfielder Ray McHale. There he registered almost a goal every three matches over 129 League and Cup games spanning three seasons. Established as a regular goalscorer, Billingham-born Tommy favoured a move south, with Southend the winners of his signature in return for a £100,000 cheque.

The move doesn't appear to have been a great success. After just 14 outings that brought five goals, Mooney was loaned to Watford in March 1994, a deal that was made permanent that summer. The move was to be the point at which he went from promising youngster to confirmed first choice. Almost 280 matches followed in the Hornets colours and Tommy banged in 63 goals. This was not prolific, but a healthy return. His forward play was recognised by his fellow strike partners as one of selfless running and powerful hold-up play that created chances for his colleagues.

When, in the summer of 2001, Birmingham City manager Trevor Francis was looking to bolster his strike force for a crack at promotion to the Premiership, Tommy was recruited to lead the line. The manager's reasoning was sound. Thirteen goals in 34 League appearances made him City's top scorer and helped the Blues to grab fifth spot and a place in the Play-offs. A penalty shoot-out success over Norwich City at the Millennium Stadium followed and Birmingham, with Mooney, were top-flight campaigners.

It will have been a disappointment, then, that Mooney graced the Premiership just once in a City shirt, in the opening home defeat by Blackburn Rovers. Francis had been replaced by Steve Bruce just months after Mooney's arrival at St Andrews and perhaps the writing had first been on the wall back in September 2002. Loaned to Stoke City for three months, Tom was barely back in Birmingham before a similar deal took him to Sheffield United, then on to Derby County.

The nomadic striker made 26 appearances for his three temporary employers and scored just three times, an unusually low tally for him but perhaps understandable given the continued uncertainty surrounding the location of his next home ground. It was in this light that Tommy began to consider his footballing future. Then in stepped Andy King and persuaded him to try his hand in a Swindon Town shirt in Division Two. It was a deal that neither party would regret.

The 5ft 10in striker had a reputation as a useful hard man who worked his socks off up front in the cause of his team, and King couldn't hide his pleasure at landing his man. He told the *Swindon Advertiser* 'A lot of people were looking at and talking to Tommy Mooney and he received financially better offers than ours. I take it as a great compliment to this football club that he has signed for us. I tried to sign him last year without success but I'm delighted that I got him the second time around. He's not come here for the money. He's come because he wants to enjoy his football and help us achieve success. His attitude is superb and his experience will help bring on Sam Parkin.'

'He was top of my list, so to get my first choice is unbelievable,' King continued. 'He has pace, power and great goalscoring ability, and he is proven. The lad was playing in the Division One Play-off Final last season and so he could be a great asset at this level. It also means that the burden is taken away from Sam Parkin and together I am hoping that they can forge a lethal partnership.'

Tommy seemed equally impressed with his new club.

'It wasn't a difficult decision to make to be fair' he said. 'I'd been in contact with Andy last summer and so when he expressed interest this time around the wheels were already in motion. In the end, despite receiving a number of offers, this one made sense, not only from a personal perspective but also from a footballing perspective. I had a miserable last year going out on loan on three separate occasions. I didn't get to see my family much and I couldn't settle. This move combines the closeness of my family with a settled position and the manager has made me feel wanted, which is very important.

'Swindon is a big club and its history speaks for itself. Everyone knows they used to be an established Division One side that flirted with the top flight on more than one occasion. Not only that but the training facilities are as good, if not better than many that I've used before and they are a great bunch of lads here. Sometimes when you walk into a club you can see the cliques and thankfully that hasn't been the case here. It's a jovial atmosphere, but everyone seems to have that desire to win.

'I'm confident I have made the right move and I am excited about the challenge ahead. I have enjoyed three promotions in the last five years, it's a great feeling and I want that again. I think the Second Division will suit my game. I don't have a set target of goals for the season but I don't want to be outside the division's leading goalscorers.' Talking about his new strike partner, Tommy continued 'I'm sure the same applies to Sam Parkin. Second Division defenders will know they've played against Tommy Mooney and Sam Parkin, goals on the board or not. Sam had a tremendous season last year and I'm looking forward to striking up a partnership with him.'

He added 'I haven't come here to draw my pension. For the last 12 months I haven't enjoyed my football and I'm determined to put that right. A sense of being wanted is a massive part of my reason for coming to Swindon. There was an interest from Andy King last year but I was under contract to Birmingham. Now that's been sorted out I hope this move will prove of benefit to both myself and Swindon Town.'

A foot injury initially hampered Tommy's involvement in pre-season training. He commented 'I've been lucky with injuries throughout my career so I'm a nightmare when I do occasionally pick one up. I'm tremendously impatient.' His patience wasn't tested for too long, as the striker overcame the knock for the start of the Division Two campaign.

Optimism always reigns at the start of a new season and the opening day of 2003–04 brought a match that would still have been the subject of much anticipation had it occurred months into the campaign. Newly-relegated Sheffield Wednesday's fans travelled to Wiltshire to swell the gate at the County Ground with what would be the second-highest attendance all season. A total of 10,573 witnessed Wednesday take a 3–0 lead inside the first 15 minutes before Town clawed back to end on the wrong end of a 3–2 scoreline. If that was disappointing, the real story of the day was far more tragic.

Jimmy Davis had signed on a three-month loan from Manchester United for the start of the previous season. Making an immediate impact with his trickery on the flank, he had been taken into the hearts of Swindon supporters over his 13 appearances in a Town shirt. The youngster had formed a good understanding with Sam Parkin before returning to Old Trafford with much praise ringing in his ears.

A Bournemouth defender about to experience the Mooney effect.

And the Cherries' goalkeeper doing the same.

Looking to build on his experience, Jimmy agreed a year's loan at Watford and was on his way down to Vicarage Road for the opening day of the new season when a car crash ended the promising life and career of the England Youth and Under-21 international. He had been just 21 years old.

His death affected the three clubs of United, Watford and Swindon, but all of Jimmy's professional appearances had taken place with Town and the news stunned everyone at the club. There can be no doubt that the players' minds were elsewhere for the first game of 2003–04.

Swindon fans had seen enough fight from Mooney in the second half comeback to suggest he might be just what had been missing the previous season, and before League competition recommenced there was the matter of a Carling Cup tie at Southend United, one of Mooney's old clubs.

Town came from a goal down to edge the game with another 3–2 scoreline, this time in Town's favour. With what was plainly typical for Tom, he claimed the last and decisive goal. 'It was great to get on the score sheet in the first week. Having said that I always score against my old clubs,' he commented in the club programme afterwards.

Town's first away League match was back to Essex the following Saturday with a trip to Colchester United, and the legacy of King's astuteness in the transfer market was beginning to reap dividends. Tommy grabbed the only goal of the match with just three minutes remaining. Swindon's points total was off the duck, Tommy was doing what he did best and the season was under way. It's a measure of the early impact he was making that the *Swindon Advertiser* already described him as a cult, and his nickname of Tommy 'The Gun' Mooney was to become a common accompaniment to the announcement of yet another Mooney goal. King was pleased. 'I think Sam

Parkin now has competition to be the fans' favourite. The fans love Mooney's attitude and I like the attitude he has brought to this club.'

So, two matches into the 2003–04 League campaign and Town had tasted both defeat and victory. 23 August brought a glimpse of things still to come when Notts County arrived at the County Ground. Both Mooney and Sam Parkin were on the mark as further goals from Sammy Igoe and Matt Hewlett resulted in a convincing 4–0 win.

The home fans had seen what a combination Tommy and Sam could be, and it left them wanting more. Tommy netted five times before August was out. It was just what Town supporters had hoped for and nothing less than a confident Mooney would have expected.

The first game of September brought a trip to Brighton, where a 2–2 draw ensued. Parkin grabbed both Town's goals but Mooney hit the crossbar, something that would be the cause of some déjà vu come May. By the end of the month, Mooney's contribution was recognised when he was named the club's Player of the Month for September, and then he was rewarded with the PFA Fans' Second Division Player of the Month award as well.

Swindon were now into a 10-match unbeaten run that took until October to end, by which time the club sat second in the table. Then, local rivals Bristol City halted the Town train with a 2–1 win at Ashton Gate. Unsurprisingly, Tommy notched Town's goal, already his eighth in a Swindon shirt. City's goalscorers Lee Peacock and Aaron Brown were both to become Town players in the future.

There were times during Mooney's run that Sam Parkin looked a little lethargic in comparison to his deadliness in front of goal the previous season. Despite hitting eight himself, there were indications that his head would drop if the chances weren't coming his way. Instead of feeling the relief of playing alongside someone capable of lifting the burden of goalscoring from his shoulders, perhaps Sam was feeling the disappointment of having to share the crowd's adulation with his new partner.

It was in the midst of an injury crisis that Town travelled to Championship side Leeds United for a Carling Cup tie on 23 September, with King forced to make a number of changes, among them Mooney. Andy Gurney gave Swindon the lead a minute before half-time and with 16 minutes of the game remaining, Parkin struck again. Ian Harte pulled one back for Leeds three minutes later and with 'keeper Bart Griemink dismissed from the field with minutes to go, United and future England goalkeeper Paul Robinson came up for the corner that looked like being the last action of the match to head the equaliser deep into stoppage time. The Elland Road side then went on to complete an incredible recovery with a win on penalties. At the end of the season, Town might reflect on their lack of success from the penalty spot on more than one occasion.

Just as the first two months of the season had been so successful, October produced a reality check, and worryingly a goal drought for Tommy coincided with an injury to Sam Parkin. Four games were surrendered in succession as the month yielded just two points from six games. The sequence plummeted the club down the table and when the last game of the month brought a 0–0 home draw with Port Vale in front of the season's lowest crowd of 5,313, Town sat 14th in Division Two – the lowest position they would occupy all season.

The return from injury of Parkin sparked hopes as November commenced. Town had failed to score in the previous three matches and the loan acquisition of Portsmouth striker Deon Burton on 17 October failed to adequately fill Parkin's boots. The season was wavering when King moved to sign Rory Fallon from Barnsley for £50,000 on 11 November.

Parkin's first full appearance in six matches at Oldham in mid-November produced his first goal for almost two months and secured all three points, followed by another four goals before the end of the year. Mooney's goals had dried up completely and, just as in the previous season, Town were over reliant on Parkin to hit the net. Then Mooney hit his second purple patch of the season and the campaign took off all over again.

Two and a half months had passed since Tommy's last strike in the middle of October, but in the first match of 2004 Mooney hit the brace that won the game at home to Bournemouth. Town were sixth and in a Play-off place, and Mooney was hungry for more goals. Each of the next three games saw a goal from Tommy as Town took seven points from nine. The results helped cement a top-six place, and a run of 11 games without defeat did no harm either. A draw at Blackpool at the end of January was followed by four home matches in five, an ideal opportunity to force home the advantage.

By 6 March Town had won the lot, including a three-point haul from the trip to Stockport County in which Mooney scored another couple. The double took Tom's total to 17 all told and reaffirmed Town's place at fourth in the table. Then a trip to Division Two leaders Plymouth Argyle saw the traditional Tommy Mooney goal, but at the final whistle Town had gone down by two goals to one through an uncharacteristic mistake from 'keeper Rhys Evans.

But there was trouble ahead. When Mooney struck twice in a 2–0 home win over Grimsby with 10 games of the season left, few Town supporters would have guessed that they had seen his last goal in a Swindon shirt. Just as his rich vein of goalscoring form at the start of the season had unexpectedly petered out in October, so his shooting boots were to show their fallibility in the closing stages of 2003–04, and the loss of his goals was to cause a stutter in Swindon's Play-off hopes.

Just three points were taken from five games, but the last of those matches over the Easter weekend produced a piece of magic that would become a seminal moment for another of Andy King's strikers.

Rory Fallon, who had patiently waited his chance, came off the bench to replace Andy Nicholas in the home game with Bristol City, with Town trailing 1–0. His spectacular overhead kick from the edge of the penalty area 15 minutes from time had the Town End behind the goal on their feet in celebration. The goal equalised a strike from future Wiltshire Robin Christian Roberts, who had turned in a cross from Lee Peacock in first-half added time. Town had conceded three goals against Bristol City during the season and all of the scorers would sign for Town in the future. The fact that Peacock's ball came from a mistake made by future City player Matt Heywood compounded the irony.

A point had been claimed against Town's closest geographical rivals and boy did it feel good. Fallon was on the mark twice more in a 3–0 win at Luton Town two days later on Easter Monday, and another 3–0 win came at Wycombe Wanderers on 17 April. Town might be missing Mooney's goals, but Fallon was coming on stream fast and that was something that might help determine the shape of Town's squad in the summer.

With three games of the season left, Town were sitting fourth in the table. Another point or two would surely secure a Play-off spot, so how typical of Swindon that another Fallon goal in the home match with Oldham would be insufficient to gain any points, and that a trip to Loftus Road on 1 May should result in no reward either. With one game to go, Swindon had still not guaranteed themselves a finish in the top half a dozen.

Town and Hartlepool United started the day both on 72 points and in fifth and sixth place respectively. Meanwhile, in the Potteries, Port Vale were enviously eyeing a Play-off place from seventh in the table and suspiciously considering the possibility of a stitch up. With Swindon and Hartlepool facing each other on the last day of the season, a draw between the sides would leave Vale needing a high-scoring win to make up the goal difference to claim a top six finish at the expense of either of them.

In the event Vale did all they could, winning 2–0 at Rushden and Diamonds but missing out on goal difference, but despite the almost inevitable draw between Swindon and Hartlepool, anyone at the County Ground that day would reject any thoughts of a conspiracy.

Mooney shoots for goal against Bristol City.

Sammy Igoe struck for Town in the seventh minute, a lead that was held until the 71st when Adam Boyd equalised for Hartlepool. If the foot was lifted off the gas by both teams then, it was no more than might have been expected at the end of an arduous season.

Tommy Mooney had played in all bar one game of the 46, rested through illness by Andy King for that very last match of the regular season. With 19 League goals to his name and that strike in the Carling Cup against Southend United, he had hugely justified King's confidence in him 10 months earlier. Matching Sam Parkin almost goal for goal, The Gun had endeared himself to the County Ground to such an extent that while playing no part in the last Division Two match of that campaign, he was to have a busy day anyway. By kick-off, Tommy had swept the board with the end of season awards, collecting every one of the trophies on offer. Along with the award for Player of the Year, he was also honoured with the awards from the Supporters' Club and the Supporters' Trust.

After the game Mooney said 'We left it a bit close at the end. Hartlepool were always going to come back. They are not sixth in the League through fortune. They're a decent side and they showed that. They got the goal and we were a bit edgy. I had not trained all week and I was on the bench just in case of an emergency but fortunately I wasn't needed.'

After that, the Play-offs were surely made for Tommy to rubber stamp his status as the Town hero. He had already taken part in Watford's 1999 Play-off success when they beat Birmingham City, before despatching Bolton 2–0 at Wembley. Then came the adventure for Birmingham in 2002. Mooney could again make his experience pay. If his early season barren scoring streak was anything to go by, he was due to break his current duck, stretching back to the middle of March, and grab the goals that would lift Town into Division One.

If only reality had lived up to the fairy tale.

On 16 May Town hosted fourth-placed Brighton and Hove Albion in the first leg of the Division Two Play-off semi-final. A 72nd-minute goal from Richard Carpenter gave Albion the upper hand and took the visitors back to the Withdean Stadium a goal to the good.

Town had had their chances. Mooney had fired wide of the right-hand post after being put through by Sammy Igoe in the 35th minute. Then Igoe himself hit the same upright after he had again combined with Tommy. Mooney went wide again after 55 minutes before he came even closer to breaking the deadlock nine minutes later. Released by substitute Grant Smith, Tom smashed a shot against the woodwork, something that was becoming a bit of a tradition for the striker against Albion. Mooney said afterwards 'We were the better side but the better side doesn't always come out on top. The best team lost here. Clearly Albion have come here for a draw and they've been very fortunate to get a win. Even their lads were embarrassed by the result at the end, and that tells a story.

'This was a very difficult match for them and in fairness you have to give them some credit for having one shot in the game' he said with a touch of sarcasm. Talking about his performance, he stated 'I missed a good chance with a header and then I thought I just had to get a good contact and it hit the bar.' And of the second leg to come, 'It will be like playing on a neutral ground because there is no atmosphere in that ground at all. Hopefully that will be enough for us to go and win it.'

The Sky TV cameras were on the south coast four days later, with the smart money on Brighton capitalising on their slender lead and home advantage. This season had one last twist, though, and it would take until the 81st minute for the drama to unfold.

In the 78th minute Tommy Mooney had performed his by now traditional feat of hitting the crossbar with a 25-yard left-footed drive and with the game still deadlocked and Brighton 1–0 up on aggregate, Sam Parkin followed up a Stefani Miglioranzi effort to slide the rebound home from close range. With the scores now level on aggregate, extra-time was to follow and it was Town fans who were jubilant first. Seven minutes into the added period, Mooney set Rory Fallon free and the big New Zealander poked the ball home via Albion 'keeper Roberts's hand. It was the first time Town had been in the lead for 187 minutes over the two matches, but with the game in stoppage time and Town within touching distance of the Millennium Stadium, Danny Cullip knocked on a long throw for Adam Virgo to score with a diving header.

Forty-six games and 210 minutes of Play-off action saw the season boil down to penalties to decide who made the Millennium Stadium Final. The game was turning into a re-run of that Carling Cup match at Leeds United. Parkin and Heywood made no mistake from the spot, but Mooney's effort was saved by the Brighton 'keeper Roberts. With Richard Carpenter, Chris Iwelumo and John Piercy all on target, Rory Fallon kept Town in it, only to see Adam Virgo add to his tally from the spot.

All the pressure was on skipper Andy Gurney, who saw his spot-kick crash off the post. Town were out. Days later Mooney seemed scarred. 'Several times a day I'm still getting a sick feeling. I've never missed in a shootout before. I struck it well but the 'keeper went the right way.' It would have been little consolation that the *Swindon Advertiser* voted Tommy Town's star man. Perhaps the most telling statement came from Brighton manager Mark McGhee. 'We've been absolutely hammered. Andy King must be devastated. I don't know if I'll have to apologise to him. We're obviously delighted but I feel for them so much. We've mugged them. The support, the players, they put in a magnificent effort. I'm not patronising them. For us it's fantastic. For Swindon...I do feel sorry for them. We've got to be the luckiest team on the planet tonight.'

Andy King was keen to tie up his out-of contract players as early as possible to build on the successes of 2003–04, but the manager was not prepared to wait indefinitely. If players were to leave, it would take the summer to find adequate replacements and deadlines were set for the team to respond to the new contracts in front of them.

One of the procrastinators was Tommy himself. His option for a contract extension had been

Mooney misses his penalty in the Play-off shoot out against Brighton at the Withdean Stadium, Brighton 2004.

triggered, but there was a rumour that he had been offered a better deal during the season than that which was eventually placed on the table in the summer. Sam Parkin would have liked the partnership with his strike colleague to continue. In the match programme he had commented 'I've really enjoyed playing with Tommy. I've picked up so much from him. Mind you, I've never known anyone to have so many illnesses. Imagine what he could have done if he had been training more than once a week.'

As had been heard before, Andy King was among the greatest fans of the strike duo. 'Parkin and Mooney are awesome and the best in the division without a doubt', he had remarked during the season, but perhaps the emergence of Rory Fallon gave King the confidence that the loss of Mooney might not be the end of the world.

The likelihood of Tom signing a new deal seemed in doubt on 25 May. Mooney said 'I don't think the club know exactly what they want.' Referring to the Play-off match at Brighton, he said 'I wouldn't want that to be the last part I play in a Swindon shirt. It makes me even more determined that I want to finish with a medal. I've thoroughly enjoyed my year here.' Pouring cold water on rumours that King and Mooney had fallen out, Mooney added 'People who suggest there is a gap between me and the manager couldn't be further from the truth.' Manager King agreed, but suggested that Tommy might have another agenda. 'My relationship with Tommy Mooney is very good and the relationship he has with this football club is fantastic, but if someone has made Tommy a better offer then it is his decision.'

Ahead of the start of pre-season training on 19 June, King announced 'I'm not waiting. Although Tommy has been good for the club he hasn't done it all on his own. Tommy has options. He scored 20 goals and made others aware of what he can do.' Ten days later saw Tom admit that he wouldn't be re-signing, with the headline 'Mooney Leaves Town'. There was a rumour that

Bristol City might move in, but for some the outcome might have seemed even worse. On 8 July the *Advertiser* headline read, 'Mooney signs for Oxford'.

'I'm confident that I can score a lot of goals and I'm looking forward to the challenge' said Tommy, after putting pen to paper for Town's greatest rivals one day before the anniversary of signing for Swindon. 'I spoke to a few people about manager Graham Rix before making the decision and people had a lot of good things to say about him as a coach. I haven't joined Oxford in order to spite anyone at Swindon Town.'

So, ultimately, there was no end-of-season glory for Tommy Mooney, but his 12 months in a Town shirt were a complete story in themselves. It's not often the case that the Swindon career of one of Town's Players of the Year can be summed up in just one campaign. Worthy winners usually take either longer to win the affection of the crowd, or stay longer having done so.

Among the reasons that Tom had mentioned for joining Swindon was family commitments, and one can guess that perhaps the commute to the Kassam Stadium along the M42 from his Birmingham home was easier than that to the County Ground.

After a year at Oxford United, though, during which time Tommy struck 15 League goals and finished top scorer, it was time to move on once more. League Two Wycombe Wanderers were just up the road and a fresh challenge appealed to Mooney all over again.

One season as the Chairboys' top scorer produced an unsuccessful Play-off campaign, during which Tommy scored against eventual winners Cheltenham before a contract extension turned The Gun loose on League Two once more.

Typically, Tommy chose the 90th minute to score against Town in September 2006, denying Swindon three points at Adams Park, and throughout the season Wanderers again found themselves challenging towards the top of the table. Mooney, of course, found himself contributing his fair share of goals.

A 12th-place finish did not consummate the hopes that had been raised earlier in the campaign, but Mooney had done his best, finishing second top scorer, 11 goals behind Jermaine Easter's 24. In the summer of 2007, Mooney, now 35 years old, was ready to pledge his future to the Chairboys for a third season. Out of contract, the club captain was looking to talk with manager Paul Lambert to finalise a new deal.

But there was almost one ironic twist to the story. Even as Wanderers manager John Gorman was trying to entice Tommy to travel to Adams Park from Oxford, news came that former strike partner Sam Parkin had left Swindon for Ipswich Town. Tommy picked up the phone and tried to broker his own deal that would see him return to the County Ground as a direct replacement for his ex-colleague.

This time Andy King declined the chance to add 'The Gun' to the playing roster. Perhaps returning with Oxford United on his CV would have been too much even for Town supporters to forgive.

Rhys Evans
(2005–06) ~ Homeward bound

A long-running story throughout several weeks of the summer of 2003 had involved a Swindon-born goalkeeper who had tried his hand elsewhere. Born in January 1982, Rhys Evans had once been in the Highworth Town youth set up but had decided to move on to Chelsea at the age of 17.

The Blues could certainly offer some excellent coaching for an up-and-coming young 'keeper, and it must have been an inspiration for Rhys to train with Carlo Cudicini and Ed de Goey, both expert proponents of the goalkeeping art. But the benefits on the training field could only lessen the chances of ever making progress on the first-team pitch. With the arrival of Roman Abramovich and the roubles that he brought with him, it became even less likely that Rhys would be offered a first-team chance.

The Swindon man with the Welsh-sounding name had already made steady progress through the England international ranks, gaining caps at Schoolboy, Youth and Under-21 levels. Rhys finally made his League debut in February 2000, during a loan spell at Division Two Bristol Rovers. A 4–1 away win at Oldham Athletic for the Pirates was an encouraging way to start a football career, but more importantly for a goalkeeper, the two clean sheets against Wycombe Wanderers and Bury would have brought great satisfaction. The four-match spell at the Memorial Stadium saw Evans help Rovers to remain unbeaten and claim eight points from 12. Rhys had officially announced his arrival on the footballing scene.

Rhys Evans poses for the camera.

Then, in November 2001, when Queen's Park Rangers' boss Ian Holloway was looking for a short-term solution to offer further goalkeeping cover at Loftus Road, he remembered the young 'keeper whom he had brought to the Memorial Stadium while manager at Bristol Rovers and gave Rhys his next taste of League action. Pulling on the 'keeper's shirt newly vacated by Fraser Digby in February 2002, Rhys played the last 11 matches of the season and helped the Hoops to an eighth-place finish in Division Two. Five clean sheets and just two defeats continued to demonstrate the ability of the increasingly confident young custodian. 2002–03 began with seven games at Division Three outfit Leyton Orient.

When that campaign ended without any further outings and with Carlo Cudicini, Ed de Goey and now Mark Bosnich all ahead of him in the goalkeeping pecking order at Premiership Chelsea, Rhys came to the conclusion that it was time to move on from Stamford Bridge.

It was Fraser Digby's trained eye that had spotted the potential of an ever-improving Evans while at Loftus Road, and it was he who alerted Town manager Andy King to the ability and the availability of the 21-year-old.

On the face of it, a move back to Swindon looked like a match made in heaven, but Evans wanted to consider all his options, and his procrastination about joining his home-town team led some Town observers to wonder whether he was confident or cocky.

Interest had also been shown by West Ham United and Bolton Wanderers, but while both clubs had a more senior status than Swindon, it would be worth little if Evans once more found himself playing second fiddle to a more established man.

Intent on making the right move to increase his first-team chances, Rhys was not ready to jump for the easy option without careful consideration. The deal took some weeks to complete, eventually concluding on 16 July. 'I signed for Chelsea when I was 17 as an apprentice, before signing two professional contracts that took me to the end of last season,' Rhys told Nick Judd for the match-day programme as his first season as a Town player got into full swing. 'I worked with Eddie Niedzwiecki (Chelsea's goalkeeping coach), and when I signed for Swindon I knew there wasn't a specific goalkeeping coach. I spoke to Fraser (Digby) over the summer about the options available to me. It is great to have him as a coach because he has not long finished playing so is aware of how the game is played now.'

Of his international record Rhys said 'I have played right from the age of Under-15. Someone told me recently that I am the most capped young England goalkeeper. I have played about 46 games for my country and I think I've played more international games than I have in the League.' With that total topped up with Under-21 caps against Serbia-Montenegro and Slovakia in 2003, it was League action that the goalkeeper now sought.

Five games into 2003–04, Evans ousted Bart Griemink in the fight for the first-team 'keeper's shirt, making his Town debut in a 2–2 home draw with Blackpool, and Griemink's Swindon career was as good as over. From then on, Rhys missed starting in just one League game, as he stamped his authority on the back of Town's rearguard and assisted a dash to the Play-offs.

The following season Evans continued as he started, surrendering just one League start to back up 'keeper Steve Book and showing a consistency that made his name the first on manager Andy King's team sheet. By the time 2005–06 loomed, Rhys had made huge inroads in his fight to gain League experience. His 86 starts for Town, when added to his loan spells while still on Chelsea's books, took the 'keeper's career total well past a century.

So with that position secure, as the season kicked off all eyes were focused at the other end of the pitch and on the new strike partnership of Jamie Cureton and Tony Thorpe, who had both arrived from QPR.

Looking back at the previous campaign's goal getters, the inevitable departure of top scorer Sam Parkin, who signed for Ipswich Town in preference to an approach from Watford, and the move of Sammy Igoe to Millwall, highlighted a worrying loss of firepower in front of goal. Grant Smith, who had hit double figures the previous campaign, had joined Matt Heywood in a move to Bristol City, midfielder Brian Howard, who had claimed five strikes, had signed for Barnsley, and Darius Henderson's five had come before his return to Watford way back in September. Alarmingly, alongside three-goal Rory Fallon, the Town man with the most goals to his name the season before was centre-back and skipper Sean O'Hanlon.

It was little wonder that expectations (and hopes) were pinned on the new striker pairing hitting it off as soon as the season started.

Under a little less pressure were the twin Bolton Wanderers signings of defender Charlie Comyn-Platt and wide midfielder Ricky Shakes. Right-back Jack Smith arrived from Watford and

Another striker denied by Evans.

experienced midfielder Gareth Whalley signed from Wigan Athletic. Completing the summer transfer activity, Nicky Nicholau came in from Southend and defender Steve Jenkins made the journey from Peterborough.

Evans had actually looked likely to move on during the summer when Leeds United expressed an interest in taking the 'keeper to Elland Road. The two-year deal that he had signed back in 2003 had expired and the Swindon man was free to go. Neil Sullivan had joined Leeds from Chelsea the previous summer and while Evans could now feel satisfaction about his progress of the last two seasons, perhaps he felt the process wasn't quite complete. Playing deputy to Sullivan wouldn't further his aims, and Rhys chose to sign another 12-month deal to stay in Wiltshire.

Evans's own back-up, Steve Book, had left the County Ground, and young reserve 'keeper Matt Bulman, without a start to his name, was the only other stopper on Town's playing roster. So it was hardly ideal preparation when a knee injury picked up pre-season meant that Rhys was forced to play in the early fixtures while less than 100 percent fit.

Four matches into the campaign, Town had taken just four points. Successive defeats in the first two games had given way to a morale boosting 2–1 home win over Nottingham Forest, but it wasn't until a draw at Bloomfield Road that Town's defence kept a clean sheet. By then it had become clear that Evans's problematic knee needed attention, and with Matt Bulman still considered ill-prepared for League One action Andy King was forced to tour the loan market while Evans faced exploratory surgery.

Rhys was understandably disappointed, but pragmatic. 'It seems the best option to me,' he told the local newspaper. 'I'm not comfortable with it and it's stressing me out. The pain can come on quite quickly and it's very, very uncomfortable. I'd rather be missing three or four games now than later in the season, especially when I've only got a year on my contract.'

Surgery was delayed until after the trip to Blackpool, then King moved to bring in 21-year-old Manchester United 'keeper Tom Heaton to plug the gap, and he was accompanied by fellow Old Trafford youngster, attacking midfielder Colin Heath. Ever strapped for cash, the arrival of the pair hung in the balance until United's boss Alex Ferguson agreed to pay a proportion of his players' wages for their three-month terms at the County Ground.

Evans could be satisfied with the part he'd played despite his problems with injury, but a penalty save at Barnsley on the opening day had failed to help gain any points.

The first-ever League meeting with Yeovil Town produced a 4–2 win and with it the hope that Town could start to climb the table from 14th place. The season was just five games old and the goals had already been flowing at both ends of the pitch in equal number, but even with a relatively healthy eight strikes on the board so far, there was an indication that all was not good up front for Town.

Altogether, seven Swindon players had found the back of the net and Yeovil's Terry Skiverton had helpfully added an own goal too, but the much hoped for injection of goals from the new

Evans in unusual action in the opposition's box at Leeds United.

strike partnership of Tony Thorpe and Jamie Cureton was failing to set supporters' imaginations alight. Thorpe had netted in a 3–2 home defeat by Oldham, but the return of Rory Fallon from a suspension held over from the previous campaign cost him his place. What fans did not realise at the time was that they had witnessed the only goal he would ever register in a Town shirt. Given another five-match run in the autumn, by December it looked best for all concerned to draw a line under Thorpe's County Ground career.

Released from his contract, he joined Colchester United on a short-term deal, with little further success. As for Cureton, without a goal in the first eight matches of the season patience ran out in September, as he was consigned first to the bench and then shipped out to Colchester in his own loan deal in the second week of October.

But before either departed for Layer Road came a disastrous run for King's men, one that would be a rude introduction to League football for new loan 'keeper Heaton, and which would have inevitable repercussions in the Town manager's office.

Starting with a single-goal defeat at Tranmere on August Bank Holiday Monday, Swindon were to suffer eight straight League defeats and the reins of the club were to be torn from King's grasp for the second time.

Through September, home reverses at the hands of Southend and Bradford City, coupled with losses at Walsall, Bournemouth and Doncaster, dropped Town deep into the relegation zone. Each match had been relinquished by the margin of a single goal, but with the exception of a strike from defender Steve Jenkins, Rory Fallon was the only other man to make the Town score sheet.

By then, the damage to King's position had already been inflicted. The last straw came on 24 September when two goals from Fallon were insufficient to claim a share of the spoils against Bradford and save his manager his job. Ironically, the win for the Bantams had been engineered by Colin Todd, the man who had brought King to the County Ground five years previously. Fans demonstrated after the final whistle, calling for the manager's head, and three days later King was consigned to history again.

Stepping into the firing line came Iffy Onuora, who had started the season as the head of youth development and had impressed during a spell when his profile had been increased through sickness to King and injury to coach Alan Reeves. He was told the job was his 'for the foreseeable future', and everyone hoped for a turnaround in fortunes.

Onuora, a likeable ex-striker who had played 80 times for Swindon, was perceived as worthy of his chance, but the appointment of a man from within saved the need for another significant addition to the wage bill. Fingers were crossed.

On 1 October Fallon was again on target, but this time there was a two-goal disparity in favour of MK Dons and Swindon had dropped to the bottom of the table. A week later and Port Vale came to the County Ground to inflict the eighth League defeat in as many games, and the third loss on the bounce for Onuora's leadership.

At last came a point at Brentford and with it the first clean sheet in 10 games, followed by penalties from Christian Roberts and Andy Gurney – who was back on loan from Swansea City – in successive matches, claiming a point apiece against Scunthorpe and Huddersfield. Three draws after eight defeats seemed like victories in comparison.

Manchester United goalkeeper Heaton had been given a torrid introduction to League football and if the object of the exercise for Sir Alex Ferguson had been to allow his young player the opportunity to hone his shot-stopping skills, he couldn't have picked a more suitable team to loan his man out to. Far better for Heaton to spend his time in 90 minutes of rearguard action, than to patrol his untroubled box as his temporary team spent the match encamped in the opposition's half.

Little wonder that the United boss was prepared to pay for the privilege of loaning Tom to Swindon.

On Friday 11 November Swindon entertained Bristol City and, not counting a 2–0 win over Conference side Stevenage Borough in the LDV Vans Trophy, Heaton was to finish on the winning side for the first time since his League debut against Yeovil back in August. The victory came through a strike from Neale McDermott, the first of his career and on loan from Fulham. That equalised a fourth-minute penalty for the visitors that had initially been saved by Heaton before the referee concluded that the 'keeper had moved before the ball was struck and ordered a retake.

On the half hour Fallon hit his ninth of the season and the lead was successfully protected until the final whistle. There were jubilant scenes on the bench as the coaching team of Onuora, Reeves and Ian Woan celebrated victory for the first time.

A local derby win is always sweet and this victory had been long overdue, but it would be the return fixture at Ashton Gate that Town supporters would have reason to remember when the season concluded.

Either side of the win over City, Town had played two games with Boston United in the FA Cup. The first, a 2–2 draw at the County Ground, led to a replay at York Street, where Heaton was sent off for bringing down Julian Joachim 20 minutes into the match. Already a goal down by then, Matt Bulman stepped between the posts and saved the resultant spot kick and then leapt to his feet to turn away the rebounded effort, but his heroics were to little avail. When the curtain came down on the game it did so on Town's FA Cup campaign as well, as Swindon trooped off 4–1 losers.

Rhys Evans claims a catch at home to Bournemouth in January 2006.

That gave Onuora a decision to make. With Heaton now facing suspension, should he stick with 19-year-old Bulman or turn to the loan market once more to fill the goalkeeper's shirt?

In the end, the boss needed to do neither. Rhys Evans's recovery from surgery had seen a huge improvement over the previous 10 days. He had started the season not fully fit and declared himself ready to take to the field once more, perhaps a little earlier than might have been expected, but with his further rehabilitation not considered at risk. The trip to Port Vale on 19 November saw Town's first-choice goalkeeper back between the posts for the first time in three months.

And his return almost coincided with back-to-back League wins.

Leading by a 66th-minute strike from loan winger Hameur Bouazza, Town appeared on course for their first away win of the season, but with four minutes remaining, Vale substitute Michael Husbands bundled home from close range after Evans had been unable to hold a shot, and a triumphant return for the goalkeeper had been denied. Rhys was pleased with the reception he was given by the travelling Town supporters. 'The welcome I got from the fans was great and it really gives you a boost when you hear that behind you,' he said after chants of 'England's number one' had greeted his return. And talking of his knee problems he said, 'I wasn't in discomfort and hopefully there'll be no reaction. I'd like to think that no one watching would have been able to tell that I hadn't played since August.'

Unable to do anything about the late equaliser, he said 'They had a corner and as the guy hit a volley I've gone to my right. It's taken a deflection, gone to my left and Husbands has been in the right place to put it in the net. I think anyone who wasn't familiar with this League would have been hard pressed to say we looked bottom of the table.'

But with just 14 points from 18 games, bottom was exactly where Town were, and already six points from the safety of 20th place.

Three days later defeat at Peterborough ended involvement in the LDV Vans Trophy, leaving Town with just their League performances to concentrate on a full six weeks before New Year's Eve. Then Barnsley visited the County Ground, scoring three times and taking three points. The match witnessed the last Town appearance for Tom Heaton, back from suspension and on his way back to Old Trafford a wiser, perhaps battle-hardened man. Rhys Evans was now back in control of the number-one shirt, and after a ground-breaking reserve-team outing to prove his fitness, he would wear it until the end of the season.

But it was time for the council to throw a spanner in the works in an off-the-field development.

The scheme to redevelop the County Ground with a £50 million makeover was thrown into disarray when the local authority told the club to rethink its plans. Apparently reliant on the council gifting the football club a package of land for the construction of hotel facilities, the legality of handing over what was effectively an asset of the ratepayer was called into question. Plainly the asset of League football in the town of Swindon didn't seem to figure very highly with the council, and the threat of moving out of the borough was perhaps the only card the club had to play.

Back on the pitch, Town took the trip to Rotherham with Evans back between the posts, and the double good news of the third clean sheet of the season and a single strike by Fallon gave Town their first away victory, which had been denied them at Port Vale. The last time Swindon had won on their travels had been in February of the previous season. Iffy Onuora announced that 'Rhys Evans was outstanding in goal. He commanded his box well and made two or three great saves.' Millers' boss Mick Harford was also impressed. 'Their goalkeeper was the Man of the Match, the best player on the pitch' he had to say afterwards.

It was 3 December and the win took Swindon off the bottom of the table for the first time in two months. Adding extra reason to celebrate, it was local rivals Bristol City who replaced Town at the foot, and Town were in the middle of their best run of form of the campaign. Inclusive of that win at Rotherham, Swindon were now to remain unbeaten for seven games, something that hadn't been achieved since February 2004. A home Boxing Day win over Colchester United came through a 90th-minute Fallon goal, and all told the defeat at Barnsley back in November was to be the only loss in 13 matches.

But over the same period Town would win just three times and the resultant sequence of drawn games wouldn't help Swindon as much as would have been hoped. Iffy Onuora's stewardship seemed to be slowly swinging the ocean liner around from its collision course with the rocks of relegation, but the season was running out as the foghorn sounded ominously.

On the verge of a new year, a 0–0 draw with second-placed Swansea City on the last day of 2005 still left Town 23rd in the table, but now the team keeping Iffy's men from the foot were MK Dons. Bristol City had lifted themselves clear of the relegation zone and shown Swindon what had to be done to avoid the drop. The Swans had been given a close-up view of Rory Fallon, and while the club denied an agenda, the January transfer window was about to open and by the end of the month, Fallon would be resident in South Wales.

Rhys had been nominated Town's Man of the Match. With his fourth clean sheet in six matches he had been in outstanding form and was already looking to 2006 with renewed optimism. 'If you had looked at the fixtures pre-Christmas you'd probably have said Swansea would have been our stiffest test and the one you might not expect to get a lot out of. We have to be happy with a clean sheet against the team second in the League. Personally I'm happy. Where I've come from to where I am now are complete opposites.'

The transfer window brought selection problems as no fewer than six players became unavailable. The loan signings of Heaton and Heath had returned to Manchester United, while Bouazza, McDermott and Patrick Collins had also departed to their own respective clubs.

But Andy Gurney's return to Swansea City was to be brief. Already set on a permanent switch back to the County Ground, the defender would miss the first two games of 2006 but be back in harness on a longer-term deal by the middle of January.

Starting the new year with consecutive away fixtures, Fallon's 13th strike of the season claimed a point at Hartlepool, then the undefeated run came crashing to an end with a 3–0 capitulation at Gillingham. Rhys admitted his part. 'It was probably my worst game of the season but I'm not going to hang myself on the basis of one match. As a team performance it was in complete contrast to the last few weeks. I suppose you could see it as a kick up the backside. There's still an awful lot of work to do.'

Onuora's choices had been further limited with the news that Christian Roberts had booked himself into the Sporting Chance clinic after announcing a dependency on alcohol. His successful rehabilitation would limit his appearances as Town continued to fight their own battle: that of relegation to League Two.

Then the TV cameras arrived at Town's Wanborough training ground, and with them came Ron Atkinson as filming began for a fly-on-the-wall documentary due to be shown in the summer. The wisdom of allowing media access to the intimacy of Swindon's behind-the-scenes activities seemed a little misplaced, and many worried about the distraction it would cause. The potentially undermining effect that a programme reported to be called *Ron Atkinson: Football Manager* would have on Onuora's leadership gave real cause for concern. Even the six-figure sum that was reported to be coming Town's way as part of the deal would be little compensation if filming hindered the relegation fight, and within weeks common sense prevailed and the show was switched to London Road, Peterborough.

Rhys Evan in action at Doncaster.

Iffy's squad needed the boost of additional numbers and midfielder Paul Smith was recruited from Gillingham, immediately before Town's trip to Priestfield took him back to Kent for the day. Jamie Cureton's three-month spell at Colchester had also come to an end, but when striker Lee Peacock arrived after being released by Sheffield Wednesday, supporters eyed the signing with some trepidation.

Rory Fallon scored in a 4–2 win over Bournemouth with 10 days of January's transfer window still to run, and said 'It's up to the club what they do with me. Someone might come in with some good money. I've no decision to make unless they say "Do you want to go?".' A fresh deal was on the table for the New Zealander, but, left unsigned, Fallon would soon be free to go for nothing. Under those conditions, when a £300,000 bid came in from Swansea City there were resigned shrugs of the shoulders as the man with 14 goals to his name moved west along the M4.

The victory over the Cherries had not only witnessed the final appearance of Fallon, but the first for Peacock, who scored on his debut, and, at last, the first goal for Jamie Cureton in a Swindon shirt.

The season was more than halfway through its fixtures and even with the departure of the leading scorer, it was about to give supporters some hope that the drop could still be avoided. After losing at Southend, the next three home games were won, and in mid sequence came a draw at Bradford City. By mid February a 1–0 home win over Gillingham meant Town's superior goal difference left the club at the head of a pack of four on 38 points. Up to 16th in the League One table, Swindon seemed to have given themselves a realistic chance of evading the trapdoor to the division below. Even better, Cureton had found the net twice more and Rhys Evans had presided over two clean sheets. Things seemed to be looking up at both ends of the pitch.

That is, until the trip to the City Ground to face Nottingham Forest.

In the third minute, Evans's line was breached by Nicky Southall to give Forest the lead, and with 65 minutes gone, referee Clive Oliver waved a red card and Jerel Ifil was off for his third early bath of the season. In between, the former European champions had added a further six goals as Town were unceremoniously outclassed.

Ironically, down to 10 men and with all hope of dignity extinguished, loan signing Trevor Benjamin scored with 14 minutes to go to lend the final scoreline the head-clutching proportions of 7–1. Rhys Evans summed up the day. 'I can't think of another occasion where I've stood there and felt embarrassed to be part of a team. At 5–0 I was thinking it was the lowest day of my professional career and that it couldn't get much worse, but it did.' Perhaps responsible for keeping the home side's tally below double figures, Rhys added 'We were in a tough situation before the match and all that performance has done is to pour petrol on it. I think people have to look at themselves and ask themselves if they have the appetite for the fight.' And, prophetically, Evans concluded 'If they haven't, then we know what's going to happen.'

All the good work of the previous two months was about to be unravelled. A month was to pass before a 2–0 home win over Chesterfield brought the first three-point maximum in six attempts, a spell when the only other point claimed was from a goalless draw at Yeovil. A 1–0 defeat at promotion-chasing Colchester United was particularly painful as former Town striker Tony Thorpe was adjudged to have been upended by Evans, and Chris Iwelumo fired the resultant spot kick past Swindon's Man of the Match to settle the game.

Evans was adamant that he was innocent. 'Knowing that Tony is a clever, intelligent player, when I came out I tried to stay up, knowing that if I went to ground too easily he could make more of it. I didn't touch him at all and the lads were all very disappointed with the decision.'

Unable to score for Town against the club for whom he had registered seven goals that season, Jamie Cureton was quiet. April began, and Town had seven matches to protect their League One place. Just one would produce maximum points and it would be necessary for Town supporters to travel to Scunthorpe to see it. A season defining defeat came at home to MK Dons, when a Clive Platt goal gave the away side a win. The visitors were still the only team beneath Town in the table, and their victory was just the third of the season on Dons' travels.

The final, embarrassing moment was to be reserved for Ashton Gate. Facing Bristol City in the penultimate game of the season, Town knew the situation was almost irretrievable. Despite a 1–1 draw, results elsewhere doomed Town to a spell in League Two, and the ignominy of concluding the fight in such a manner at the home of their closest rivals of the season was difficult to stomach.

After the win at Scunthorpe, Iffy Onuora had said about his goalkeeper 'I hope he chooses to stay. He's been outstanding for us and I can't remember a single bad game he's had. He's kept us in games at important times and he's been a credit to himself.'

Now, as fans set about determining which of their players had performed best in a disappointing season, Evans was about to receive another pat on the back. The last County Ground fixture of League One for at least 12 months took place on 6 May, with Huddersfield Town the opposition and with both teams already sure of their fate. A Play-off place awaited the Terriers, League Two awaited the Robins and a 0–0 draw ensued.

On the same day Rhys Evans took to the pitch for the last time in a Town shirt before seeking pastures new, although that wasn't apparent at the time. Pictured on the back of the *Adver* with the Player of the Year trophy in his hand, Rhys had been voted the fans' favourite for 2005–06, and only Goal of the Season had evaded the clutches of the 24-year-old 'keeper.

Accepting the silverware Rhys said 'This award is voted for by predominantly Swindon people, so to be voted for by Swindon people as a Swindon person myself is a great honour. This is for the people who were there for me early on in the season and propped me up when things were tough. My name will now go down on the trophy with some great players and hopefully one day I'll be regarded in the same manner. The *Adver* award will definitely take pride of place next to my England caps.'

Trophy in the net. Rhys Evans with the Player of the Year silverware.

But talking about his future, a one-year deal was still unsigned on the table and it seemed Evans was seeking improved terms. 'The club are going to have to look at the contract because at the moment it isn't quite what I'd want it to be. The big question for me is whether I take the easy option and stay. When I do speak to the manager I will ask for certain things. If I go it will be a massive wrench for me and my family, but if I move and it's seen as a positive step, I hope people will understand that. I have to ask myself, is it time to challenge myself again?'

There had been some who were still ready to doubt Evans's reasons for joining Swindon three years previously, to question his commitment to his home team and to publicly wonder whether the goalkeeper was confident or overly cocksure. They would have used some of Rhys's comments to justify their cynicism, but presumably they weren't among the 68 percent of voters who gave the Player of the Year award to their goalie.

Like Steve Mildenhall five years earlier, Evans had proved his goalkeeping skills to the fans of his hometown club, and, just as Mildenhall had, he departed Swindon weeks after being crowned Player of the Year. And as had been seen three years earlier, it would be a calculated plan for professional advancement that would dictate Evans's footballing destination, rather than the emotional tug of his roots.

Deciding that League Two football was not likely to serve the purpose of continued progression, Rhys declined the offer of a new contract and moved to Blackpool to resume football at League One level. There he ousted Lee Jones from between the posts to become the regular choice stopper through to February, but after 38 appearances, Paul Rachubka arrived on loan from Huddersfield and deposed the Swindonian, who was suffering hernia problems. Once in possession of the green jersey, it was Rachubka who starred as the Seasiders defeated Yeovil at Wembley to take the last promotion place, bound for the Championship, and when the summer brought the permanent arrival of the ex-Terrier, Rhys Evans knew he would have a fight on his hands to get his place back.

As for the outcome of 2005–06, Jamie Cureton had finally managed seven goals for Town but his tally could not prevent Swindon slipping into League Two. The striker managed the same number at Layer Road, and in contrast the four points gained from his goals against Yeovil and Hartlepool made the difference that took Colchester United into an automatic promotion spot.

When it was made public that Cureton had an escape clause in his contract that would allow him to leave on a free transfer should Town be relegated, there was little surprise when he pitched up at Layer Road again for the start of the U's Championship season of 2006–07. As Town's season had run its course, where would be Cureton's motivation to score for Swindon, when the choice was League Two or Championship football the following year?

There had been signs that relegation could be avoided, notably when five wins in seven had been claimed in the new year, but even though that run left Swindon outside the relegation zone for the first time for almost five months, the 7–1 thrashing at Nottingham Forest destroyed all the newly-found hope.

Town had become the first team since the formation of the Premiership to drop from such lofty environs to the basement division of the Football League.

Lee Peacock

(2006–07) ~ Peacock earns his colours

This book began 17 seasons ago, with the whole town devastated by the news that football's authorities deemed it appropriate that Swindon Town should be denied the promotion to the top flight that a Wembley Play-off win over Sunderland had been expected to bring. Now, Town kicked off at the very basement of the Football League again, a level that the club had last occupied 20 years previously.

As the summer began, manager Iffy Onuora started to shape his squad for the following campaign. Trimming Stefani Miglioranzi from the playing staff, many thought that a more revealing indicator of the security of the well-liked boss's job would be whether he was allowed to bring any new faces in. That speculation was over before May was out.

'I'll give it my best shot,' said Dennis Wise, as he was announced as Swindon Town's new manager for the coming campaign. The ex-Chelsea, Wimbledon and England midfielder left the playing staff of Coventry City to take the manager's office at the County Ground, bringing with him his old teammate from Chelsea, Uruguayan defender Gus Poyet, as his number two. 'We've come here to achieve something', the man who had led Millwall to the 2004 FA Cup final during

A happy Lee Peacock after his goal at Macclesfield in January 2007.

an earlier managerial reign said. With both men signing playing contracts, the moved looked likely to breathe fresh air into the backroom and playing staffs in equal measure. 'We haven't come here just to sit where we are in this division,' Wise concluded prophetically.

Consequently, the speed of the playing staff turnover increased. Central defender Sean O'Hanlon pledged his commitment to Swindon, but fellow full-back Steve Jenkins was told his services were not required for 2006–07. Midfielder Paul Smith soon followed as the summer gathered pace.

Travelling towards Wiltshire were Fola Onibuje, Andy Monkhouse and Jamie Vincent. Paul Evans and Royce Brownlie also augmented the playing staff, then on 4 July came the news that O'Hanlon had sought his own independence after all, jumping ship for MK Dons and turning his back on a three-year deal offered by Swindon. A fee of £170,000 was eventually agreed for the 23-year-old, but the change of heart left a sour taste in the mouth of many a Town supporter.

Curtis Weston had become the FA Cup's youngest finalist when Millwall manager Dennis Wise had given the then 17-year-old his place in the 2004 Final, and it was Wise who brought Weston west on a mission to pad out the depleted midfield in July. Central defender Adi Williams, newly-arrived from Coventry, was handed the captain's armband as the new campaign beckoned.

One undecided man was Aaron Brown, who first proclaimed his intention to quit Swindon and then stated his desire to stay, sending confusing signals that produced equally mixed responses from the stands. O'Hanlon had done the same, but in the reverse order.

Two star signings for which Swindon supporters would thank the managerial duo 10 months later were the arrivals of goalkeepers Peter Brezovan and Phil Smith, who came in to fight for the place vacated by last season's Player of the Year Rhys Evans. The Slovakian came in on a year's loan from Czech outfit FC Brno, while Smith came from the somewhat closer to home source of Crawley Town.

All the changes of the summer, coupled with the arrival of fresh investment from new director Bill Power as the previous campaign had drawn to a conclusion, brought a new sense of anticipation to the club. Town might have sunk to the lowest level of the Football League, but the depression that had followed had been swept away by the excitement of a new challenge. Season ticket sales were up and players and supporters alike were ready for the fight for an immediate return to League One. And the first test would be against Hartlepool, surely expected to be one of the most difficult away days Town would face all campaign.

Lee Peacock struck the first goal of Swindon's season from a Ricky Shakes cross after 11 minutes, but by then debutant Brezovan had already saved a second-minute penalty and blocked the follow up. Then, 70 minutes after the first, Brezovan pulled off his second spot-kick stop of the afternoon to give Town a win over one of the sides that had accompanied them down from League One. Peacock was pleased to have opened his goalscoring account for the season, but had more to say about the events at the other end of the pitch. 'It's the best goalkeeping display I've ever seen in my life,' the striker said about the performance of Town's new keeper. 'He's pulled off some world-class saves. He's just been amazing. The size of him scares you.'

But while that seems dramatic enough, as the evening progressed a different drama was to unfold as news came through of an event that would make the heroics of Town's efforts pale into insignificance.

Liverpool legend Bill Shankly has often been quoted as saying that 'football is not a matter of life and death...it's much more important than that.' The passage of time since the 1960s and the events of Hillsborough, Heysel and Bradford have turned that phrase from one of amusing folklore to one that can be seen as far too glib.

A plane crash that involved the Town backroom team of director Bill Power, marketing manager Mike Sullivan, chief executive Mark Devlin and his son Stan as they travelled back from Hartlepool by private aircraft threatened the lives of everyone on board. All were to need lengthy recuperation, but thankfully all four, and the pilot, were to make successful, if painful, recoveries.

Back on the pitch, the Dennis Wise revolution was to take the start of the League Two season by storm. Straight wins in the first six matches of the League campaign left Town setting a blazing trail at the top of the table. By the evening of 1 September Town were already four points clear of second-placed Lincoln City, as a Friday night match at Chester brought a brace of goals from Peacock and maximum points for Swindon.

'I'm happy to get on the score sheet as it's been a few games since I've scored,' said the man who had last registered on the opening day. With 20 minutes to go, defender Jerel Ifil had been sent off for a second yellow card, but four minutes later Peacock's second goal of the night had secured the points for 10-man Town. 'It was another test for the lads, down to 10 men against a big strong team, and to be honest I still don't think we're firing on all cylinders,' the goalscorer concluded.

Not surprisingly, Wise was named League Two's Manager of the Month for August, as all the hopes of the close season looked like being consummated.

One story that had been running since the summer was the rumour that ex-Manchester United, Liverpool and England midfielder Paul Ince might take the chance to join his friend Dennis Wise at the County Ground, and after weeks of speculation it was finally announced that the guv'nor had signed a one-year deal as a player-coach. The deal heightened the expectation among Town supporters even more. Everything was going according to plan and Town looked destined to annihilate all whom they faced. How could things fail to get even better?

A home win over MK Dons in September was followed by defeat by Peterborough at the County Ground, then four straight 1–1 draws dented the charge for the championship. By the middle of October, Bill Power's injuries had forced the new director to leave his position, Paul Ince had departed to take over as boss at Macclesfield after just three appearances in a Town shirt, Dennis

Wise was being connected with the managerial post at Leeds United and club benefactor Sir Seton Wills was threatening to walk away after falling out with the supporters' group TrustSTFC, who had announced plans to contact the departed Bill Power with a view to making a bid for the club.

If that wasn't bad enough, the sequence of draws dropped Town down to fourth and out of the automatic promotion places. Supporters raised their eyebrows. Only at Swindon Town could things change so dramatically and so quickly.

Three goals had brought three points against Grimsby in the middle of the month, but a broken arm suffered by new star goalkeeper Peter Brezovan with 15 minutes remaining overshadowed the day. The injury brought the curtain down on the entire campaign for the big Slovakian. Lee Peacock scored his second in consecutive matches in the win over the Mariners but, just as on the opening day of the season, the striker's thoughts were of his goalkeeper. 'It's a massive shame. Straight away it looked bad as I heard a massive crack. Peter is a gentle giant and seeing him in such agony was hard to take for any of us. He is going to need us to keep his head up and we will all rally round him.'

Lee wins a header against Darlington in February.

Peacock's 88th-minute goal was celebrated with a spot of breakdancing that lightened the mood, as emergency keeper Adi Williams held on for a clean sheet. Then came the setback that most supporters thought had been averted. On Saturday 21 October Swindon recorded a 2–1 win at Shrewsbury, and by the following Monday the club were looking for new manager.

Old Chelsea chairman Ken Bates, the man who had presided over the Blues while Dennis Wise had been a player at Stamford Bridge and who was now at Leeds United, decided his ex-midfielder was just the man to lead Leeds United away from danger near the foot of the Championship table. The man who had poached Glenn Hoddle from the County Ground for Stamford Bridge back in 1993 had returned to Wiltshire to steal another Town boss for his own needs.

Fans were stunned. Wise had remained tight-lipped throughout all the weeks of rumours and many thought the storm had been weathered. What now for Town's season?

Commenting on 'an unnamed individual connected with Swindon Town' whom he found difficult to work with, Wise offered little further explanation for his departure. 'It was a pleasure to work with Mark Devlin and Bill Power. I will say no more than that. I'd like to say thanks to the fans who made me feel so welcome during my time there.'

What was known was that director Bob Holt had resigned after telling the media that Wise was staying with Swindon, and that Wise had been upset that such confidential discussions had been made public. Wise had been in charge for just 17 games, and Poyet joined his boss in the move to Elland Road.

Youth set-up head Dave Tuttle initially accepted the mantle of caretaker boss, and then a day later reneged on the agreement. Then skipper Adi Williams agreed to step in and steady the ship as everything that had happened so far was thrown into confusion.

As in all similar cases, speculation regarding a permanent managerial replacement was rife. Among those reported to have their hats in the ring, and with varying levels of expectation of landing the role, were ex-Swindon midfielder Luc Nijholt (the Dutch star from Town's year in the Premiership), Paul Sturrock (recently axed by Sheffield Wednesday) and Town mascot Rockin' Robin.

Traditionally, Lou Macari was the first to be nominated as the fans' choice before the man himself declared that he was flattered but not available, then on 7 November Sturrock was unveiled as the man to carry on where Wise had left off.

The man known affectionately as 'Luggy' had cut his managerial teeth at St Johnstone and Dundee United, then enjoyed two promotion successes in four years at Plymouth Argyle before moving on to Southampton to replace Gordon Strachan in the summer of 2004. There, after an extraordinarily short spell of 13 games, he was shown the door, but a month later was appointed boss at Sheffield Wednesday.

At Hillsborough Sturrock took the Owls to the Championship via the League One Play-offs, then, incredibly, the former Scottish international was sacked just five weeks after signing a new four-year deal. Football's mechanisms often defy logical explanation.

'Here to Stay', the *Adver* headline announced as the newest man to take Swindon's helm put supporters' minds at rest regarding his long-term commitment to the County Ground. Stand-in chief Adi Williams had seen his temporary charges capitulate in both his games in charge and might have had mixed feelings as he handed the office keys to his new boss, and there might have been some trepidation when Lee Peacock learned that Paul Sturrock was to become his next manager.

The Paisley-born, ex-Scotland Youth and Under-21 player had come through the ranks as a Carlisle United trainee, signing his first professional contract in March 1995. Making his League debut as a substitute in April 1994, the Cumbrians grabbed a Division Three Play-off place but were unable to overcome Wycombe Wanderers in the fight for a place in Division Two.

Over the next three years Lee established himself as a first-team regular at Brunton Park. Coming off the bench five times in seven League appearances during 1994–95, Lee helped his side to the championship of Division Three and also helped overcome a troublesome central-defensive problem. The early career of a young Peacock had still to shape his future. Of 22 appearances the following season, almost half were made as a substitute, the rest with defensive duties to the fore.

Lee started the third League match of 1995–96 at home to Swindon Town when an Eddie Murray goal gave Lee's future employers a victory. Carlisle were destined for relegation once more as Swindon were on course for the Division Two trophy, and his goalscoring pedigree had yet to make itself evident. That all changed in 1996–97 when he was thrust up front to begin the campaign as a striker.

He failed to make the score sheet until 12 October, but then a goal at Rochdale brought a point and left Carlisle third in the table. Four games later, his brace at home to Chester City indicated the converted defender was learning the art of goalscoring. By May, United had regained their Division Two place and Peacock had missed just two games and had scored a respectable 10 goals. Then, in October 1997, Steve Parkin splashed out a club-record £90,000 to take him to Mansfield Town and back into Division Three.

Five goals in 32 appearances that season perhaps didn't bring the return that the fee justified, but injury played its part as Lee settled in Nottinghamshire. The following year he missed just one League game as he finished the Stags' top scorer on 17. Lee's goals weren't enough to earn his team a Play-off spot, but they helped gain the respect of a Field Mill crowd who could recognise the honest enthusiasm of the powerfully-built striker.

In the summer of 1999 Bill Dearden replaced Parkin, a managerial change that didn't seem to pay instant dividends. Just one goal was scored and just one point was taken in the first five matches

Peacock accepts his teammates thanks. Lincoln City, March 2007.

of the season, then, as Lee found his shooting boots and fired in seven goals in six games, the new boss decided it was time to cash in the asset he had inherited. Manchester City boss Joe Royle offered a cheque for half a million pounds and Lee made the step up from Division Three to Division One in November.

While Royle was to lead City back to the Premiership six months later, Peacock found first-team opportunities few and far between. Shaun Goater was becoming a legend at Maine Road and proved difficult to shift from the forward line.

Lee made just four League starts, coming on as a substitute in a 3–0 home win over Swindon in December, and he failed to find the net at all. In August 2000 and with City poised to pay over £3.5 million for West Ham United striker Paulo Wanchope, Peacock moved to the West Country to sign for Danny Wilson's Bristol City for £600,000.

Back in Division Two Peacock set about demonstrating his eye for goal once more. Teamed up with another future Swindon striker Tony Thorpe, the pair scored 38 goals between them, with Lee

Lukas Jutkiewicz helps Lee celebrate at Lincoln.

claiming 15. A year later he registered the same number again, including one in a 2–1 win over Swindon at the County Ground in January 2002. A 77th-minute goal at the Millennium Stadium helped City to the LDV Vans Trophy in 2003 at the expense of old club Carlisle United, as Peacock scored his traditional 15 goals. Defeat in the Division Two Play-offs, however, denied City a Cup and promotion double, and when Play-off failure against Hartlepool 12 months later again disappointed the board, the winds of change were blowing through Ashton Gate.

Out went boss Wilson, and in July 2004 Peacock left for League One side Sheffield Wednesday on a free transfer. He had bettered his usual scoring tally by one during his last season as a Bristol City Robin. Lee signed for Wednesday boss Chris Turner, but in September, after a run of three draws and two defeats, the Hillsborough board panicked and Turner was axed and replaced by Paul Sturrock.

A goal in the Play-off semi-final win over Brentford led to ultimate success at the Millennium Stadium over Hartlepool. Wednesday were in the Championship and Peacock had made it up through the Play-offs at the third consecutive attempt. A period of consolidation followed, and Lee found it difficult to match his striking rate of earlier seasons. Just three goals had been claimed as the transfer window of January 2006 opened, and Sturrock told his striker that his contract would not be renewed in the summer. With 10 days of the trading month to run, he signed on a free transfer for Iffy Onuora to become a Swindon Town player ahead of interest from a Paul Merson-led Walsall.

Peacock had taken advice from someone who knew a bit about Swindon Town. Adam Proudlock, one of Lee's former Wednesday teammates, was by then at Ipswich Town, where he was paired with ex-Swindon star Sam Parkin. A quick dialogue through all the parties resulted in Lee hearing Sam's assessment.

'The word I got back was, get yourself down there, you'll love it, they're brilliant,' Peacock said after signing for a club in the midst of a relegation battle. 'If I go part way to filling Parkin's boots I'd be happy. I can't believe the position they're in, looking at the players on board. It's a great club and I'm looking forward to getting down to business.'

Sam Parkin told the *Adver* 'Lee was someone who always worried us when we played Bristol City. I hope he enjoys success at Swindon.'

A goal on Peacock's debut helped Town to a win over Bournemouth and immediately showed Town supporters what their new man could do. 'Scoring was a massive bonus. I don't think I have scored on my debut at other clubs. Hopefully it's a good omen,' said the goalscorer. Lee's Swindon career had got off to a good start, but relegation would follow and by the following November he would be once again under the charge of a man who had previously told him he did not feature in his plans.

Sturrock was obviously facing a tough challenge when he took the reins at Swindon Town. The arrival of Dennis Wise in the summer and the success that early results had promised had raised the bar. Nothing less than promotion would be considered acceptable in Wiltshire come May.

It was a relief when Sturrock started his period in charge in a manner similar to that of the previous manager back in August. League Two wins over Torquay and Bury, interspersed with FA Cup successes against Carlisle and Morecambe, gave Sturrock four successive victories to start his period in office. When December continued with a 2–0 win at Walsall, the first home reverse to be suffered by the League Two leaders, Town were back to second in the table and had the seven-point gap between them and the Saddlers in their sights.

By then a story had already broken that Town had owed creditors £100,000 since June, as part of the creditors' voluntary agreement that took Town out of administration four years previously, and another £900,000 was due imminently. Welcome to Swindon Luggy.

The opening goal at the Bescot Stadium, Walsall, had been struck by a young man with the world at his feet, the second by someone who had undergone quite a test of his resolve. Seventeen-year-old Lukas Jutkiewicz registered his first senior goal and started to attract the attention of footballing suitors, and Christian Roberts, soon to announce the successful completion of his first alcohol-free 12 months for some time, rounded off the afternoon's scoring from the penalty spot.

Back in August Roberts had been challenged by his manager to score 20 goals, and the fact that Wise had subsequently left for Leeds did not appear to affect the promise of a free holiday if he achieved the feat.

Jutkiewicz was at it again a week later with the goal that equalised a Richard Walker opener for Bristol Rovers at the County Ground. Then another youngster opened his Town scoring account when 19-year-old Curtis Weston's thundering drive cannoned off the crossbar and over the line before Aaron Brown followed up to make sure.

So it was four wins in five League attempts for the team now led by Paul Sturrock. For the second time in just four months, Swindon had a new manager who looked capable of turning around years of underachievement. There were some new kids showing their faces on the Swindon goalscoring block. Time for an old hand to make a reappearance.

Two days before Christmas, Lee Peacock grabbed a goal that was insufficient to claim a point at Macclesfield Town, a team who had looked cast adrift at the foot of League Two but were resurgent since the arrival of Paul Ince. Then on Boxing Day ex-Town hero Tommy Mooney was in Swindon for the visit of Wycombe Wanderers, and the young and not-so-young combination of Jutkiewicz and Peacock sent the Chairboys home without a festive point to show for their day in Wiltshire. Paul Sturrock was encouraged by his strike force, but had reservations about the rest of his team. 'The last 20 minutes was like the Alamo. We allowed ourselves to be dragged back by not defending properly, high enough up the pitch,' said the boss. But of his front men, he said 'I felt Lukas and Lee gave us presence up front. Lukas looked more like himself, whereas on Saturday (at Macclesfield) he looked a bit leg weary. As for Lee, that's two in two games. I thought he was fantastic in our box as well.'

Perhaps this was an indication that the boss had plans for Peacock that would use his skills elsewhere on the field of play.

Lee was at it again to usher in the new year. A single goal on the half-hour at second-placed MK Dons gave Swindon all three points against their promotion-chasing rivals. 'Jamie Vincent tried to claim it but he actually booted the back of my leg. I don't think it would have reached otherwise,' joked the man credited with the goal, scored from loan midfielder Michael Timlin's corner. 'I thought he was excellent in both boxes' said his boss. 'That's three goals in four games for him. He's that non-scoring striker everyone keeps telling me about,' continued a happy Sturrock.

At the back, goalkeeper Phil Smith's performances had interrupted Sturrock's search for a replacement for the injured Peter Brezovan. Attempting to emulate Brezovan's opening-day blinder, Smith had blocked an Izale McLeod penalty just four minutes after Town had taken the lead. So impressive had the ex-Crawley stopper been that he was handed the League Two Player of the Month trophy for December, and the first-team shirt was his for the rest of the campaign.

Swindon were in the midst of a seven-match unbeaten run and it would be February before defeat was tasted in the League again. The only blot on the landscape was a highly-creditable 2–1 defeat at Championship-side and promotion-chasing Crystal Palace in the FA Cup. The 17 points collected from the 21 on offer would go a long way to defining Town's destiny as three further successive victories, at Boston and at home to Wrexham and Macclesfield, continued the good sequence.

Lee Peacock's second-half free-kick doubled the lead over Paul Ince's Macclesfield and gave Swindon some breathing space. The man who nursed the Man of the Match champagne at the end of the afternoon said 'It was good to get one over them because we let ourselves down last time,' referring to the defeat at the Moss Rose Ground just before Christmas.

Manager Sturrock had announced his intention to play Lee in a midfield role and the boss was delighted by the way he had contributed to the play. 'I thought Peacock was immense. He was the best player on the park by a mile. He really dictated the way the game was going to pan out.' Meanwhile, Lee himself said 'I'll play anywhere as long as I get across the line.' But if the manager was to move his in-form goalscorer away from the forward line, was there sufficient firepower up front to keep the promotion push on track?

A 1–1 draw at Peterborough brought the curtain down on January and a goal for the manager's son Blair. The boss celebrated the League Two Manager of the Month award and Town were back up to second in the table, just one win away from Walsall and four points higher than Lincoln City. Once more, supporters turned their attention to the chance of some silverware. That sort of optimism is a cue for Town supporters to be forced into a rethink. Over the next seven matches Town did a good impression of a team who had trouble believing their own good press. Two wins and just seven points threatened to whip the promotion party carpet from under their feet.

The stutter began when Andy Monkhouse, shown the door at the County Ground almost as soon as Sturrock arrived, returned with Hartlepool and scored the goal that won the match. When the midfielder had left for Victoria Park, a clause in his contract excluded his eligibility to play against Swindon. Paul Sturrock magnanimously waived that condition and Town paid the price. Then, two more points were dropped at home to Darlington, and by the time Swindon travelled to Sincil Bank on 25 March to play Lincoln City in front of the TV cameras, they were as low as fifth in the table, facing the team that sat one place higher by the slim margin of goal difference.

Ahead of the match Sturrock had brought in Sheffield Wednesday striker Barry Corr, a 6ft 3in target man. Just two men had found the net since January, with defender Andy Nicholas claiming a brace and colleague Jack Smith doing likewise with two spot-kicks. Goals from the forward line had dried up completely.

Donning his lucky coat, Peacock joins in the promotion celebrations.

The Imps started the brighter of the two teams and opened the scoring in the 12th minute, but Christian Roberts levelled four minutes later. Just after the half-hour, Corr marked his debut with the goal that gave Town the lead, turning home a loose ball after a Jack Smith shot had been blocked. Then, three minutes into the second half, Corr's clever footwork in the six-yard box presented a chance to Peacock who opened up a two-goal cushion. A second goal for the home side's Mark Stallard with a quarter of an hour remaining brought about some nervous moments, but Swindon held on for the win that lifted them above their hosts.

Now a confirmed midfielder, goalscorer Peacock said 'You will make mistakes as you are learning a new role, but I'm loving it in there. You're involved in so much, winning headers, tackling, making runs, you really feel like you're contributing and getting your teeth in.' But it was the contribution of Barry Corr that caught the eye.

The win started the third seven-match spell, all of which had distinct character. Seven without defeat from the new year had given way to the same number of very variable results when promotion aspirations looked at risk. The win in Lincolnshire launched another run of five wins and two draws as the season reached its climax.

Corr was on target again in a 2–1 win over Shrewsbury, then successive 0–0 away draws were followed by nine points from nine, starting on Easter Monday at home to Torquay United, who were almost doomed to the drop.

The end was in sight.

April ended with the news that Town man Lee Peacock had been nominated the PFA's Fans' Player of the Year for 2006–07, then came the chance to consummate the season. Two matches remained, the first at the Memorial Stadium to face Bristol Rovers and the second the last fixture of the campaign against Championship-chasing Walsall at the County Ground. A point from either would leave Swindon out of reach of MK Dons, the only team who could pip them to third place.

A disappointing first-half display in Bristol in front of a huge Town following was punctuated by a spectacular 30-yard goal from Pirates' Rickie Lambert. With Town still unable to find any form reminiscent of earlier in the season, an inaccurate rumour that MK Dons were failing to win at home to Wycombe Wanderers sparked premature and ill-founded celebrations in the stands. At the final whistle, reality set in as everyone found out that the season was going to go right to the wire.

Back in August, as fans had perused the newly-published fixture list, one match had looked particularly appealing. The visit of the Saddlers to Wiltshire, for what would be the last game of the regular season, looked as though it could be important. For once, supporters' expectations went true to form.

On 5 May almost 15,000 fans packed into the County Ground to watch the two teams battle it out for the all-important last positional shake-up. As long as Town didn't lose, third place was guaranteed, while Walsall would take the championship if they bettered second-placed Hartlepool's result at home to Bristol Rovers.

There was to be no repetition of Swindon's shaky performance the week before. A sparkling first half of surprisingly tension-free football saw Town take the game to the visitors, but led to a 0–0 score line at half-time. Then, with seven minutes of the second half gone, Zaaboub swung in a corner and Jerel Ifil powered home a Shaun Taylor-esque pile driver of a header to give Town the lead. It was the powerful central defender's first League strike of the season, and a good time to break his duck.

Still the game was played at a high tempo and with an open spirit, and as the match entered injury time Saddlers striker Dean Keates unleashed an unstoppable shot past Town keeper Phil Smith's outstretched left arm. The Walsall supporters on Stratton Bank went wild, while their Swindon counterparts nervously conferred that it made little difference to them.

It's not often that both sets of supporters are joyous in equal measure at the final whistle. Hartlepool had gone down 2–1 at home to Bristol Rovers, confirming Walsall as League Two champions, while Town's point had secured the automatic promotion place that they had toyed with all season. The pitch became a sea of jubilant red and white-clad fans of both persuasions.

But before all that, Lee Peacock had kept an appointment to get acquainted with the Player of the Year award. More than 50 percent of the votes cast had nominated the man who had seen his role redefined as the season progressed. Lee seemed pleased.

'It's massive for me. This will be my proudest season when we get promoted,' Lee proclaimed. 'The fans who voted for this are the people watching you week in and week out and paying your wages. I'm absolutely over the moon. I can't say how much it means, as the fans are the heart and soul of the club. I think the fans here just appreciate a bit of hard work. I don't pretend to be the most skilful player in the world. What I have is old-fashioned determination.'

Injury had occasionally threatened to limit Peacock's appearances, but he was made of stern stuff. Forty-four games throughout the campaign had produced 10 goals.

As the celebrations following Town's elevation back to League One continued, Lee did something that the fans' elected Player of the Year hadn't done for three seasons. With a year of his contract to run, the popular striker-turned-midfielder announced not only his desire to stay with Swindon Town for its duration, but his intention to request an extension to tie him to the club until the end of his career. The last player to trot out to start a fresh campaign three months after being elected the Player of the Year had been Sam Parkin in 2003.

Of course, not everything had been sweetness and light.

Throughout the season, the dialogue between the club and the Bill Power-led takeover bidders had stolen the limelight from the main show on the pitch. After some tit-for-tat point scoring, the

The fans bestow their recognition.

club called for the consortium to prove their financial credentials in January. The consortium offered to do just that, and responded by hijacking the colour orange and suggesting that anyone wearing one of their free woolly hats would be showing their support for Power, rather than just trying to keep their head warm.

Bob Holt was back hosting Town's AGM by December, and in February former chief executive Mark Devlin announced his own departure from the County Ground, citing 'other opportunities' as his reason for going.

A February panic came when it was revealed that Town were due to make a further payment on the CVA, and a fans' forum brought denials that the club intended to move out of the borough to Chippenham. The club were on the verge of a promotion season, and there appeared to be doubts about whether the club would stay in Swindon. Things are always interesting at STFC.

By the end of March it seemed that meaningful discussions had still not taken place between the club and Bill Power's team, and patience seemed to be wearing thin at TrustSTFC, who were fully behind Power's struggle. Then, even as the close season began, news broke that another unnamed potential investor was ready to step in and secure the club's future. If true, the development would be most welcome, but few Town supporters would be holding their breath in anticipation. There had been far too many plot changes in the soap opera that is Swindon Town Football Club.

But as the summer of 2007 approached, everyone who held Swindon dear to their hearts had a lighter step. Seventeen seasons previously, Town had looked on course to take their place on the highest stage of English football before the Football League intervened. Succeeding in making the step up three years later it had then been an almost relentless plummet, until Town found themselves back at the level from which Lou Macari had launched his stratospheric revival back in the 1980s.

While unable to capture the Championship trophy that had been claimed the last time Town had been in the bottom division, at last Town were moving upwards again, once more led by an ambitious Scot who seemed to relish a long-term challenge. The players, officials and supporters of Swindon Town Football Club were on their way back.

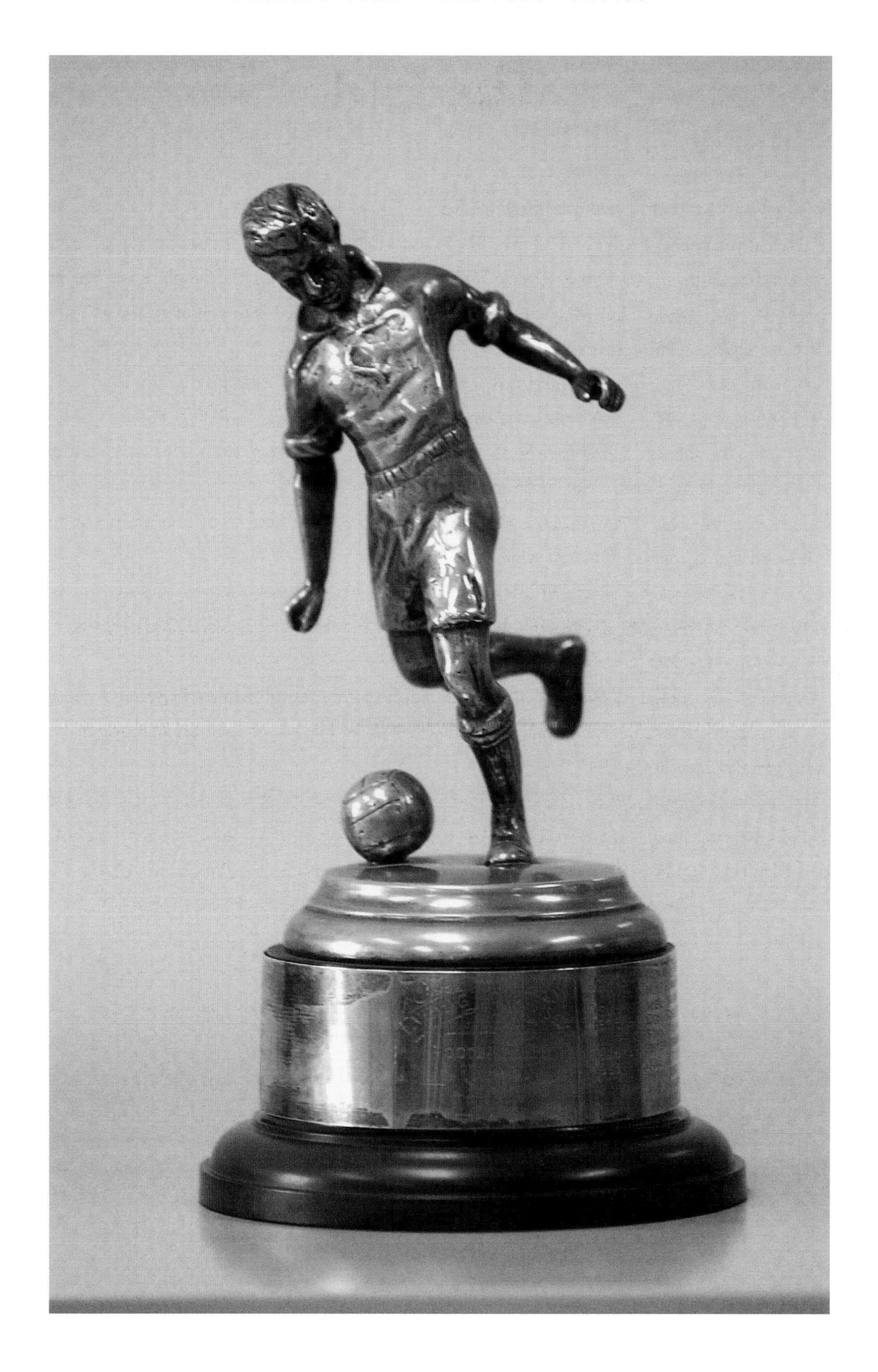

The End

So, what is it that makes a Swindon Town Player of the Year?

Well, if you're a striker it doesn't hurt to score a sackful of goals. It is not a bad idea to score the winner that claims promotion or fends off disaster, but, curiously enough, if you're a goalkeeper, your chances of gaining the award seem enhanced if you have conceded dozens of goals and Town have been less than successful on the pitch.

It is worth noting, however, those that have not been granted the award.

Only seven players can claim to have scored for Town at Wembley, with Roger Smart among them. Even though seven of the players that took to the field in the League Cup Final of 1969 won the Player of the Year award, Smart was never one of them.

Even Don Rogers, surely Town's star of stars, won the award just once, and that was two years before the much-celebrated League Cup win.

Craig Maskell was responsible for the goal that put Town two goals to the good against Leicester City in the Play-off Final of 1993, but he is also absent from the roll of honour. It would appear that Swindon supporters are not easily impressed by one moment of inspiration.

Perhaps Glenn Hoddle, the third Town Wembley goalscorer not to win the Player of the Year, failed to gain the accolade because supporters felt he would get enough credit through his managerial success at the club.

Once the trophy has been handed out, there is a high probability that the recipient is about to take to the pitch in a Town shirt for the last time, and it is for that reason that after the photo shoot on the pitch, the characteristic figurine of a 1960s footballer is whipped away from the winner's grasp and replaced with a less charismatic trophy for the newly-crowned Player of the Year to keep.

Otherwise, come the start of the following season, the silverware that has been handed out for over half a century might have been boxed up and taken to the other end of the country, as the fans' favourite moves on to pastures new.

Swindon Town supporters are a discerning crowd. Anyone who has been chosen as the best player of the season, and whoever gains the award in the future, can feel satisfied at having gained the approval of such a learned and dedicated team of football critics.

For Town players, the demands can be high, the rewards not great, but the respect that is demonstrated when the fans vote in their Player of the Year is heartfelt and hard won.

Roll of Honour

Matthew Arnold
Brian Birch
Ken Bridgeman
Ken Brown
Paul William Brown
David William Brown
Norman Cambray
Ronald Carter
Claire Colbert Martin
Mick Collin
Matthew Colsell
Andy Cooper
Adam Brian Davies
Owain John Davies
Malcolm Davies
Ian John Davies
Paul Davis
Wendy Dilkes
Toni Dilkes
Craig Douglas
Alan J. Drayson
Don Drew
Robert Drury
Keith Evans
Harry Fitchett
Amber Giles
Kelly Giles
Barry Giles
Dennis Goulding
Michael John Grzesiak
Ross Hancock
Ozzie Hancock
Mark Hancock
Edward Hanson (Turkish) SN8
James Haville
Bob Haville
Ralph Haville
Carrie Hayward
Steve Hayward
Harold Hibberd
Malcolm Howell
Alexander Ide

Maureen Large
Fred Large
William John Law
Tom Lee
Naomi Leonard
David Mallender
Keith Marsh
Andrew Mears
Gary Parker
Brenda Peachey
Lee Porter
Tim Preedy
Geoffrey Price
Joe Ranger
Terry Ranger
Susan Reeve
Denis Reeves
Grant Robinson
Kevin Russell
Craig Samuels
Stephen K. Simmonds
C Spencer
Paul Stevens
Paul Stoneham
Jon Stump
Adam David Tanner
Andy Tyrer
Paul Van Der Waal
Mrs J. Wallis
Eric Wallis
Paul Wells
Marlene Wells
Isaac Wells
Tim Westcott
Luke Westgate
Adam Williams
Paul Willis
Ian Woolford
Paul Wynn
Michelle Wynn
Joseph Wynn-Davis
Thomas Wynn-Davis